D0529481

WHO SHALL LIVE

WHO SHALL LIVE
THE WILHELM BACHNER STORY

SAMUEL OLINER AND KATHLEEN LEE

ACADEMY CHICAGO PUBLISHERS

© 1996 Samuel Oliner and Kathleen Lee

Published by
Academy Chicago Publishers
363 West Erie Street
Chicago, Illinois 60610

All rights reserved.
No part of this book may be reproduced in any form
without the express written permission of the publisher.

Printed and bound in the U.S.A.

Library of Congress Cataloging-in-Publication Data
Oliner, Samuel P.
    Who shall live? : the Wilhelm Bachner story / Samuel Oliner and Kathleen Lee.
        p.   cm.
    ISBN 0-89733-437-X
    1. Jews—Persecutions—Poland. 2. Holocaust, Jewish (1939–1945)—Poland—
    Biography. 3. World War—1939–1945—Jews—Rescue—Poland. 4. Bachner,
    Wilhelm. 5. Poland—Ethnic relations. I. Lee, Kathleen M. II. Title.
    DS135.P63B328   1996
    940.53'18'092—dc20
        [B]   96-24750
                                                          CIP

On Rosh Hashana it is written
On Yom Kippur it is sealed:
How many shall pass on, how many shall come to be;
who shall live and who shall die;
who shall see ripe age and who shall not;
who shall perish by fire and who by water;
who by sword and who by beast;
who by hunger and who by thirst;
who by earthquake and who by plague;
who by strangling and who by stoning;
who shall be secure and who shall be driven;
who shall be tranquil and who shall be troubled;
who shall be poor and who shall be rich;
who shall be humbled and who shall be exalted.

Yom Kippur morning service

Contents

Photographs between pages 112-113

ACKNOWLEDGMENTS

This book would not have been possible without the help of many individuals who gave us their time, knowledge and encouragement. First, a special debt of gratitude is owed to Wilhelm and Cecile Bachner, whose courage, compassion and action saved so many lives, and who before their deaths patiently shared with us their detailed knowledge of World War II, especially the events on the eastern front and the tragedy that beset the Jews there.

A very special thanks to Hilde Bachner Balhorn, Wilhelm Bachner's sister, and her husband Herbert Balhorn, of Moraga, California, not only for long hours of interviews and the provision of letters, photographs and documents, but also for their loving patience and encouragement during the long process of researching and writing this book.

We gratefully acknowledge the contributions of Gerda Reichenbaum Buchen, interviewed in Moraga, California, during a visit to this country from Australia; Hania Teifeld Shane, a resident of Southfield, Michigan; Jadwiga Finder Bloch, Nina Lurie Hudzik and Heniek Buchführer, who were interviewed in Israel. Also thanks to Ruth Stamberger Stroynowski of Cologne, Germany, and Elsie Dunner, of Vancouver, B.C. These individuals, who survived the

Holocaust with the help of Wilhelm Bachner, devoted hours to multiple interviews and provided a wealth of information to the Bachner story.

Thanks to our spouses, Dr Chris Lee, who proved to have hidden editorial skills that helped us a great deal, and Dr Pearl Oliner, who offered many helpful suggestions during the long process of research and writing.

Dr Lewis Bright, Dr Jack Shaffer, Judy Shaffer, Dr Jerry Krause, Professor Jack Norton and Shirley Ohrenstein read the manuscript in its early stages and offered helpful suggestions. Joanne Sullivan made helpful editorial suggestions. The Drs Janusz Reykowski and Suzana Smolenska from the Polish Academy of Science in Warsaw provided insights from the Polish perspective and encouraged us to write what they considered an important book.

Jerry Jacobs and Nancy Baker Jacobs have made helpful suggestions and given constructive criticism.

Kim T. Griswell has done detailed editing of the entire book and rewritten many sections, greatly improving the text. Linda Hall-Martin deserves thanks for proofing and typesetting the book.

Barbara Merker of the Potsdam Bundesarchiv provided us with materials about the Reichsbahn and Bauzüge in the German war effort, and Professor Steven Fox directed research on the war on the eastern front.

We are grateful to Erich Schimps, Dr Mark Shaffer, Dr Kay LaBahn, Ruth Neumann Block and Ursula Osborne for helping with translation from the German, and to Vasco de Sena and Melissa Peterson, Melanie Coddington, Jonathan Mermis-Cava and Ian Oliner for their assistance in transcribing interviews and other materials related to our research, as well as some first-rate proofreading.

I am sure there are many others we may have forgotten to mention. But this oversight does not mean we are any less grateful to them.

FOREWORD

I knew the Bachners when they were congregants at Temple Beth Abraham in Oakland, and I was its rabbi. Who would suspect that this taciturn couple had lived through such incessant nightmares, possessed of such singular courage? Heroism does not speak with a loud voice.

I want my grandchildren to read this book, if for no other wisdom than that of Cicero who noted: "Not to know what happened before you were born is to remain forever a child." Children must grow up; to raise them unknowing is to condemn them to a fatal ignorance.

I want them to read this book so that they understand the reality of evil without ignoring the reality of goodness; so that they understand that the mystery of goodness is no less awesome than the mystery of evil.

I want them to read this book so that they may be helped to balance the lopsided views ranging from Callicles down to Nietzsche and Freud, that dark view that human beings are essentially exploitative and entirely selfish.

The body of empirical evidence accumulated by Sam and Pearl Oliner in their significant study of *The Altruistic Personality,* and here substantiated by the exploits of Willi Bachner, have much to teach our post-Holocaust generation. That generation is in desperate need of moral heroes, not men and women with iron fists whose prowess is found in humiliating and torturing the weak, but persons of blood and flesh who did not compromise their human decency. It is important that they learn what the historian Frederick Woodbridge once wrote: "There are times when one ought to be more afraid of living than of dying." Beneath the myriad of statistics surrounding the research on the Holocaust, there is the incarnation of goodness of tens of thousands who, like Willi Bachner, "turned themselves into hiding places from the wind and shelters from the tempest." For the sake of the record, for the sake of my grandchildren's morals and morale, for God's sake, this story should be known.

—Harold M. Schulweis
Founding Chairman
Jewish Foundation for Christian Rescuers, NY

PREFACE

In 1983, as part of the Altruistic Personality Project, a study of the rescuers of Jews in Nazi-occupied Europe, we made an appointment to interview Wilhelm and Cecile Bachner of Moraga, California. Their names had been given to us as Holocaust survivors who were rescued by Gentiles. The interview had barely begun when it became obvious that Bachner had not been saved through the actions of others, but was one of that rare group of Jews who had not only survived but had managed to save many others.

The project questionnaire was set aside and over the next two days, Bachner shared his fascinating story of surviving the Holocaust by burying himself in the German railroad bureaucracy in Nazi-occupied Poland and the USSR. Hired as an engineer by a German architectural firm doing war work, Bachner soon became a supervisor and began removing Jews from Polish ghettos. After providing them with false papers, he placed them in work crews under his direction. He saved over fifty people from almost certain death, most of whom survived the war.

The Altruistic Personality Project proved to be an all-consuming task for the next several years, resulting in the publication of

The Altruistic Personality: Rescuers of Jews in Nazi Occupied Europe.

When we returned to the story of Bachner in the fall of 1991, we discovered, to our dismay, that he had died only eight months earlier. However, his story seemed too important to be ignored.

The interview conducted in 1983 served as a starting point from which the Bachner story was assembled. Next we interviewed family members, as well as surviving members of the group of Jews that Bachner had saved. Then we began the task of reconciling the stories of these survivors with what was known about the conduct of the eastern campaign and the work of construction units such as those of the Johannes Kellner firm that employed Bachner.

In addition to the interviews and examination of materials relating to the war and occupation in the east, we studied German archival material on the Reichsbahn, or German railroad, which employed the Kellner firm for much of the war, and the rail-based construction units known as Bauzüge, where Bachner and the others spent the last year and a half of the war.

There have been many memoirs and narratives written about the Holocaust. In addition, there have been hundreds of scholarly works which have examined nearly every aspect of this horrific period in human history. What we have tried to do is present a synthesis of these two forms. The story of Wilhelm Bachner is told against the background of the historical events that surrounded it. One cannot fully understand what was at stake for Jews like Bachner unless one understands why the Germans decided to annihilate an entire people for no other reason than their ethnicity. In the same fashion, the events of the story make no sense unless they are explained in the context of the conduct of the Second World War in the east.

The story is told in a narrative style, but the persons, places and events are real. Descriptions of the places and events, the people and the words they speak in the following pages were constructed from the interviews, books and archival material we explored in our research.

Our purpose in writing the story of Wilhelm Bachner is two-fold. First, Wilhelm Bachner and the people who helped him are true heroes whose stories need to be preserved for future generations. Too many of the heroes of the Holocaust have died before they were able to share their stories with the world.

Second, the Wilhelm Bachner story is part of a growing body of evidence which refutes the commonly held belief that Jews went to their deaths without resistance, "as sheep to the slaughter."

The myth of Jewish passivity came about for a variety of reasons: Allied guilt over its failure to act, the desire of the new state of Israel to contrast the heroic Israeli Jew with the cowardly European predecessor and persistent stereotypes of the cowardly and conniving Jew. Once established, this myth has become very hard to dislodge.

In recent years, many examples of Jewish resistance during the Holocaust have been described, such as involvement in partisan struggles, an underground railroad for smuggling Jews across borders and individual resistance like that of Wilhelm Bachner. Bachner and those he saved refused to give in. When the opportunity came, they seized it, spending nightmarish years hidden among those who sought to murder them, fearful that each day could be their last.

This book is dedicated to the memory of Jews like Bachner who lived to tell their stories of individual resistance, as well as to the millions who did not.

1 THE DEVICES OF THE WICKED

WHY, O LORD, DO YOU STAND ALOOF?
   WHY HIDE IN TIMES OF DISTRESS?
PROUDLY THE WICKED HARASS THE AFFLICTED,
   WHO ARE CAUGHT IN THE DEVICES THE WICKED
   HAVE CONTRIVED.

                    PSALM 10:1-2

The voice coming from the radio was frequently drowned out by the shrill whine of falling bombs and the muffled thunder of buildings exploding as the furious bombing raid continued to cause fire, brick and stone to rain into the streets of the city. Those crowded around the receiver no longer winced with each blast. One could get used to anything, Wilhelm Bachner realized, if it went on long enough, even the destruction of Warsaw. After weeks of constant German bombardment, the city crumbled beneath the weight of Hitler's fury. Now, in the third week of September, the Poles still resisted, but they knew that the surrender of the city was just days away.

Warsaw Mayor Stefan Starzynski did his best to lift the hopes and spirits of his citizens. His voice crackled over the radio: "We will never surrender. Warsaw may be in flames, but we are proud to die bravely." Rachmaninoff's Second Piano Concerto followed the mayor's address, but the uplifting strains played for only a few minutes before a distant blast cut it short, filling the room with static.

"They must have hit the station," someone commented matter-of-factly as if describing an everyday occurrence.

Bachner had joined his fiancée, Cesia Diamant, and her family in the basement of 84 Sienna Street. They were the closest thing he had to family in Warsaw, and at such a time, one needed all the intimacy one could get. Had the war begun only three weeks ago? Bachner rubbed his forehead as he tried to recall the initial raid. It seemed so long ago.

On the first day of September 1939, after months of apprehension, the German attack had burst suddenly upon Poland like a storm. The bombing of the Polish capital followed almost immediately, becoming more intense as the outgunned, outmanned Polish forces were trampled beneath the onslaught of the Third Reich. On September 8, the Germans rolled through the gates of Warsaw. Amid the staccato burst of gunfire and the grinding rumble of tanks, Poland's most illustrious city became, as it had so many times before, a fortress besieged on all sides.

It wasn't supposed to be this way, thought Bachner. When he had arrived in Warsaw from the provinces just eight months earlier, things had gone very well for him. He found a good job and met the woman he hoped would become his wife. He was looking forward to a comfortable life in a city that was a cultural center for Jewish and Christian Poles alike. He had planned to observe his first High Holy days in Warsaw at the famous Tlomackie Synagogue, rather than huddled in a basement with the whine of bombs assailing his ears.

Today, September 23, was Yom Kippur, the most important day of the Jewish calendar, the day when Jews atoned for transgressions of the past year and reconciled themselves with God and with each other. The targeting of the Jewish section of Warsaw was done deliberately by the Germans.

"What exactly are we atoning for here?" someone in the cellar quipped as the shelling intensified.

Cesia's grip on Bachner's arm tightened, and he gave her what he hoped was a reassuring smile. When he looked back, he had to admit that the warning signs had been there for years. By the time he was graduated from the Deutsche Technische Hochschule at Brno, the Germans had already annexed Austria and the Czech

Sudetenland. Youthful optimism and a promising career as a structural engineer lulled him into a complacency which allowed him to ignore the approaching danger.

When a family friend from his home town of Bielsko offered Bachner the chance to manage his Warsaw office, he accepted without hesitation. It was just the place for an ambitious twenty-seven-year-old professional to get his start. Hitler was always lurking in the back of everyone's consciousness, of course, like a goblin in a children's story. For Jews like Bachner, the Führer presented a much more terrifying aspect. Word about Hitler's ascension to power in 1933 and his hatred of the Jews had spread from synagogue to synagogue. As stories of the Führer's mistreatment of Jews in Germany escalated, Bachner, like many others, selfishly hoped the German dictator would be satisfied with the German-speaking territories he had already annexed. Perhaps the threat of another war with Britain and France, which had guaranteed Polish sovereignty, would deter a further territorial grab.

Deep down, Bachner had to admit, he identified with Germanic culture. His home town, Bielsko, had been part of the Austro-Hungarian Empire before the Great War, and he had grown up speaking German both at home and in school. His family was assimilated into Austrian culture and Bachner admired the Germanic traits of organization and efficiency. The excesses of Nazi discrimination against Jews were appalling, but hardly reflective of German culture at large, just as the anti-Semitism of the Poles was an indisputable part of Polish history, but not something that would interfere with the career of a competent, hardworking Jewish professional such as he.

But now, with the ferocity of the German attack, Bachner began to feel the same sense of foreboding that many older Jews had been expressing for months. He looked down at Cesia beside him. Her small stature and delicate features made her seem much younger than her twenty-four years. Although still devoted to her parents and brothers, she had already begun to rely on Bachner for direction and support. Their first meeting last spring and the idyllic summer courtship that followed seemed to belong to a different age.

How could he have guessed last spring when he admired her from across the dance-club floor that he would soon find himself trying to comfort this beautiful girl in a dank cellar shaken by continuous jarring, ear-splitting explosions?

Suddenly, with a crackle of static, the radio once again came to life, not with Polish words of encouragement or the music of Chopin or Rachmaninoff, but with an explosion of guttural German. Bachner's body went rigid as he leaned forward. The Germans had either seized the station or set up a broadcast on the same frequency. As he listened, the harsh, authoritative voice informed the population of Warsaw that their paltry attempts at resistance were futile and would be met with decisive retaliation. Bachner felt Cesia's hand slip into his. He squeezed it gently, trying to reassure her.

"Don't worry. It will be all right. I won't let anyone hurt you." Even as he spoke these words of comfort, the emptiness that had overwhelmed him over the last three weeks deepened, and he felt as if he were falling into a chasm, the bottom of which he could not see through the gathering darkness.

*   *   *

The bombardment continued intermittently for the next few days. When things seemed relatively quiet, the inhabitants of 84 Sienna would emerge from their hiding place, trying to assess the damage. Little by little, through word of mouth, the inhabitants of Warsaw learned the news: "The Royal Castle has been badly damaged . . . the Soviet Embassy is completely destroyed . . . you remember Mr and Mrs Maizel, dead and buried in the debris of their building."

On street corners in the city, women set up tables to serve bread, soup and tea to the exhausted defenders of the city. It was a brave show of solidarity, but everyone seemed to be resigned to the inevitable: the Germans would soon be masters of the city. The infrastructure of Warsaw had quickly fallen beneath the barrage of German bombs; what had at first been mere inconvenience now became a matter of survival. There was no longer running water, gas or electricity.

Bachner spent much of his time in the streets trying to round up enough food to feed himself and the Diamants. As he stepped over the litter cluttering the sidewalk, he clasped a wet handkerchief over his face, trying to block out the putrid smell of garbage, backed-up sewers and rotting flesh. No matter how hard he tried, he could not block out the most disturbing sights. Though he kept his gaze steadfastly ahead, from the corners of his eyes, he could still see the severed human limbs which lay along his route. Bachner's empty stomach churned, the raw, burning acids threatening to rise into his throat.

Amid the rubble in the streets lay the rotting remains of dead horses, their flanks mutilated by scavengers before they had decomposed to their present state. Desperate with hunger, some had carved out chunks of horseflesh. The image, at first so unsettling to Bachner, now seemed commonplace in this surreal war-torn city, where meat of any sort was virtually impossible to come by. The burden of finding enough food to feed the Diamant family weighed heavily on Wilhelm, yet he readily accepted the responsibility. Occasionally, Cesia's brothers, Abraham and David, stopped by to make sure their parents and little sister were all right. If they had enough for their own families, they would drop off some foodstuffs. But whenever life began to assume some strange sense of normality, the drone of bombers would be heard and they all scurried back into shelters and basements to brace themselves for yet another attack.

On the afternoon of September 27, the gunfire and shelling tapered off, then finally stopped. When Bachner and the Diamants emerged from the cellar, they found the streets crowded with people, and rumors were flying thick and fast. Either the Germans had taken the city or the Poles had successfully beaten them back. Some said France and England had come to the rescue of Poland as they had promised; others claimed that their allies had capitulated to Hitler's seizure of Poland. Everything was either all right now or terribly wrong, depending on whom you talked to. At any rate, the bombs had stopped and that, in itself, was something to be grateful for. It was in this mix of confusion, apprehension and relief that Willi and

Cesia tried to sleep through what was to be their last night free from the Nazis.

They awoke the next morning not to the sounds of siege but to those of occupation. Thousands of Germans paraded through the streets of Warsaw, marching and singing as they followed hundreds of trucks and motorcycles. The Germans distributed free bread to the citizenry—an encouraging sign. Maybe now that Poland had surrendered, the worst was over, many hoped. True, Poland was occupied, but Poland had spent the last few hundred years being carved up among Prussian, Austrian and Russian princes and dictators. It had survived then and it would survive now—or so many thought.

Even more than most Poles, the Jews of Warsaw felt a shadow of foreboding shroud the land as the Germans advanced, a feeling which was justified all too quickly by the actions of the victors. The Jews were ordered to begin cleaning rubble from the streets. Not only Orthodox residents, easily identifiable by their frock-coats and sidelocks, but assimilated Jews and non-Jewish Poles as well. Anyone who, to German eyes, lacked the proper "Aryan" features was conscripted into these impromptu work crews. The more sadistic Germans not only forced the Jews to work, but tormented them as well. Taunting soldiers especially targeted Orthodox Jews for abuse. Beatings became common. There was outrage in the Jewish community over humiliating public displays like the shaving of beards and sidelocks of Orthodox men unfortunate enough to be caught in the streets by German soldiers. But few dared voice their objections.

*   *   *

"Sind Sie ein Jid?" (Are you a Jew?) rang in the streets of Warsaw day and night. An affirmation meant immediate impressment, but most often, so did a denial. In the occupied city, the Germans became the ultimate arbiters of ethnic identity. The trick was to avoid being questioned in the first place. Bachner, though dark-haired and brown-eyed, was not noticeably "Jewish" in appearance. Putting on his best "German" demeanor, he walked stiff-backed; filling his five-

foot-four frame with a semblance of authority, he forced himself to maintain eye contact whenever accosted. By this method, he usually succeeded in avoiding impressment.

Christian Poles were not spared the perils of defeat either. As Slavs, they were considered inferior, although a step higher on the Nazi ladder of racial purity than their Jewish compatriots. They became the chattel of the Reich. Intellectuals, politicians and cultural leaders who were not Nazi supporters were arrested and imprisoned. Thousands were rounded up and sent to Germany as forced laborers. Yet the Jews were not to have even this limited role in the Third Reich. They lived in limbo, unsure of their place in the Nazi world. But their increasing mistreatment at the hands of the Germans foreshadowed Hitler's intent: to find a way to free Europe of them, permanently.

Although anti-Semitism had a long history in Germany, it took Adolf Hitler and the National Socialist philosophy to bring the tradition of hatred to its most horrendous manifestation. Hitler returned to Munich after World War I, already despising the Jews and holding them responsible for Germany's defeat. There he met some of the recent Russian émigrés, who brought with them *The Protocols of the Elders of Zion*, which promulgated the myth of a Jewish conspiracy to rule the world. Russian Bolshevism was seen as a manifestation of the Jewish assault on European Christian civilization and implicit proof of the truth of *The Protocols*.

In *Mein Kampf*, Hitler described the Jews as international anti-German conspirators, criminals and a life-threatening pestilence. During his rise to power, Hitler did not emphasize the anti-Semitic aspects of the National Socialist program. However, it was a useful tool in mobilizing German dissatisfaction with the status quo. Democracy, socialism and internationalism became synonymous with "Jewishness," and millions of European Jews were transformed into unpardonable enemies.

As the Germans set out their policy for the Jews of Warsaw, they used the long-established Jewish Council as their conduit. This civic group, which had previously represented Jewish interests with the government, was revised to specifically carry out German decrees. At its head was Adam Czerniakow, an engineer who had been appointed by Mayor Starzynski to fill the post left vacant when the previous chairman fled the country at the beginning of the war. By using this Jewish council, called the Judenrat, the Germans managed to make the Jews of Warsaw and all other occupied areas participants in their own oppression. Czerniakow, though he was to demonstrate a tragic myopia regarding the intentions of the Nazis, was no traitor or collaborator, but a dedicated man who repeatedly refused to escape Warsaw and took his duties as spokesperson for the Jews very seriously.

It was through Czerniakow and the Judenrat that the decrees regarding the Jews of Warsaw were made known to the populace. On October 6, the Führer's resettlement policy for the Jews was announced. Much of Western Poland was to be annexed to the Reich and it was to be Judenrein, free of Jews. Jews in Germany, Austria, Czech Sudetenland, Pomerania and Silesia were to be deported to occupied Poland, which was known as the Generalgouvernment. At its head was Hans Frank, who had thrown his lot in with Adolf Hitler in the 1920s and had gone on to become Commissioner of Justice and Reich Law Leader. Having lost its west to the Reich, its eastern lands to the Soviet Union and its center to an occupying force, Poland had, as twice before in its troubled history, ceased to exist.

In early October, it was announced that all Jewish-owned firms were to be "Aryanized" by the Germans, that Jewish assets in Polish banks were frozen and that all radios were to be turned in to the German authorities. All Jewish men between the ages of 14 and 60 were ordered to be available for forced labor and Czerniakow was to conduct a thorough census of the Jewish population. Jewish schools were closed and worship at synagogues restricted.

To Bachner, these challenges were to be met with the same determination that had marked his academic and professional careers. He had always overcome the obstacles that anti-Semitism had placed in his path by charming his teachers or employers with hard work, efficiency and polished manners. Now that the engineering firm of his mentor Josef Hornrock had been closed, he found what work he could, frequently relying on the skills he had learned from his craftsman father in Bielsko. Cesia's father also had to adjust to his new status. With his business and inventory seized, he was no longer a prosperous textile merchant, and was forced to find whatever manual labor he could.

Although the situation for Jews in Warsaw was deteriorating daily, it was anxiety over the fate of his family that troubled Bachner the most. His two young sisters, Anna and Hilde, had been in the Polish city of Lwów when that area was annexed by the USSR in early September of 1939, and had not been heard from since. His parents and little brother, Bruno, were still in Bielsko, now part of the Reich and soon to be free of Jews. After writing repeated letters, he finally learned that his parents and brother were safe, though reluctantly planning to leave Bielsko, and he learned from his parents that Anna and Hilde too were, at last word, safe. In the midst of all this uncertainty, Willi and Cesia made the decision to marry. After all, who knew what would happen? If they were going to go through hard times, if they were not going to survive, at least they would face their ordeal as husband and wife. The wedding on October 11 was a small, subdued affair. A rabbi came to the Diamants' apartment; a ceremony in a synagogue would risk the unwelcome appearance of the Nazis. Only a few of their friends, Cesia's brothers and their families attended. But for a few moments as they shared the wine and crushed the glass under a makeshift canopy, surrounded by cries of "Mazeltov!" the grimness of their lives receded and they could dream of a long, bright future filled with children and grandchildren.

*   *   *

Throughout October and November of 1939, Jewish refugees displaced from the Reich streamed into Warsaw and the other major cities of the Generalgouvernment. The destruction of the Jewish quarter by September's bombardment, left still unrepaired, and an ever-increasing population resulted in crowded conditions in refugee centers. The Jewish community was expected to pay for the housing and feeding of refugees, even as Jewish assets remained frozen and money unavailable. Communicable diseases began to take their toll among the weakest victims, the very old and very young. By mid-November, the Jewish areas of Warsaw were marked with signs warning *Achtung! Seuchengefahr. Eintritt verboten.* (Attention! Danger of Epidemics. Entry Prohibited.) The census conducted by Czerniakow showed that as of November there were 359,827 Jews in Warsaw.

The terrorization of Jews continued, with beatings, arrests and random shootings. In retaliation for the fatal shooting of a Polish policeman, fifty-three men from the apartment building from which the shots were fired were arrested, even though the single culprit was identified. A ransom of 300,000 zlotys was demanded of the Jewish Council. The community struggled to raise this huge sum and presented it to the German authorities on November 28, only to be told that the men had already been shot. The Germans took the money anyway. But the impact of all the restrictions, seizures, curfews and haphazard harassment was not as devastating as the announcement of November 23, 1939, in which Governor Frank decreed that "All Jews and Jewesses over the age of nine throughout Generalgouvernment must wear a four-inch arm band in white, marked with the star of Zion on the right sleeve of their inner and outer clothing." The star was to be yellow except in Warsaw, where, for some inexplicable reason, it was to be blue. The penalty for failure to comply was imprisonment. For the Jews it was notification that they could no longer see themselves as Polish citizens; they were marked for special mistreatment by their Nazi overlords.

The practice of marking Jews with an identifying badge was not new: Having begun in medieval Islam, it spread to Christian Europe in the 14th and 15th centuries. But yellow badges and confinement to Jewish areas had never been a Polish practice and the revival of this archaic discrimination dredged up the aura of centuries of mistreatment and injustice.

To Bachner, the arm band was a degrading reminder of what he had heard from so many Jews while he was growing up. "Don't even try to assimilate. You are a Jew and to the Gentiles, you will always be a Jew." If he wanted to work, he would have to wear the arm band. Still, every morning when he put it on before leaving home, he felt diminished by this strip of cloth.

Many refused to wear the arm band because they feared it would make them more vulnerable to German malevolence. Others refused on matters of principle. Everyone had heard the story of Janusz Korczak, a physician, author and radio personality in Warsaw. Korczak, who ran a large Jewish orphanage in Warsaw, was a veteran of the Great War and insisted on wearing his Polish uniform without an arm band. He managed to move about town soliciting donations for his orphans, but despite his seemingly cavalier attitude, he always kept a wary eye on the occupiers. Whenever he became the object of German scrutiny he mumbled gruffly to himself or sang loudly, looking for all the world like a demented old man.

In response to this flagrant noncompliance with a direct order, the Germans instituted a fine of 100 zlotys for anyone caught without an arm band. The Judenrat was fined and Czerniakow added this burden to the already insurmountable one carried by the Jewish community.

*   *   *

On a cold January morning in 1940, Bachner was seized at a corner near Sienna Street and shoved into a ragtag group clearing the previous night's snowfall from the street. Although he had managed to avoid most of the forced labor gangs, no one could escape entirely. Even Chairman Czerniakow had been seized on several occasions and was not always successful in convincing the guards that he was exempted from such duties.

Hunched over, shoveling snow in a bitter wind, Bachner observed the German guards pacing back and forth, stamping their feet and rubbing their hands together. As they tried to keep warm, they kept one eye on the Jewish laborers. There was something about one that seemed familiar; his walk reminded Bachner of someone. Then, as the soldier turned, Bachner saw his face full on. It was

Heinz Hoinkes. They had gone to school together in Bielsko. Although not close friends, they had a nodding acquaintance and had shared many classes together. Now Heinz had traded his school uniform for that of the German Army and was standing guard over his former classmate. For a fleeting moment Bachner considered calling out, but he realized that even if his old classmate wanted to help him, Heinz had never been the type to risk the consequences of coming to the assistance of a Jew. Bachner looked down at the band encircling his arm, the shovel he held in hands gone numb with cold. What would Heinz think if he saw Wilhelm Bachner, the most promising student in his class, working in the street like a common laborer? No, it was best for both of them that he say nothing. As Heinz walked past him, Bachner pulled up his coat collar, pulled his cap down over his eyes, turned away and continued shoveling the dirty snow.

When he returned home to his apartment at 54 Zlota Street he found his wife huddled on the couch, her face streaked with tears, hands cold and trembling. His concerned inquiries only brought fresh tears.

"Come," he said taking her by the hand and sitting down on the sofa. "Calm down, Cesia. What is so terrible that you can't tell your husband?"

Cesia took a shuddering breath and wiped her eyes with her damp handkerchief. "Today I was at the market and I saw my friend Sarah. She told me that last night Germans came to the apartment down the hall from her. They somehow learned that the man was a diamond merchant and—and they wanted some."

Bachner shook his head, gathering his wife into his arms. It was a familiar tale to Bachner; numerous Jewish families had lost most of their belongings to Germans who forcibly entered their homes, frequently after being led there by Polish thugs who enthusiastically participated in the looting.

"Cesia, Cesia . . ." He squeezed her shoulder gently. "There is nothing new in that. Why has it scared you so?"

Cesia sat silently, her lips pressed together, face pale. After a moment, she began to speak, softly, slowly. She described how the German officers demanded the family's money, jewels and goods. After they forced the father and brother to load their belongings into a waiting truck, they turned to the two daughters. Cesia's shoulders shook. Her words came in short, hesitant bursts.

"They locked the parents and the brother in a room. Then they made these two young women strip naked. They made them dance." Cesia buried her face in her handkerchief.

Willi waited patiently. The muffled words filtered through his wife's clenched fingers as she finished the story. The sound of the girls' parents' pleas for mercy mixed with the music of the gramophone, Cesia told him. The torment continued for what seemed like hours, until one of the girls collapsed and the Nazis, becoming bored with their sport, left.

"Willi." She sobbed. "What if they come when you aren't here? What will I do? I would rather be dead. What is going to happen to us?"

"Don't worry." He patted her hand reassuringly. "They are after bigger fish than us. Do we have jewels and silver? Who would want our old sofa and broken chairs? We would have to pay a beggar to take them off our hands." Willi chuckled. "It will be fine, don't worry."

Bachner found it easier to brush off Cesia's anxieties than to still his own fears, but he dared not share those fears with his emotionally fragile wife. The world had been turned upside down. Old rules no longer applied. Though he had always prided himself on being able to tackle any situation and land on both feet, he began to realize that his future and that of his family was now completely beyond his control.

Throughout the fall and winter, decrees continued to decorate the walls of the city as the Germans tightened the noose around the Jewish population. On January 21, the Gestapo ordered the registration of all Jewish property; on the 26th, all Jewish congregational worship was forbidden—even outside the synagogue. Jews were forbidden to travel by train, forbidden to use public libraries and forbidden to purchase goods from Aryans. As demands for labor increased, the random roundup of labor crews became more ruthless, including those to whom hard physical labor was a death sentence.

Czerniakow, hoping to lessen the hardship, offered to organize labor crews in return for a cessation of the roundups. The Germans agreed and set a daily quota of 350 to 400 workers. Those who agreed to work in the fourteen labor camps around Warsaw were mostly those who had no choice: the very poor and the refugees deported from western Poland. Czerniakow kept a diary in which he recorded the increasing difficulty of meeting the work quotas, and the near impossibility of scraping together a meager wage to pay these workers. An exemption from labor crews could be purchased from the Council for 100 zlotys. From this source, Czerniakow made futile attempts to provide workers with enough money to survive the harsh conditions in the labor camps.

The oppression came in so many forms it was hard to keep them all straight. The first encounters the Jews had were with units of the dreaded Schutzstaffel, better known by its initials, SS. Headed by Heinrich Himmler, the black-uniformed SS had infiltrated all areas of the Nazi regime. They were Hitler's personal bodyguard, an elite fighting group in the army, and they encompassed all aspects of policing the Reich: Kripo (Criminal Police), Sipo (Security Police), Orpo (Order Police) and Gestapo (Secret Police). It was the Gestapo special mobile units, Einsatzgruppen, which set up the Judenrat and enforced Frank's decrees.

*   *   *

Hans Frank's Civil Administration was headed in the Warsaw District by Ludwig Fischer. But it was the Plenipotentiary for the City of Warsaw, Ludwig Leist, who was primarily responsible for overseeing Jewish affairs. In addition to the Civil Administration and the SS, there were German Army personnel based or on furlough in Warsaw and numerous German businessmen who came to Warsaw to take advantage of the business opportunities provided by the rape of Poland. Most of the Civil officers in Warsaw were members of the SA, the "Brownshirts," who had lost to the SS in a power struggle during the early days of the Nazi regime. They were jealous of their power in Warsaw and resented SS interference.

Thus the Civil Administration was smugly satisfied when, in the spring of 1940, Berlin decided that they, not the SS, should oversee Jewish affairs. However, the fanatical SS was there on the sidelines ready to involve itself in Jewish affairs whenever an opening appeared.

In early April, the SS saw its opportunity. A wall was to be constructed around the Jewish sector "to defend the Jews against excesses" and to quarantine the increasing incidence of communicable diseases. While the Germans denied that the wall was to enclose a ghetto, the Jews were not fooled. The name "ghetto" came from the area of Venice to which the Jews were confined in 1516. Like the other ghettos of Europe, the one in Venice was designed to limit Jewish "contamination" of the Christian population. Although Jews could leave the ghetto freely during the day, they were locked in and patrolled by Christian guards at night. Jews were also confined to the ghetto during Church festivals such as Holy Week, when the anti-Semitic fervor of the populace (often exacerbated by fiery preaching of the clergy) led them to seek revenge against the Jews for the crucifixion of Christ.

Ghettos had long been abolished in Europe; they had never been present in Poland, but rumors that the Germans intended to revive this vile medieval practice had been rampant since the war began. When the official announcement finally came, the dispirited Jews greeted the news with resignation. To make matters worse, the Nazis informed the Judenrat that it would be their responsibility to provide both materials and labor. The project would proceed under the direction of the SS.

2 THE YOKE OF FOREIGNERS

OUR INHERITED LANDS HAVE BEEN TURNED OVER
  TO STRANGERS,
  OUR HOMES TO FOREIGNERS
THE WATER WE DRINK WE MUST BUY,
  FOR OUR OWN WOOD WE MUST PAY
ON OUR NECK IS THE YOKE OF THOSE WHO DRIVE US.
  LAMENTATIONS 5:2-5

April 13, 1940, dawned bright and sunny after several days of rain. In various locations around the Jewish section, ill-fed and ill-clad workers began excavation for the wall under the watchful eyes of sleek SS officers in black and silver. On that day, a middle-aged man, his wife and son warily made their way through the streets of Warsaw. There was nothing remarkable about the trio. They wore the same mismatched clothing, had the same rabbit-scared eyes as the thousands of other refugees wandering aimlessly through the streets, trying to avoid the rubble of buildings demolished by German bombs. They had heard that lucky refugees managed to find a relative with enough room to share; those not so fortunate crowded into refugee centers vying for meager rations in communal kitchens maintained by the Judenrat.

These three refugees only appeared aimless; they had a specific destination in mind. When they found 54 Zlota, they hurried into the building, located the apartment they sought and apologetically introduced themselves at the door to a surprised Cesia. She bustled them inside, checking to make certain no inquisitive eyes watched. Keeping up a nervous stream of idle chatter, she busied herself preparing hot tea, assuring her visitors that Willi would be home soon.

Bachner trudged through the door a few minutes later, with two loaves of bread and a head of cabbage with drooping leaves. "You would think I was buying golden bread and silver cabbage for what these cost me."

"Willi," Cesia interrupted, looking uncharacteristically pleased with herself. "Don't carry on so. We have visitors." She spread her hands toward the couch.

Bachner turned. His confused expression soon gave way to a surprised look of recognition. "Mama, Papa! What are you doing . . . I mean . . . How did you get here?" He didn't wait for a reply but gathered both his parents into a wide embrace. Next, he turned toward the boy, still seated on the couch, smiling shyly up at his older brother. It had been so long since Willi had seen those wide round eyes staring trustingly up at him.

"Bruno." He pulled his brother off the couch into a rough embrace. "You must have grown a foot since I saw you last." Willi held his brother so tightly that the boy tried to wriggle free, complaining that he couldn't breathe.

Willi sniffed, blinking the tears from his eyes before his young brother could see the desperate relief washing over him. He hastened to clear the dark cloud from the air, to change the atmosphere to one of celebration.

"I almost forgot, Bruno. Congratulations on your Bar Mitzvah! How does it feel, Mama, to know your baby is a man now?"

"It makes me feel very old, but not as old as it does to have a married son and to think about soon being a grandmother," Helena Bachner replied with a wink at Cesia.

"Speak for yourself, Mama. I am not old. I get younger every day."

"Congratulations to you both," added Bachner's father, Heinrich. "But what was the hurry, you couldn't have waited for your family to come to your wedding?"

Bachner put his arm protectively around Cesia. "Don't blame me, Papa, it's the Germans who convinced us not to wait. You know what they say here in Warsaw, 'Hitler is a *schatchen*.'" Hearing Hitler described with the Yiddish word for matchmaker caused them all to break into laughter.

"So, tell me, what made you decide to come to Warsaw?" asked Bachner. "Not that I'm not glad to see you." He held up a hand. "But your last letter said that you had moved to Osweicim."

"What choice did we have but to go there when all the Jews were forced out of Bielsko?" asked Heinrich. With a groan, the elder Bachner settled back onto the couch, patting the seat at his side for Willi to join him. "You remember our cousins there? We stayed with them."

"They were wonderful," said Helena. "They even helped us with Bruno's Bar Mitzvah."

Heinrich agreed. "They said 'War or no war, a thirteen-year-old needs his Bar Mitzvah.' But a few weeks ago we were told that we must leave again. The Nazis are building one of their prison camps at the old army artillery barracks outside of town. It's not even Osweicim anymore." Willi's father rolled his eyes. "It is to be a German town with a nice German name, Auschwitz. So, where should we go? We go to Warsaw to see our son, the famous engineer."

"Hardly famous, Papa, and not even much of an engineer anymore. More like a street sweeper or a bricklayer." He gestured toward the bread and cabbage. "Or a scavenger of food. For Jews, life is not so good in Warsaw these days."

"Nor in Bielsko," said his father, shaking his head.

"You should have seen them, Willi," Bruno said, overcoming his initial shyness. "All of our neighbors, the parents of my friends from school." The young boy shrugged his shoulders. "At least I thought they were my friends, they came day after day to our house to buy everything. 'Oh, isn't it too bad you Jews must leave! You can't take all these things. Let us help you, we'll buy them from you!' they'd say, like it was the marketplace or something." The torrent of words came to an abrupt halt as he added despondently, "Only no one in the market would have sold them for what we got."

"All of our things, Willi," his mother said, her voice breaking and her eyes filling with tears. "They said they were buying them, but we had no choice. Even if they didn't pay us. Everything our family's had for generations . . . all that is left is what we could carry away on our backs. These few bags are all we own in the world."

Willi noticed for the first time that his mother's hair no longer had the dark, healthy brown sheen he remembered. What had been mere streaks of grey when he left home such a short time ago now bled together like rivers of despair washing over her.

"Now don't start again, Helena. You can't change anything now. What's done is done," said Heinrich. "Now we have to find some place to stay."

"You will stay here, of course. We have four whole rooms. We practically get lost in them, don't we, Cesia?"

"Yes, you must stay with us," Cesia said, although her hesitant tone told Willi that she found the prospect of living with unfamiliar in-laws somewhat intimidating. She smiled, nonetheless, as she graciously offered his parents more tea.

Helena returned the younger woman's smile, but placed a hand over her teacup.

"No, thank you, my dear." She shook her head.

Bachner hesitated before broaching the next subject. "Hilde and Anna?" he queried tentatively. "Is there anything new?"

Helena's smile faded to a look of worry as her husband related the last word on the two Bachner sisters.

"We got a letter from Hanka just before we left Bielsko," he said, using the family nickname for the elder Anna. "It turns out you aren't the only one with love in your eyes. She is married to a fellow named Salek Hirschhorn and they were moving to live with his people in the Ukraine, a village called Boguslav. As for Hilde . . . she wrote us in November to say that she had signed up to return to Poland and that she couldn't wait to get home. But since then," he held up empty palms, "nothing."

Bachner tried to reassure his parents that sixteen-year-old Hilde had probably heard about conditions for Jews in Poland and decided to remain in the Soviet Union. "You know Hilde, she and her violin could charm Stalin himself," he said, smiling.

Hilde's sunny disposition and musical talent always seemed to make her welcome wherever she went, but the reminder of the circumstances that had brought them together darkened the mood of the reunion. Bachner knew the storm clouds gathering over them could not be lifted by facile reassurances and forced smiles.

With feelings of joy over their reunion, and anxiety for those still far away, the new family members settled in. Willi and his father took whatever jobs they could to make ends meet. The elder Bachner's skills as a painter allowed him to get some work in the ongoing repair of Warsaw and so the family eked out its existence through the spring and summer of 1940.

Meanwhile, outside Warsaw, the Germans occupied more and more of the Continent. On April 9, they invaded Denmark and Norway and repelled the British, French and exiled Poles who tried to stop them. On May 10, the Wehrmacht, the German war machine, rolled over Belgium, Holland and France. Up until that time hardly a shot had been fired in the west. The British called it "the phony war," the Germans the Sitzkrieg, the "sit-down war." But the Sitzkrieg was replaced by the Blitzkrieg (lightening war). After the disastrous retreat of British forces at Dunkirk, the Germans turned toward Paris. A little more than a month after the invasion of France, the French capital was under the control of the German Army.

Warsaw learned of the German victories from both the occupier's propaganda and from clandestine reception of the BBC. The news only served to deepen the gloom. The French and British had been the fragile hook by which the Polish people had hung onto hope. Now any thoughts of a quick end to the war had to be forgotten. With the United States and the Soviet Union remaining staunchly neutral and Mussolini's Italy coming in on the side of Germany, the Third Reich was beginning to look invincible. On August 1, 1940, Governor Frank announced that the Jews of Krakow were to be dispersed to Warsaw and other Polish towns. During the first two weeks of August, nearly 30,000 Jewish inhabitants and refugees were forced to leave. One of these refugees soon joined the Bachners in Warsaw. Late one afternoon, a knock on the door of 54 Zlota announced the arrival of Bachner's eighteen-year-old cousin, Heniek Buchführer.

Heniek, with his bag slung over his shoulder and his cap clutched in both hands, seemed too large for the doorway as he stood peering down at his short uncle. "Hello, Uncle Heinrich, do you remember me? I'm Heniek, Leo's son."

"Of course, Heniek, come in, come in. Helena," he called to his wife, "it's Heniek, your brother's boy."

Helena dropped her sewing on the chair and hurried over to embrace the boy. "Heniek, what are you doing here? How did you find us? . . . Wait, your mother, where is your mother?" She stood on tiptoes, trying to look over her nephew's shoulder. "Is she coming too?"

"Give the boy a chance, Helena, he just got here." After beaming up at his nephew for a full five seconds, Papa Bachner pulled the boy into the apartment, sat him down at the table and took over his wife's questioning.

Heniek eagerly accepted the bread and tea his aunt bustled off to prepare for him.

"Mama is still in Bielsko. They allowed a few hundred Jews to stay. She did get your letter, though. That's how I knew where you were. How I got here is a long story—it will take all night, maybe two nights." He looked around at Cesia peering out of the back room and then inquisitively at his aunt and uncle.

"Oh, excuse me," apologized Helena, reaching over to pull her daughter-in-law into the room. "Cesia, this is my nephew Heniek. Heniek, this is Cesia, Willi's wife."

Heniek stood abruptly, nearly spilling his tea, as he awkwardly offered greetings to his cousin's wife.

"Willi has spoken of you often," Cesia said, smiling shyly. "I know he'll be so glad you are here."

Indeed, Heniek was one of Willi's favorite cousins and the affection was mutual. Willi admired the boy's ability to land on his feet no matter what the situation. He had seen him hold his own against Polish thugs who harassed Jews in Bielsko. It was no surprise that the burly youth could have found his way alone to the Jewish quarter of Warsaw.

That night after Willi returned home, Heniek filled the Bachners in on the events of the past year. Cesia served tea and thin slices of coarse, dark bread to the family members clustered around the kitchen table.

"When the Germans came to Bielsko, our neighbors told Mother to keep me inside." Heniek began. "Jews were being beaten and rounded up for work. But in October, the Germans said every Jew from seventeen to fifty had to report to the train station on the morning of the twentieth. Our neighbors, our *German* neighbors," Heniek raised his bushy eyebrows for emphasis, "knew I was there. I had to go." The young man took a sip of his tea before continuing.

"They told us we were going to Lublin to build camps for the Jews to live in. I thought we would go by train, but they piled us into trucks. When they ordered us out a couple hours later in Katowice, they made us walk through town to the train station. The townspeople spat at us and called us 'Jewish swine.'" Heniek lowered his eyes and nodded when his aunt drew an angry breath.

"At the station there were other Jews from Ostrava. They made Czech Jews leave too. Thirty of us in one freight car. We had no food, hardly any water. Anyone who complained was beaten. For three days we traveled east; no one knew where they were taking us. When we arrived at the Nisko train station near Lublin, we thought we would be taken to work, but no, the SS had other plans."

Cesia stopped trying to force more tea on Willi's cousin and sat down beside her husband, reaching for his hand.

"We got out of the train. Some of us could hardly stand. The Nazis surrounded us and one officer said, 'Jews! At the order of

Heinrich Himmler you have been sentenced to death.'" Heniek's hand shook as he lifted his teacup; it clinked against the chipped saucer, the noise amplified in the silent room where no one dared to speak, even to breathe. The family waited as Heniek took a sip of tea, cleared his throat, and went on.

"'We are giving you your lives,' the Nazi said. 'Giving you your lives,'" Heniek repeated, shaking his head in disbelief. "'But first, any valuables—gold, diamonds, money you must hand over immediately. Anyone found with these items will be shot.'" Wilhelm sat stiff-backed listening to his cousin's story, his face impassive. He could not allow the emotion surging through him to show for fear of frightening his wife. Cesia's small hand had turned ice-cold in his. An icy fear coursed through Willi as well, but it was accompanied by a red-hot anger that threatened to flush his cheeks.

"We had five minutes to turn over these valuables," Heniek continued, "and six hours to get to Russia. We were at a station in the middle of nowhere, with forest all around us. One of the Ostravans said to us, 'Boys, I will lead you. Follow me!'"

"As we ran into the forest, we heard shots. I—I turned to look." A sob caught in Heniek's throat; his eyes glistened.

Bachner again felt anger surge through him; he had never seen his bear of a cousin reduced to helplessness. Never. Not in all the years of their youth. He silently handed Heniek his handkerchief. After a moment, Heniek collected himself enough to continue.

"Two people from Bielsko lay dead a few feet behind me. One of them—his face, it was gone. The SS shot them. Like animals." Heniek shuddered; he paused for breath.

"So then?" prompted Willi, hoping to distract his cousin from the vivid, terrifying memory. "You were in the forest, what then?"

"We fled deeper into the forests. We tried to stay away from the Germans. At the villages we bought food and asked for directions to the Russian border. Finally, at the end of November we got to Brest and crossed the border."

"Why in the name of all that is holy didn't you stay in Russia?" interrupted Heinrich. "You would be safe there."

"Uncle," Heniek patiently explained, "I tried. Three times I tried. Three times I crossed into Russia. The first time we met some militia. They even spoke Yiddish. A lot of good it did us. They put us in prison, asked us about German defenses. Two weeks we spent in dirty cells with rats, lice, fleas. Then they take us back to the border and say so nice to the Germans, 'Here are your Jews.'

"The Germans say 'We don't want Jews, we sent them to you.' And they laugh. But soon, the Russians march us across the border to Belzec. Twice more we cross into Russia, twice more we are caught and sent back. Well, I was getting a little tired of it. I felt like a football, being kicked back and forth across the border." His uncle nodded sympathetically.

"So," he shrugged, "I gave up and went back to Lublin. The Jews there were already wearing the yellow star. I spent seven days there and talked with people from Bielsko before I decided to go to Krakow. I knew some people there and I wanted to see Mama. So I started out on foot."

Bachner's neck muscles felt like iron as he listened tensely to the rest of Heniek's journey. At Deblin, the young man had to cross a German pontoon bridge—the old bridge had been blown up. He heard rumors that if the Germans caught Jews, they threw them into the Vistula River. Heniek got lucky; he had his identification papers from school carefully tucked in an inner coat pocket. The crumpled papers gave his name, but did not divulge that he was a Jew. The Germans reluctantly let Heniek pass and he went to Krakow.

"What about your mother?" queried Helena. Wilhelm noticed her hand tremble as she lifted her teacup to her lips.

"I last saw Mama in December," replied Heniek. "I was in a refugee center and had an appendicitis attack. Mama got permission to come and visit me for a few days. She brought what was left of my things." He added wistfully, "Since then, only a letter here and there when they manage to get through.

"I got a job at a factory in Krakow, at a dieworks. It was all right, I slept at the factory and had enough to eat. But earlier this month the Nazis said all refugees must leave Krakow and whoever stays will be sent to labor camps. So I wrote Mama and asked 'What should I do?' She said 'Go to Warsaw and find your aunt and uncle,' so here I am." He lifted his shoulders wearily, as if the world rested there. Willi felt that weight on his own shoulders as well.

Despite the fact that Heniek was the sixth person to crowd into the four-room apartment, the other five inhabitants found him a welcome addition. A sturdy and willing laborer, the young man frequently accompanied his Uncle Heinrich out of the Jewish section as the master painter's assistant. The family's financial situation vastly improved when Bachner managed, with the help of an engineering acquaintance, to get the painting contract for the rebuilding of the Italian Embassy in the center of Warsaw. Willi relaxed somewhat, knowing that now he, his father and his cousin could count on steady work for the next few months.

Around them, the walls continued to grow, yet German officials assured the Judenrat that there were no plans to construct a ghetto: the walls were for the Jews' protection. Nevertheless, as the walls went up, their shadow fell upon a nervous populace. Then, on August 7, the Warsaw Plenipotentiary, General Leist, issued a decree stating that Jews entering Warsaw could take up residence only within the walls, that Warsaw Jews could change residence only by moving into that area, and that non-Jews could not move there.

Warsaw Jews living outside the Jewish area were seldom given any choice about moving during this period. The practice of commandeering Jewish homes had become common. No longer content with merely removing selected items, the Germans now entered apartments at will, throwing out the Jewish owners with nothing but the clothes on their backs. These unfortunates had no choice but to enter the Jewish section and compete with the ever-increasing number of refugees for the scant charity of the Judenrat.

Czerniakow vocally protested increasing restrictions on Jewish movements, just as he sought to have Jewish funds released to pay for food and housing for refugees and workers. He was soon reprimanded for his outspokenness in a memo from the Gestapo: "On August 1, 1940, you allowed yourself to criticize the orders of SA Brigadier General Leist. May I call to your attention that any repetition of such conduct will be answered with the severest penalties."

Outside of Warsaw the war escalated; the Germans seemed unstoppable. Hitler had predicted that the British would seek a peace with Germany after the fall of France and stated that for all practical purposes, the war was over. But he underestimated the resolve of Winston Churchill and the English people. When Britain refused to surrender, plans were drawn up for "Operation Sea Lion," the German invasion of Britain across the English Channel.

However, the military's lack of enthusiasm for the prospect of attempting a sea invasion of the highly fortified island led to a strategic change in tactics. The Germans decided that an aerial bombardment of English cities would so demoralize the populace that they would surrender. So began the Battle of Britain and the London Blitz. The plans for an invasion were cancelled. Bombing of English and German cities became almost a nightly occurrence. The first anniversary of the war passed with the Führer in his Berlin bunker while RAF planes rained down death on Berlin.

Although London and Berlin were far away, the events outside Warsaw were keenly observed by its Jewish inhabitants. For the first time, the Germans had not rolled over their opponents as their Panzer tanks rolled over Europe. And for the first time, Germans were being killed in the very capital of the Reich.

On October 12, 1940, the Jews of Warsaw observed the second Yom Kippur of the war. Although congregational worship was forbidden, devout Jews attempted to conduct what observance they could in the privacy of their homes. Heinrich Bachner stood in the middle of the room, prayer shawl around his shoulders and prayer book in his hands. His wife, two sons and daughter-in-law stood at respectful attention as he recited in Hebrew the morning prayers for Yom Kippur:

> Not for ourselves alone do we pray,
> Not for ourselves alone,
>   but for all your children.
> Knowing all our failings,
>   let us be patient with those of others

> Knowing our will to goodness,
>> may we see in others a dignity that is
>> human, a beauty inviolate forever.
> Every soul, Lord, is precious in your sight,
>> and every life is your gift to us.
> Yet one stands poised to strike the next;
>> armies uproot vines and fig trees,
>> as war and war's alarms make us all afraid.
> God of pity and love, return to this earth.
> Go not so far away, leaving us to evil.
> Return, O Lord, return. Come with the d—

Papa Bachner stopped mid-word, his hand paused above the prayer book as heavy footsteps pounded up the stairs. Before he could expel his breath, Heniek crashed through into the room. "It's finally happened," he said between gasps. "The Germans are going through the streets with loudspeakers. There's to be a ghetto." Wilhelm started to speak, but his father interrupted.

"Heniek! I don't expect the Germans to leave us in peace on Yom Kippur," Papa Bachner said in a stern voice, "but I must say I expect better from you."

"Uncle," protested the young man, "it's terrible. Everyone is running around trying to figure out if they have to move. Even the Christians are going . . ."

"It can wait." Papa Bachner motioned Heniek to stand next to his cousins. Feeling like a young boy, Wilhelm stole a glance at Heniek, as though he could glean some information just by looking at him. His instincts told him to move, to head into the street to see what plans must be made to protect his family, but he forced himself to stand rigid.

The sounds of confusion on the street below fought for attention with the ancient Hebrew text as Papa Bachner once again turned to his book and continued calmly reading in Hebrew:

> Come with the light, that we may see once more
> Across this earth's uncomfortable floor
> The kindly path the old and loving way.

Let us not die of evil in the night.
Let there be God again, let there be light. . . .

Papa Bachner's final "Amen" hung in the air for a few seconds before Willi turned to Heniek. "Now, cousin," he said with an exasperated glance at his father, "what is happening in the outside world?"

The pent-up words spilled out in a rush. "The Germans say all Jews in Warsaw must move into a Jewish quarter by the end of the month. It's madness out there! Christians, Jews, everyone running around like chickens with their heads chopped off. They have to move out, businesses, homes, everything!"

"Where are they supposed to go?" Wilhelm asked, pulling up a chair to face Heniek, who had collapsed onto the couch.

"The Jews are trying to find houses here, in this quarter. The Christians must find homes in the Polish quarter." Heniek shoved a hand through his disheveled brown hair. "No one can move furniture, only what they can carry on their backs. We won't be able to leave the Jewish quarter unless we have a pass to work."

"But what about us, Heniek, where is the boundary?" asked Bachner, leaning forward. Cesia came up behind him and put a hand on his shoulder.

"No one knows for sure. There must be five different maps of the Jewish quarter. That's why everyone is going crazy out there."

"Heniek," said Bachner, separating every word to make sure his cousin understood, "do we have to move?"

Heniek glanced around. Bachner's gaze followed his cousin's; each face held a different version of the same worried frown. Willi patted Cesia's hand.

"Oh . . . us . . . well . . . um . . . I'm afraid so," he mumbled at first, then the words began to tumble out faster and faster. "You see, we just missed it, just by one street. Zlota will be the boundary. In fact the boundary will go right through the middle of this block. We will have to find somewhere else to live. The ghetto will be inside the walls that have been built so far. In this neighborhood that's Zelazna, Zlota and Zielna streets."

A sigh, somewhere between resignation and despair, rose from them as each family member realized that they would not be spared this particular hardship. Their four rooms on the third floor might be crowded and spartan, but they could do far worse. Now they would have to join the throngs of people frantically seeking new lodging.

"Well, Heniek," said Bachner, grabbing his coat and heading for the door, "let's go and see about your ghetto."

Bachner knew he had no time to waste. He knew a Christian building contractor who lived on Sienna Street, in what was to become the Jewish ghetto. If he moved fast enough, he might be able to manage a direct trade of accommodations. The apartment exchange was negotiated in short order, Bachner's acquaintance being more than happy to accept an exchange of similar flats in the same neighborhood.

The Bachners wasted no time arranging for a horse-drawn cart to move their sparse belongings the few blocks to their new quarters.

*　　*　　*

Those without Christian acquaintances or those who put off moving were not so lucky, but moving early was also risky. The Germans continued to readjust the ghetto boundaries even as people struggled to comply with the directives. A family might manage to find an apartment to move into, only to find that their new lodgings had been drawn out of the ghetto. With the stroke of a German pencil on a map, the search would have to begin again.

Over the next few weeks, utter chaos and misery swept through the Jewish quarter like a storm held within the bounds of Hitler's hastily built ghetto walls. The numbers involved created a kind of inertia in the midst of the furor—people milled about on the street, many with all the belongings they could manage to salvage piled high in their arms or strapped across backs bowed with despair, praying feverishly for God to grant them some small space to lay their heads. Of the nearly 400,000 Jews who lived in or near

Warsaw, approximately one-third lived outside the quarantine area of the "Jewish Quarter." During the six weeks that followed, 138,000 Jews hastened to fill the inadequate spaces in the quarter left by the 113,000 Christian Poles forced to move out.

The ghetto proclamations headed with the black eagle and swastika, which the Germans plastered on the sides of nearly every building, were quickly surrounded with small white cards advertising apartment exchanges between Christians and Jews.

A few days after the announcement, Willi and Heniek stood near the three-way intersection of Zelazna, Twarda and Zlota streets, observing the pathetic transmigration. They had little else to do; the city had virtually shut down as it tried to absorb and adjust to the latest German proclamation. German guards had been placed at the gate to the intersection. From their behavior one would have thought the people were traveling from one country to another rather than through familiar city streets.

The guards in their somber black uniforms demanded identification papers from everyone entering the gate, cross-examining all Jews to ensure compliance with Nazi directives. Failure to display the white arm band with the blue six-pointed star in the prescribed manner meant immediate arrest, and attempts to bring in forbidden furniture resulted in confiscation.

Most of those entering their new prison came with decrepit pushcarts filled with pots, pans, bedding and clothes; nothing the Germans would be interested in. Bored guards searched each cart nonetheless, throwing the meager belongings into the mud and debris along the road, frequently overturning entire carts, simply for the sadistic pleasure of watching the Jews scramble for their pathetic belongings. Having run the Nazi gauntlet, the "immigrants" had to begin another ordeal, the search for shelter. The area set aside for the Jewish quarter contained mostly apartment houses, separated by narrow streets with very little open space. Families pushed their carts along, stopping at every doorway with the same inquiry, "Have you any room?" The air was filled with the sounds of lost, crying children and frantic parents, those begging for food and those begging for shelter. A third of the city's population jammed into 2.5

percent of the area of Warsaw. By the end of October, 50,000 home-less Jews huddled in doorways and straggled along the streets of the new ghetto.

On November 4, word spread through the ghetto that Czer-niakow had been arrested. The Judenrat leader was held by the Ge-stapo at Pawiak Prison, a red brick fortress built in czarist times to house political prisoners. The Gestapo found its location in the cen-ter of the ghetto ideal for their purposes. The Germans charged Czerniakow with making disparaging remarks about the SS and ad-ministered a severe retaliatory beating and held Czerniakow over-night. Although barely able to walk, the Judenrat leader resumed his duties the following day. Despite the fact that he, too, had been forced to move, his apartment and belongings confiscated by an envious Pole, Czerniakow seemed determined to continue the struggle to lead his people, ignoring his own pain.

Twice, the Nazis extended the deadline for the exchange of populations, but the end of November was the final date. From that point on, the gates of the ghetto were closed to Jews unless they left under German guard. Those who left did so only to work in facto-ries in the "Aryan" sections of Warsaw, where they essentially worked as slave labor, receiving only miniscule pay but at least be-ing fed once a day. The markets outside the ghetto were closed to Jews and many common items disappeared from ghetto stores. Many Christian Poles brought bread for their Jewish acquaintances, but after several Poles were killed for throwing sacks of food over the walls, the smuggling of food became more difficult.

Czyste Hospital, the main Jewish medical facility, was found to be outside the ghetto boundary, as was Janusz Korczak's orphan-age. Neither was able to find comparable facilities in the ghetto. Korczak eventually exchanged facilities with a trade school on Chlodna Street and one day in late November marched his orphans under the orphanage's green banner to their new location, but not before the Germans confiscated the wagons of supplies Korczak had so painstakingly assembled. When he protested, he was arrested and charged with the additional crime of not wearing his arm band. Imprisoned in Pawiak Prison for a month before his release could be arranged by a substantial bribe, the selfless Korczak returned to the orphanage's new location, once again taking up his attempts to feed and clothe 170 Jewish children.

For Bachner, day by day the degradation grew. A proud man who did not consider his pride a flaw, he had always been slightly embarrassed by Jews who had not assimilated. He was ashamed to admit to himself that he probably had thought himself superior, with his stylish clothes and German manners. Now he realized that the Germans saw no distinction between him and a hassid, between an engineer educated at one of their own universities and an uneducated rag-seller from the Warsaw market.

Every time he had to step off the street to let a German pass, every time he struggled to find food for his family and every night when he returned to the crowded apartment where he and his wife had no privacy, he wanted to smash his fist into the arrogant face of the Führer, glaring down at him from posters plastered throughout the ghetto.

On Christmas Eve, 1940, Willi Bachner lay awake, listening to the sounds outside his window. The Jews were, of course, all in their homes as it was well past curfew. However, German revelers were not to be denied seasonal sport. Groups of drunken SS drove through the deserted streets yelling insults at the darkened buildings, shooting randomly. Bachner heard the tinkle of glass breaking in a window and the staccato ping of bullets hitting metallic surfaces.

"Peace on earth, goodwill to men," he thought ironically as Cesia stirred beside him in her sleep. What could he do? The question had grown in intensity until it almost consumed him. It was with him every waking moment and now plagued him long into the night as his eyes grew dry from staring into the darkness.

What could he do? How could he get out of the situation that fate and Adolf Hitler had put him into? How could he spare his family the daily indignities and the slow starvation that was the ghetto's only promise? He had never faced anything like this. He had sailed through life with his intelligence, charm and hard work, but this ghetto, this hatred of Jews . . . it would take more than an engaging smile and quick wit to conquer Hitler's racism—it would take courage. His courage had never been tested; the world had seemed in love with Wilhelm Bachner until now.

Now that he could no longer get engineering work on the outside, he would be forced to choose between legal unskilled labor or the illegal professions of smuggler and black marketeer. Neither provided any long-term hope. As a physical laborer at one of the camps, it was only a matter of time before his health failed and he succumbed to the poor diet and rampant disease of the ghetto. Unlike his tall cousin Heniek, he had never been very good at physical labor. As for the black market, if he chose that route, it would be only a matter of time before his luck ran out and he found himself on the wrong side of a firing squad. And then what would happen to Cesia, to his parents, to Heniek and to poor little Bruno? They all depended on him.

Before falling into a fitful sleep, Bachner realized he had no choice but to resign himself to God's will. "Help me think of something. Show me some way we can survive."

3 Out of Captivity

All her people groan, searching for bread;
   They give their treasures for food, to retain
   the breath of life,
Come all you who pass by the way, look and see
   Whether there is any suffering like my suffering.
                    Lamentations 1:11-12

The last week of December 1940, was bitterly cold in Warsaw. The snow in the ghetto was deep, but not deep enough to cover the squalor of too many people crammed into too small an area without adequate food or shelter. There were now nearly 400,000 people confined to about 22 square blocks, a population density of 146,000 per square kilometer.

The first weapon of the Germans had been the segregation of the Jews. Now they began to use their second weapon, famine. The German policy was clear. The vast bulk of the food produced in Poland was exported to Germany. The Poles were to be kept alive; the Jews were to get the leftovers. The official food ration for ghetto residents in late 1940 was around 800 calories a day, an allotment incapable of sustaining life without augmentation by food obtained illegally through the black market. Whatever food was available was sold at inflated prices, forcing the Jews who had any remaining assets to dig deeper and deeper into their ever-diminishing reserves of money and possessions in order to survive. The typical ghetto diet consisted of a few slices of dark bread, a grain-based cereal, a tiny amount of sugar and, occasionally, a small head of cabbage or a handful of potatoes.

The Germans seemed intent on extracting all wealth, labor and energy from Poland's Jews. In order to feed themselves, Jews were forced to work in German factories for little or no pay. Some labored day after day, knee-deep in rank, muddy water, digging canals and drainage ditches, only to return in wet clothes to unheated labor camp barracks at night. Jews had become the Reich's expendable labor force, to be used and abused until all vitality had been drained from them. Those who fell beneath the weight of their labors, sickened or died, were discarded like chaff in a wheat field, and others took their places.

As Wilhelm Bachner slowly navigated his way down Zelazna Street toward the marketplace, he couldn't help noticing that the plight of many ghetto inhabitants was far worse than his own. The Bachner's apartment was in the area known as the "Little Ghetto." Once a wealthy residential area, it had become home to prosperous Jews forced to move from the Aryan side. Bachner considered it very lucky that, despite his family's modest finances, he had been able to arrange to stay in this "affluent" neighborhood. Most Jews were crowded into unheated apartment buildings with as many as ten persons per room. Others had been unsuccessful in finding any sort of shelter and now were forced to brave the Polish winter out in the open.

The sight of the children bothered Bachner the most. He was forced to walk by them continuously: small, frail shadows of children, wrapped in filthy rags, holding out skeletal arms as they wailed their pleas for food or money. As Bachner came to the corner of Zelazna and Leszno, he was grabbed suddenly from behind.

A woman with vacant, sunken eyes and sour breath clung to his arm with surprising strength. "Please, sir," she entreated, "a few zlotys to buy bread for my son. He's so hungry, please, you must help me."

Bachner stared at the misshapen bundle of torn, dirty rags in the woman's thin arms. The child was dead, his arm outstretched in rigor, his skin a bluish grey. The child's dark eyes stared through the film of death toward the grey winter sky. Bachner's chest tightened until he could barely squeeze a breath past the pain, past the hopelessness of this mother whose mind would not allow her to see that her child was beyond help. Bachner pried her hand loose from his arm and placed a few zlotys in it, as much to relieve his own pain as to help the poor woman. Bachner hurried away, head down, trying not to see that it was the same on every corner: the children, the mothers, the emaciated men, crying out for assistance; the bodies of those who had ceased to call out and had succumbed to the cold of the Warsaw night. At this time in the morning, there were also the burial crews. The Chevra-Kadisha came every morning to collect those who had died in the last twenty-four hours. Bachner quickened his pace, trying not to see the emaciated bodies being lifted from where they had fallen in the streets and gutters. Old men whose toothless mouths hung open, young children whose round cheeks had sunken toward their prominent cheekbones—all were piled haphazardly on carts for an unceremonious trip to the overflowing Zydowski Cmentarz, the Jewish cemetery.

The dizzying sounds of wildly conflicting music accompanied the scene, a funereal concert played from the depths of chaos. On one corner a Hasidic cantor sang in Hebrew; down the block a man played a Mozart violin concerto; on still another corner, Yiddish folk songs intermixed with a classical aria. The vigorous entreaties of those who sought to stave off death by hawking whatever possessions they still owned—clothes, candlesticks, furniture, rags, arm bands with the Blue Star of David, half-baked bread and rotten onions, watches and old mattresses—assaulted the ear like some demented polyphonic symphony which increased in volume as Bachner drew nearer to the central ghetto market on Leszno Street.

The crush of the crowd grew more intense. Bachner could barely make his way; at times it seemed he was almost standing still. He could not help thinking of this daily ordeal as his penance for living so well, compared to others in the ghetto. The ghetto market was now the only place where the family could hope to obtain their meager amounts of food. Hoping to spare Cesia and his parents, Willi and Heniek had taken responsibility for daily "shopping." Had there really ever been a time when one could stroll leisurely into bright, well-stocked shops, chat with friendly merchants and go on one's way? The memory seemed more incredible every day. And then, he saw her. Her blond hair caught his eye at first, the pale gold a vivid contrast to the monochromatic grey-brown of the ghetto. The child who clutched her hand had the same flaxen curls spilling out of her hat and down the back of her navy wool coat. It was not unusual for Christian Poles to come to the ghetto to snatch up bargains to sell at a profit on the Aryan side, but this woman was so striking that the melee of the crowd seemed to part a bit to allow her to advance. As she turned his way, their eyes met and recognition dawned.

"Annia!" His mouth formed the name, but the ghetto noise swallowed the sound. It was his cousin, his Jewish cousin, Annia Meyer. She wore no arm band, and he realized that she was "passing," playing that dangerous game of avoiding confinement to the ghetto by masking her Jewish identity. She gave him a warning look that silently pleaded for him not to approach her under the concentrated scrutiny of the two ghetto policemen in the market. He nodded his understanding and drew back into a doorway, all the while keeping her in sight. He drew from his pocket a scrap of paper and hurriedly wrote his address on it; then he emerged from the doorway to examine a stall containing small household articles.

"How much for these candlesticks?" he inquired, putting his palm on the counter. As he pretended to be surprised at the exorbitant price and made an attempt to bargain with the merchant, Annia came up beside him and began to finger some tattered linens. Bachner good-naturedly told the merchant his prices were fit for nobility while his goods were fit only for beggars and turned away, leaving a slip of paper on the counter. As the merchant turned to another prospective customer, Annia reached up and snatched the paper, put it in her pocket and strode away from the stall as well.

Shortly after a meager supper that evening, Bachner responded to a tentative knock on the door. Annia quickly entered the apartment along with her child. Helena pushed past her son to be first in line to hug her niece, but Annia had to run the gauntlet of warm, welcoming embraces from all her relatives before they allowed her to take a seat on the couch. "I don't have long," she said, declining Cesia's offer of tea. "I must be out of the ghetto before curfew." No Jew was allowed on the streets between the hours of 9 p.m. and 5 a.m. Last spring the running joke was that the Prophet Elijah had gone to Krakow to get a pass to allow him to be on the streets on Passover. If Annia were to return to the Aryan side, she would have to do it at a time that would not raise suspicions.

"Annia, what are you doing here?" asked Bachner, "How did you manage to stay outside the ghetto?"

"I came to Warsaw last summer," she replied. "A friend helped me." The attractive Annia had never lacked for "friends," and had more than one Polish boyfriend.

"He got me a job as a governess for a rich Polish family. I have Aryan papers, nobody knows who I am. At least they didn't. Lately, they've started asking me all kinds of questions about my background. I think they are getting suspicious."

"What are you going to do?" asked Bachner. Annia's dilemma was much the same as the one which had been plaguing him for weeks.

"I've already done it. I quit yesterday. I heard that a German architect was looking for a secretary. So I went to his office this morning and applied. He has just arrived from Dresden to do repair work for the German Army. He gave me the job; I start tomorrow."

Annia crossed her legs and rested her hands on her knee. "That's why I was able to come shopping in the ghetto today. What a coincidence I should see you here." She smiled warmly at her cousin.

For a time, the talk diverted to catching up on the whereabouts of various relatives and the hardships they had endured since the war began. Suddenly Annia turned to Bachner, "Willi, you should get a job there."

"Outside the ghetto?" he asked incredulously. "How?"

"It isn't so hard," she replied. "You speak German, you don't look that Jewish . . . and you have that fancy engineering degree from a German university. What could be more perfect?" She spread her hands expansively. "Believe me, this Johannes Kellner will hire you in a minute. I get the idea he's not the most organized person in the world and he'd welcome some help."

Helena protested that it was too dangerous and Cesia agreed with her mother-in-law. But Bachner dismissed their fears. "What choice do I have? We can't go on the way we have been. Annia, how do you get in and out of the ghetto?"

"That, I know," interjected Heniek. "Getting in is easy; it's getting out that's hard. But I heard you can bribe one of the foremen on the detail that works on the Aryan side. I don't know that you'd want to do it too often."

"I'll worry about that later. First I must get the job. Tell me Annia, what should I do?"

"Wait a few days," said his cousin, "then come in and apply. The address is Ulica Flory 5. When you come in you must pretend that you don't know me. Just ask him if he needs an engineer." Annia gathered up her coat and took her daughter's hand. "Now I must go. It's been wonderful to see you. I hope I can come back again; you're all the family I've got in Warsaw."

With a flurry of hugs, she was gone. All that remained was a scent of hope that maybe, possibly, their situation would improve. Bachner had prayed for something to happen. Now, maybe his prayers had been answered.

*　　*　　*

Shortly after New Year's Day 1941, Bachner decided to make his move. He relied on Heniek, who had more street contacts than he, to put him in touch with the Jewish foreman of a factory crew. Early one cold clear morning, his diploma in his coat pocket, Bachner waited at the assembly point with the other workers. He slipped the money into the foreman's hand when no one was looking, then inserted himself into the line of workers. Out they marched, past the Jewish policemen at the Twarda gate through the opening in the three-meter-high walls topped with barbed wire, past the bored Polish policemen on the Aryan side.

Once outside, Bachner continued to march along with the workers until they came to a row of bushes at the side of the road. There Bachner slipped out of line and into the foliage on his left. If they noticed at all, the workers gave no sign, but continued to plod along toward a day of hard work in a German factory.

Bachner waited for a few moments to make sure no one had noticed his divergence, then, removing his arm band and stuffing it in his coat pocket, he emerged from the bushes and proceeded down the street. He had dressed carefully for this interview: his dapper black suit and starched white shirt made him feel like his old self as he strolled toward Ulica Flory. Warsaw was a busy city, full of Poles and Germans, but after the crowded ghetto, the city's streets seemed positively deserted. This added to the sense of freedom that Bachner felt in his first excursion into the Aryan side since autumn.

He worried a little, as he walked down the street, that the casual glances he exchanged with passersby might somehow reveal that he was Jewish. Could they tell? If he looked furtive, it might make him more suspicious. He tried to remember what it was like to walk down a street and not think about being a Jew. He took a deep breath, squared his shoulders and tried to walk with more confidence. Of course they cannot tell, he told himself. He could fit easily into one of the Teutonic subsets that had been concocted by Nazi proponents of racial purity. Not the ideal blond, blue-eyed "Nordic," but perhaps the "Eastern Baltic" or "Dinaric" types he had seen on Nazi posters which defined acceptable physiognomy. He was German, he told himself. He must walk like a German, talk like a German and think like a German. And so, full of Germanic reassurance, he walked up the steps to No. 5 Ulica Flory.

Annia flashed him a brief smile as he opened the door to the office. "May I help you?" she asked in Polish.

"Good morning, Fräulein," Bachner answered in German. "I am here to inquire about employment."

"Just a moment. I will tell Herr Kellner."

That proved unnecessary; Kellner, hearing the exchange, came out of his office. Tall and slightly balding, the imposing Architekt Kellner walked with a limp. Bachner noticed that ironically his prospective employer did not look German at all. With his receding jet-black hair combed straight back and swarthy complexion, Kellner looked less Aryan than either Wilhelm or Annia. Kellner looked down at the much shorter Bachner. "Yes? What is it?"

Bachner straightened himself and made a precise bow. "Good morning, Herr Architekt. My name is Wilhelm Bachner and I am a structural engineer." He paused to pull out his diploma, hoping that it had not been wrinkled in his trek out of the ghetto. He unrolled the document and presented it to Kellner. "I was wondering if perhaps you needed the services of an engineer."

"Hmmm . . ." Kellner perused the diploma, "University of Brno. You are German?"

"No, Herr Architekt, I am Polish." Bachner knew if he admitted to being German he would have to explain why he wasn't serving in the Army. "I grew up in Bielitz," he added, using the German name for Bielsko. "But I speak perfect Polish as well. I would very much appreciate having the chance to once again work as an engineer."

"Well, Herr Engineer," said Kellner, "do you know anything about painting?"

"But of course," Bachner said. "My father was a master painter. I have worked with him since I was a child."

"In that case, you are hired. Our firm is to build and paint a new barracks for the Luftwaffe at the Warsaw airport. I am to go there tomorrow to make an estimate. Be here first thing tomorrow morning." With that, Kellner turned and limped back into his office.

"Yes, Herr Kellner, thank you," Bachner called to his retreating back. With a grin and a silent nod of thanks to Annia, he left the office, feeling lighter than he had in months.

*   *   *

The next morning found an eager Wilhelm Bachner at the Kellner office waiting for his employer to arrive. Upon his arrival, Kellner acknowledged Bachner, gathered up a few papers and set off for the tram with his new employee in tow.

When the train arrived, Kellner boarded the front car reserved for Germans and Bachner entered one of the rear coaches. Before long, the conductor came down the aisle asking for tickets. Bachner's hands went cold and clammy as he fumbled in his pockets. Not only did he have no ticket, he had no money either. He tried to explain to the Polish conductor that he was with a German in the front car and that his boss would pay for him. The skeptical conductor refused to accept Bachner's story, probably afraid that an attempt to coerce money from an unknown German could only bring trouble. Bachner, equally afraid that he would be thrown off the train and lose his new job, pulled a pen out of his pocket and offered it to the conductor. The man accepted the pen as payment, pocketed it and moved on.

When the train arrived at the arranged stop, Bachner hurried down the aisle, taking the two high steps down to the platform in one leap. He found Kellner waiting impatiently for him in front of the station. The architect limped toward a waiting car and Bachner kept pace, watching for any crack in his new employer's cool reserve. When they arrived at the Luftwaffe office at the Okecie Airport, Bachner took in the scene. All over the airport, workers shoveled dirt, hammered nails and filled in holes, reconstructing runways and buildings which had been heavily damaged during the attack on Warsaw.

Kellner wasted little time in the cramped office, and Bachner followed behind him, listening carefully as his boss discussed the painting of the new barracks with a Luftwaffe Oberleutnant. For the first time since the war began, Bachner found himself completely surrounded by Germans. The sight of so many uniforms with swastika arm bands and black boots undermined the sense of confidence that he had felt when he set out that morning. Suddenly realizing his vulnerability, he began to imagine the worst. If they discovered who he really was, they would not waste time transporting him back to the ghetto. They would make an example of him on the spot.

At that point, Kellner turned to him, gave him a folding ruler and ordered him to begin measuring. Bachner stepped over to a wall and fumbled with the measuring stick. In his haste, he broke the tool in half. Kellner shot Bachner a withering glare while the officer chuckled condescendingly. Muttering about Polish incompetence, Kellner pulled another ruler from his back pocket and handed it to Bachner.

With a deep breath to steady his pounding heart and shaking hands, Bachner began to measure. Tentative at first, he called out the first few numbers for Kellner to record. By some sort of unspoken agreement, the estimates of the area to be painted became somewhat inflated. The Luftwaffe officer was oblivious to what was going on and Bachner, seeing a hint of a smile on Kellner's face, became bolder. In the end, he had an estimate of an area nearly twice the size of the actual barracks.

"Well done, Herr Engineer," said Kellner as they left the airport. "Well done indeed."

*   *   *

Back at the office, Kellner told Bachner to arrange for Polish workers to construct the barracks and to obtain materials necessary to complete the job. Bachner saw the chance to ease his way in and out of the ghetto. He explained to Kellner that he had heard that brick from demolished buildings and other building materials were available at a much cheaper price in the Jewish ghetto. Perhaps if his employer could give him a pass to move in and out of the ghetto, he could increase the profit margin. Kellner agreed and drew up the necessary documents. Bachner lost no time disposing of his old identity card and replacing it with his new work papers.

He was now free to enter and leave the ghetto as an Aryan. The ghetto guards soon came to recognize him and let him pass. Once inside, he would slip his arm band on and become a Jew again, blending in with the crowd. Each night he returned to his family, usually bringing with him some food—a small slice of pork fat or a few eggs—or some household necessity, such as a cake of coarse soap, which had become more and more difficult to find inside the ghetto walls. He even managed to pay Heniek a small amount for helping him keep track of the materials the Kellner firm purchased.

Bachner continued in this fashion for several weeks, supervising the painting of the airport barracks during the day and returning to Sliska Street every night. Then, one day in February 1941, as the airport project was drawing to a close, Kellner called him into his office.

"I want to tell you, Herr Bachner, how satisfied I am with your work."

"Thank you, Herr Architekt," responded Bachner. "I am enjoying the work very much."

"Yes, well, that is why I called you in here. Our work at the airport will be concluded in a few days. I will have to close the office here and return to Dresden."

Seeing Bachner's crestfallen look, he added, "You are an excellent worker. I wish I could take you back with me, but it isn't possible."

Bachner felt as though the wind had been knocked out of him. Things had looked as if they were going to work. But now, he would have to return to the squalid ghetto once again. Frantically his mind raced to come up with a way to forestall this catastrophe.

"Herr Architekt, why don't you organize a construction firm yourself here in Warsaw? There is plenty of work to do for the German Army and far less competition than in Dresden. Just think of how successful it could be."

"That's all well and good," responded Kellner, "but how can I do that? I would need workers and tools. All I have is you and a secretary. I wouldn't know where to begin." Bachner could see that the prospect of high profits was intriguing to Kellner. He also knew from Annia that Kellner did not get along well with his wife and his in-laws in Dresden.

"Don't worry," he reassured Kellner, "I'll take care of everything for you. I'll go to the Arbeitsamt (the labor office) and get construction workers. I know how to handle these Polish workers, they're a rough lot, but I can handle them. You need tools, I'll get you tools and at a good price too. You arrange the jobs, I'll take care of the rest."

Kellner was, at this point, living the charmed life of a German in Nazi-occupied Warsaw. He had his pick of apartments in some of the most elegant neighborhoods. He already had a young Polish mistress to whom he had become quite attached. In short, he was more than willing to forestall a return to Dresden. And if there was a profit to be made, all the better.

"Well, Bachner, I suppose it can't hurt to try."

*　　*　　*

With Kellner's German contacts and Bachner's Polish ones, the new firm, Reichsdeutsches Bauunternehmen, Architekt Johannes Kellner, was immediately profitable. Bachner, who went from being an hourly employee to a salaried one, began to assume more and more responsibility for the day-to-day operations, while Kellner's role was primarily one of interacting with the German authorities. The site of the second major contract was near Bialystok, northeast of Warsaw. The city was itself in Soviet hands, having been ceded to the USSR by the terms of the Hitler-Stalin Pact. The Luftwaffe was constructing a new airport near the border. The Kellner firm was officially declared *kriegswichtig*, important to the war effort, making it easier to obtain materials and travel permits, and deal with all the other impediments set up by the bureaucratic occupying government. Bachner became the firm's Bauleiter, or supervisor. He began to hire, not only manual laborers, but skilled workers and engineers as well. The job near Bialystok required about fifty workers, who were housed in barracks. Bachner, for the most part, remained at the construction site, but also made frequent trips back to Warsaw for supplies, and to keep Kellner appraised of the job's progress.

Although the firm flourished and Bachner prospered, he remained far from satisfied; he continued to look for any opportunity that would help him to improve his family's situation. Once again, it was Annia Meyer who gave him an opening.

During the second spring of German occupation, Annia gave Kellner notice that she was leaving. Privately, she told Bachner that her Polish lover was moving to Krakow and wanted her to go with him. Bachner immediately offered to find a replacement for Annia.

He suggested to Kellner that, given the increasing business and the number of employees, it might be time to hire two office workers to replace Annia. Kellner affably told Bachner to take care of it.

Bachner did not have to look very far, for he already had two men in mind, two Jewish men. Adolf Stamberger was an accountant and a Bielsko native whom Bachner had visited often when he first came to Warsaw. He was married to a German Christian and was living outside the ghetto under the name Andrzej Staniecki. His son-in-law, Julek Schwalbe, a Jew married to Stamberger's half-Jewish daughter, was "passing" as Juljusz Stroynowski. Both were tall, blond and blue-eyed and spoke Polish without a trace of accent. Both had the credentials to satisfy Kellner. As the bookkeepers of the firm, they had the job of making out work papers for all Kellner employees. A plan began to form in Bachner's head, a contingency plan to save his family if conditions in the ghetto should worsen. He wasn't sure yet what he would do, but he knew that having the ability to provide false identity papers would greatly enhance his chances of success.

*　　*　　*

In early June 1941, having completed the reconstruction of the Bialystok airport, the Kellner construction crew returned to Warsaw. That evening, as Bachner entered the ghetto through the Leszno Street gate, he couldn't help noticing that conditions had deteriorated. He found the smell the hardest thing to block out. A stomach-churning over-ripeness permeated the air. The smell of rotten food and disease combined with the smell of decomposing corpses in doorways, propped against walls in alleys. This, on top of the smell of hundreds of thousands of people with no place to bathe or wash their clothes, took Bachner's breath away. During the spring, an additional 72,000 Jews had been forced from the countryside into the Warsaw ghetto. Bachner pulled a kerchief from his pocket to hold over his mouth and nose as he hurried along the street.

Deaths in the ghetto had now reached one hundred fifty per day. The cemetery overflowed and there was talk of building a crematorium. German sightseers came to the ghetto like carrion crows

to gawk and take pictures of skeletal corpses stacked in sheds awaiting burial. Treatment of the Jews in the labor camps had so deteriorated that a large-scale irrigation project to be built with Jewish labor that spring had to be abandoned. Inadequate food, shelter and
sanitation, and overwork in the camps forced the death toll so high
that camps outside Warsaw were closed in June. No one seemed to
move quickly anymore. The only sparks of activity came from the
thin, grimy children who were always there in the shadows, ready
to snatch a piece of bread from the hands of the unwary. As he made
his way home, Bachner joined the shuffling mass of people trudging through the oppressive June heat. He found himself shuddering
away from the emaciated, foul bodies that pressed against him. It
bothered him greatly that he was reacting to his own people this
way. Could it be that he was being contaminated by his daily contact with Nazis? With relief, he reached the less crowded Little Ghetto
area and made his way to 33 Sienna Street. It turned out to be a
double homecoming, as Heniek had just returned from a road construction job at Milejow near Lublin in eastern Poland.

Willi and Heniek spoke of their respective jobs, the dull but
adequate food and the difficulty of working under Germans who
were constantly admonishing them to work faster.

"I don't know what the big hurry is," said Heniek. "It's not
as though there aren't already roads and airports in the east. It seemed
like every day there was some Nazi big shot there slapping his little
stick against his boots and haranguing the foreman to make the 'Jewish swine' work faster."

"Something is up," replied Bachner. "Around the construction site there are rumors of an attack in the east."

"Russia? Why would they fight Russia? They have a treaty.
They're working together. Remember when I was in Belzec, the
Russians turned us over to the Germans. They divided Poland be-
tween them, why fight now?"

"Just because they both hate Jews doesn't mean they love
each other." Heinrich chuckled. "After all, everybody hates us."

"Willi may be right," Heniek said. "No sooner had we finished the road when here came tanks, soldiers, artillery. . . . What
happened to Hitler and Stalin's treaty?"

Bachner shrugged. "Treaty or no treaty, Hitler hates Communists and he hates Slavs. Russians are both of these. Stalin shouldn't be sleeping too easy at night."

*   *   *

Anyone familiar with Hitler's manifesto, *Mein Kampf*, knew that Hitler viewed Russia as a site for German colonization, or lebensraum. To Hitler and the Nazis, Russia equaled Bolshevism which equaled Jewry, and there was no distinction. "If we want to rule," Hitler claimed, "we must first conquer Russia."

In fact, the east was Hitler's true objective; his campaign against western Europe was primarily to secure his rear before he turned to his primary objective, the Soviet Union. The British, French and Dutch were enemies to be sure, but they were, after all, fellow Aryans who needed to be shown the light. France, Denmark, Norway and the Benelux countries had been conquered and Hitler was sure, despite England's stiff resistance, that an accommodation would eventually be reached with Churchill.

Planning for the invasion of the Soviet Union began in the summer of 1940. Neither the Army nor the Foreign Service were enthusiastic about such a campaign, but the former had been made fools of by Hitler for their misgivings in the French campaign and the latter had been largely discounted by Hitler as old regime reactionaries and carried little clout.

For his own part, Stalin proved to be an unwitting accomplice to Germany. In 1937, he instituted a purge against the Red Army, which he felt was becoming too independent of his control. Three of the five marshals of the Soviet Union were arrested. Thousands of officers were executed or sent to forced labor camps. The Army had begun to modernize, casting aside the practice of dual command, where both an officer and a party commissar gave orders. They had begun to augment Stalin's "offense-only" military strategy by planning defensive operations and training partisan units in guerilla warfare. All of this came to a halt with the purge of 1937–1940. Gone were the officers who were independent thinkers, unhampered by the chains of political ideology. Gone too were most of those who had waged successful campaigns during the revolutionary period. Those who remained were young and inexperienced or Stalin's sycophants. The purge was well-known to the Germans, as was seen in one strategist's comment, *"Die Rote Armee ist führerlos,* The Red Army has no leader."

Throughout the first half of 1941, Stalin refused to accept any evidence of Barbarossa, the German code name for the invasion. American, British and even Soviet intelligence provided concurring evidence of a planned German invasion. Stalin obstinately held that the capitalist world was determined to destroy the Soviet state and clung to the belief that Germany could be a useful ally, an attitude one historian characterized as "the triumph of preconceptions over reality."

Even when the buildup of German troops that Bachner and his cousin observed was confirmed by defecting German soldiers, Stalin refused to move to a defensive stance. Planes were not removed from open runways; western forces were not supplied with ammunition or supplies. All information about the probable German invasion was kept from the frontline commanders, who nonetheless were drawing their own conclusions based upon ground observations. Stalin had become absolute master of the Soviet Union, and had convinced himself that he was all-wise and all-knowing. It was impossible that he could be wrong.

But wrong he was. Early on the morning of June 22, 1941, German forces crossed the border into Russia along three separate fronts, decimating the ill-prepared troops in their path. Within the first eight hours, the Soviets lost 528 planes on the ground and 210 in the air. Within sixteen hours, two separate Soviet fronts had been broken through. Still, Stalin continued to give orders prohibiting retaliation, frantically trying to reach the German ambassador, who had suddenly become unavailable. When a change of orders finally came from the Kremlin, the exasperated front commanders found that it now called for an all-out attack. By that time any hope of an offensive maneuver was ludicrous. However, those who tried to tell the Kremlin were labeled "cowards, deserters and panic-mongers."

But try as he might, Stalin could not isolate himself from the reality of the Third Reich. The news of conquered cities came in to the Kremlin; the Wehrmacht shot straight for Moscow like a huge arrow. Lwów, a Polish city which had come under Soviet control after the Hitler-Stalin Pact in 1939, fell on June 19; the Ukrainian town of Berdichev on July 7; Zitomir on July 10; Smolensk, in Russia proper, on July 16. The leaderless Red Army was powerless to stop the advance.

In the wake of the German army came the other agencies of occupation, the SS, the civilian administrators and businessmen ready to make a profit. The Germans referred to the Soviet Union as "our India," and many who had not been very successful at home hoped to take advantage of the opportunities presented by the Nazi occupation of the Soviet Union.

One such individual was Johannes Kellner, who immediately applied and was accepted as a contractor for the Ukraine. So it was that news with which Kellner greeted Bachner one morning just as the events in the east became known in Warsaw.

"Good morning, Herr Engineer. I have good news. We are going to the Ukraine."

4 THE SNARES OF EVILDOERS

FOR TOWARD YOU, O GOD, MY EYES ARE TURNED;
    IN YOU, I TAKE REFUGE; STRIP ME NOT OF LIFE.
KEEP ME FROM THE TRAP THEY HAVE SET FOR ME,
    AND FROM THE SNARES OF EVILDOERS.
LET ALL THE WICKED FALL,
    EACH INTO HIS OWN NET, WHILE I ESCAPE.
                                    PSALM 141:8-10

The preparations for the job in the Ukraine kept Bachner occupied throughout most of the summer. Besides the presentation and approval of the designs for the barracks and support facilities, he had to arrange for the hiring of labor and the sending ahead of supplies. Bachner had also been busy arranging for the needs of his family during the months that he would be absent from Warsaw. Knowing that he would not be able to mail money directly to the ghetto without raising suspicion, Bachner arranged a go-between. A Jewish diamond merchant, named Ostrowski, was using a Pole to transport the diamonds he bought from Jews inside the ghetto to the Aryan side for sale. Ostrowski assured Bachner that the Pole, Tadeusz Kazaniecki, was completely trustworthy. He had a Jewish girlfriend who was the sister of Ostrowski's partner; he was devoted to her and determined to help in any way possible. Kazaniecki agreed to pick up money sent by Bachner to the Kellner office and take it to the Bachner family in the ghetto. It was decided that while Bachner was in the Ukraine, Cesia would go to live with her parents, who also were relying on Bachner's income for survival. Throughout the summer, Bachner returned to the ghetto nearly every night, entering the ghetto every evening as a Pole, assuming his Jewish identity by slipping on his blue and white arm band, and with the morning light emerging from the ghetto once again as a Pole.

On a morning in mid-August, Bachner followed his usual routine, removing his arm band, stuffing it in his pocket, greeting the now-familiar guards at the gate and making his way to the Kellner office. He had no sooner opened the door when he was summoned to his employer's office.

It took only one look at Kellner to know that something was very wrong. He limped back and forth behind his desk, wiping his ashen face with a large white handkerchief.

"What is it, Herr Kellner?" Bachner inquired. "What has happened?"

"I have just received a call from SS headquarters. Nieczajuk has been arrested. They say he is a Jew!"

The news that the firm's Ukrainian engineer had been arrested was just another reminder of the dangerous game that Bachner was playing. "But he's not! He may look like ten Jews but he's Ukrainian."

"Don't tell me, tell it to the SS, which is what he did, along with saying he works for me. That's probably the only reason he hasn't been shot. Now they want me to come down and identify him."

Kellner's pacing became even more furious, and the white handkerchief fluttered back and forth as he gesticulated. "Do you know what this means, to be called to the SS? What if they don't believe me, what if they accuse me of hiding Jews?"

With a sigh, Kellner ceased his pacing and dropped into his chair. "I cannot do it. Please, Bachner, he is one of ours, we cannot leave him to the Gestapo. You must go and get him."

Bachner found himself thinking, Oh, Herr Kellner, if you only knew what you are asking. The irony did not escape him of sending a Jew to the SS to negotiate the release of a Ukrainian because a German was too terrified to do it. He found himself struggling somewhere between a grin and a grimace as he realized what a dangerous task his boss had charged him with.

"Well, Herr Kellner, here is what you must do. Write a letter on the firm's stationery, identifying me as your head engineer and vouching for Nieczajuk's identity. I will go and try to get him out."

Kellner agreed, with great relief, and less than an hour later Bachner stood outside SS headquarters at 25 Szucha Avenue. There was little foot traffic in the vicinity of the grey stone building, with its huge red, white and black Nazi flag. People approaching from all directions would veer off when they came within a block of the place as though repelled by some mysterious physical force.

Bachner took a deep breath and once again attempted to cloak himself in a Germanic aura as he stepped across the threshold. His first obstacle was a supercilious sergeant who had found his true role in life in demeaning and turning away, whenever possible, those who worked up enough nerve to challenge the judgment of the Security Police. He was no match for Bachner with his perfect grasp of bureaucratic German and his document from Kellner. The sergeant sent Bachner upstairs immediately to wait for an audience with the Gestapo.

After a long, nerve-wracking wait in an almost deserted anteroom, he was ushered into the office of SS 2nd Lt. Brandt. With a click of his heels and a stiff bow he introduced himself. "Good morning, Herr Leutnant, there has been an unfortunate mix-up. As you can see from this letter from my employer, last evening one of our engineers, a Mr Nieczajuk, was arrested under the mistaken impression that he was Jewish. Herr Kellner has sent me to clear up this misunderstanding."

Brandt leaned back in his chair and regarded Bachner in silence. He glanced at the letter from Kellner, then tossed it back across his desk. "I don't care what you or your Herr Architekt say, the man is a Jew, any fool can see that."

"I assure you sir, he is not. He is Ukrainian, that is why he speaks no German and why he has an accent. Many Ukrainians are dark, surely you know this."

"You are wasting your time," replied Brandt, looking out the window and feigning boredom. "The Jew will remain here. You are dismissed."

Bachner sensed that Brandt had no real stake in Nieczajuk's fate. The Ukrainian was only one of the many seized for the crime of looking Jewish or having questionable identification. He also knew that Brandt had but to remove the man's trousers and expose his circumcision to prove he was Jewish. Unlike in Germany, where circumcision was fairly common for male infants, circumcision of Gentile Poles and Ukrainians was quite rare. But if this officious SS bastard didn't know what every Polish schoolboy knew, Bachner was not about to share that information with him. Realizing that Brandt was holding out only to avoid admitting an error, Bachner pushed a bit harder, exaggerating Nieczajuk's importance to the firm. He placed his hand on Brandt's desk and leaned toward him. "Herr Leutnant, our firm is preparing to depart for the Ukraine to construct a Luftwaffe airport. Nieczajuk's work is essential to the successful completion of this project. If he is not released, we shall have to find another engineer to replace him and delay our departure. Do you really want to be responsible for interfering with our work on behalf of the Luftwaffe?"

Brandt continued to look out the window, but Bachner knew the computation going on in his mind. If he released the engineer and he really was a Jew, Brandt could justify his actions by the fact that a German national had vouched for him. On the other hand, if he held the Ukrainian, Kellner could complain to his superiors that he was interfering with important work for the war effort. The choice was really quite simple.

"Very well, you shall have your 'Ukrainian.'" Brandt rose and called out to a guard outside to bring Nieczajuk up from his holding cell. He then returned to his desk and ignored Bachner while he busied himself with paperwork.

A few minutes later, the guard returned with a disheveled and frightened Nieczajuk. The little Ukrainian did indeed look like an anti-Semitic caricature, a fact that was not helped by his inability to speak a word of German. Upon seeing Bachner, he began to tell him in his heavily accented Polish what had happened, how he had been mistreated and how glad he was that Herr Kellner had finally sent someone to save him.

Bachner wanted to spend no more time than was absolutely necessary in SS headquarters. He managed to silence Nieczajuk, and expressed his thanks to Brandt, who waved them off without a word. They were down the stairs and out of the building as fast as they could manage without looking suspicious. It wasn't until they boarded a trolley that the two men relaxed. The conductor came by and asked for their fares. Bachner reached inside his pocket and felt the piece of white cotton with the blue star of David that had been there since he left the ghetto that morning.

"What is it, Bachner?" queried Nieczajuk. "You look like you saw a ghost. We're okay now. The time to be scared was back there."

"Oh, it's nothing," said Bachner in a hollow voice. "Just something I forgot I had in my pocket."

$$*\qquad*\qquad*$$

The train moved steadily eastward through the untended wheat fields baking under the September sun. Every so often, the pale sea of grain was broken by signs of the devastation of battle: tank tracks, bomb craters, burned-out trucks, mangled, unrecognizable pieces of metal, destroyed bridges or the remains of burned farms and villages. Then, just as suddenly as they had appeared, the evidence of the Nazi Blitzkrieg would recede and the fields would once again stretch toward the flat, distant horizon.

The Western Steppe rolled across the Soviet Union for over 2000 miles: from the base of the Carpathian Mountains in Hungary, through Ukraine to Russia, where it was separated from its eastern counterpart by the Ural and Altai mountains of Siberia. The Steppe had been both the savior and the bane of the Slavic peoples. It was ideal ground for grain cultivation and pasturage and had supported a large population since ancient times. However, it was also an ideal route for invasion both westward and eastward. The geography of the Steppe helped to explain Russia's paranoia about invasion from the west and it was the route taken by the German Army southward when it swept through eastern Ukraine in June of 1941.

Kellner had informed Bachner that the first contract for the firm in the Ukraine was to be the construction of barracks at a Luftwaffe base being set up in the town of Berdichev. The Kellner firm was subcontracting for a large German construction firm, Organization Todt, which itself was under the direction of Luftwaffen Bau Dienstelle, or Airforce Construction Service Unit. Although Bachner had never been to the Ukraine, he knew the town by reputation. Nearly half of the 60,000 people who lived in Berdichev were Jewish. It was the birthplace of the famous Rabbi Levi Isaac Ben Meir, who had introduced Hasidic Judaism to Poland. It was considered to be the quintessential Jewish town in Russian and Jewish literature.

As the train pulled into the Berdichev station, Bachner wondered how Ukrainian Jews were faring under the domination of the "Master Race." This issue overshadowed the anxiety he felt about once again having to work so closely with the German military.

Would he find a ghetto in Berdichev? What would be the fate of Soviet Jews, who were seen by the Nazis as doubly cursed for adding the sin of Bolshevism to that of their Jewishness?

Above all, he wondered about his two sisters. He had located Boguslav on the map before leaving Warsaw. It was an area southeast of Kiev, one which was currently being overrun by German forces. Bachner knew he would be less than a hundred miles away and wondered how he might be able to justify a trip to the front to see his sister Anna. As for Hilde, the best he could hope for would be to make some discreet inquiries in Lwów.

The confusion of organizing the Polish workers recruited by the Kellner firm in Warsaw and of arranging for the transport of supplies piled high at the station left little chance for Bachner to search out answers to his questions before the short ride to the airport site. Having arrived in late afternoon, he was advised by the Luftwaffe supervisor that they would be given the evening to settle in, but that they would be expected to start work in the morning.

Bachner felt entirely alone in alien surroundings. At least outside Bialystok he had been in Poland, and only a few hours from Warsaw. He always thought that if he were discovered, he would simply melt into the countryside, where his Polish and Gentile looks would serve him well. Now he was hundreds of miles from his family in a foreign land, where he didn't speak the language and where the flat, open landscape would make escape difficult. He realized he would have to increase his already intense vigilance to come through this one safely. There would have to be no more chances like the one he had taken a few days before he left Warsaw. No more reliance on blind luck.

Now, in his bunk in Berdichev, Bachner re-experienced the same wrenching fear he had felt when he realized he had gone into SS headquarters with a Jewish arm band in his coat pocket. He remembered how, as soon as he got back to the Kellner office, he had gone to the lavatory and burned his arm band, and flushed the ashes down the toilet, vowing never to wear another, never to place himself in that kind of danger, never to forget just how tenuous was his hold on life.

The next morning Bachner organized his crew and reported to the construction site. They were a coarse-looking group, their appearance as rough as their language. Those who willingly sought work in occupied Ukraine usually had a good reason for wanting to leave Warsaw: aggressive creditors, the police a little too close on their trail or simply a sharp-tongued wife. Although he spoke Polish with a German accent and was much smaller in stature than most of them, Bachner still commanded respect, and he had the reputation of being a fair boss who took care of his workers.

Bachner found their Luftwaffe liaison to be a rare breed, a boisterous and cheerful German. Oberleutnant Hans Gregor greeted Bachner with a slap on his back and a huge grin. The two of them went over the blueprints for the barracks and Bachner proceeded to instruct his workers in Polish. Throughout the day Gregor returned from the other building sites at the airport to check on their progress and confer with Bachner.

Suddenly, during one of these conferences, Gregor turned to Bachner and said, "Tell me, Herr Engineer, where did you study that you learned both perfect German and Polish?"

Bachner was forced to make one of those calculations as to whether he should lie or tell the truth, one of the hundreds that someone who was "passing" was forced to make in a split second, weighing the potential consequences without looking as if he were hesitating. He decided to go with the truth.

"I received my degree from the Deutsche Technische Hochschule in Brno."

"*Mensch!*" exclaimed Gregor in delight. "We studied together! When did you finish?"

"In '38," said Bachner, "How about you?"

"'35. I can't believe it! Do you remember Hrach?"

"Of course, and his assistant Hrych." Bachner chuckled.

The two reminisced about professors both beloved and despised, and Gregor asked Bachner what student organizations he had belonged to. This time Bachner lied. He could hardly tell Gregor that he had belonged to the Zionist group Hashomer Hatzair.

"I was in Polonia," he said, all the while knowing how the intensely nationalistic and anti-Semitic group would have rejected him, not only for his Jewishness, but for his German roots.

"Ah yes, I remember them." Gregor nodded. He turned to one of his fellow officers who was walking by. "Hans! Look what I have here." He spread his hands. "This is Willi Bachner. We went to school together."

Bachner found himself shaking hands with another smiling German while still trying to calculate if his disclosure would help or hinder his chances for survival. He needn't have been concerned. Gregor's discovery of a fellow alumnus took on more significance because he too felt out of place in Ukraine. Bachner was a connection, albeit a tenuous one, to a happier and less turbulent time. The Oberleutnant continued to tell anyone who would listen that the little Pole was a friend of his from school. Bachner was gratified to see that all this attention being bestowed upon him by the Germans did not escape the eyes of the crew, who, even though they could not understand what was being said, realized that their boss was someone of no small importance.

Two weeks later, Kellner came from Warsaw to check on the progress of the project. He asked Gregor, "So, are you satisfied with the work of my Bauleiter?"

"I am most satisfied," exclaimed Gregor. "But what would you expect? We know each other from college and we college mates stick together, you know."

Kellner once again congratulated himself on finding such a splendid employee as Bachner. Not only was his firm bringing in more income than it ever had, and he was nearly completely free from the tedious day-to-day operations, but he had a Polish supervisor who managed to impress even the Luftwaffe. He rewarded Bachner with a raise—a small one, so that the engineer would not forget his place—and returned to Warsaw a happy man.

*   *   *

It was late October before Bachner learned the fate of the Jews in Berdichev. He had been searching for signs of the large and thriving Jewish community since his arrival. The only hint had been the ruins of a burnt-out synagogue near the center of town. But he had not spoken of it when he rode by with the Poles in his crew, and he had remained silent when he heard a few of them joke about it. Who could he ask—Hans Gregor?

No, he could ask neither his college mate nor any of the locals without his questions being met with others such as "Why do you want to know? What interest is it to you? Why do you care about what happened to the Jews?" But the unanswered questions nagged at him and he never stopped trying to find out.

The unwelcome answer came from an unlikely source. Bachner asked Gregor where he could get a haircut and was directed to an address near the center of town. He was puzzled at first when he approached the area. It was under guard, entirely surrounded by barbed wire. As he drew closer and noticed a few souls shuffling around in the yard, he saw why. They were Jews! Under guard in this mini-ghetto were skilled workers the Germans felt were necessary to guarantee a decent quality of life in this Ukrainian backwater: a tailor, a bootmaker, a blacksmith and a barber, all at the beck and call of the Nazi occupiers. Bachner fought the urge to rush up, pull one of these pale men aside and demand to know the fate of the Jews of Berdichev. Instead, he calmly informed the guard he had been told he could get a haircut here. He was shown into a little room with a barber chair tended by a small balding man with sad brown eyes. The barber said nothing, simply handed Bachner a hand-mirror and turned the chair to face the blank grey wall.

While the guard was still in earshot, Bachner instructed the barber on how he wanted his hair cut, but as soon as they were alone, he whispered to the man. "*Amchu*," he said in Hebrew, identifying himself as a Jew. He continued in Yiddish, "They do not know who I am. Please. You must tell me what happened to all of you."

The man, as if realizing that the time might be short and that this might be his only chance to let the outside world know what had happened in Berdichev, began to tell Bachner of the events of the past summer in a low voice as he cut his hair.

"The Germans came on July 7, early in the morning. First the soldiers, then the SS. They wasted no time rounding up Jews. The Ukrainians helped them. All of the men were rounded up and brought to the center of town. Anyone who refused was shot on the spot. The Ukrainians beat those who remained, raped the women and looted the houses.

"They made us lie face down in the dirt in the middle of the square. They went among us taking our money, our jewelry, even our clothing. Some of the Germans decided it would be great fun to trample on our bodies where we lay. We did not dare move, even when their boots dug into our backs. Anyone who tried to get up was shot or their heads bashed in with a rifle butt. Right in front of me was a man I knew. His skull was crushed; I could see his brains, his eyes were staring at me all day as I lay in the sun, without water. God! The smell, the heat, the flies, I cannot tell you . . ."

Bachner's entire body felt numb, as if all energy had been drained from his pores. He listened. Silence hung in the room for a long while to be broken at last by the clip of the scissors. Bachner felt the barber's hand tremble as he struggled to maintain control and continue his tale.

"They asked for all the doctors, lawyers and writers to stand and step forward. A lot of people stood up, they thought they might be able to save themselves. They were marched away. A short time later we heard shooting, shooting that seemed to go on forever. Then the Germans ordered all craftsmen to stand. What was I to do?" The insistent snip-snipping of the scissors stopped as the man shrugged. "I decided that being shot was better than dying face down in the dust staring at the smashed brains of my neighbor. When I told them I was a barber, they brought me to the prison. I stayed there for three weeks, in a dark hole.

"Then they brought me here and I have been here ever since, cutting their hair and shaving them, trying to decide if I should try to stay alive or just satisfy myself with cutting one of their throats before they kill me."

Bachner felt the sting of the towel against his neck as the barber slapped away the stray hairs on the back of his collar.

"But the others," interrupted Bachner, "what happened to all the others?"

"The few here in our little ghetto are all that remain of the Jews of Berdichev."

Bachner jerked around, causing the barber's scissors to rip an uneven clump from the hair on the right side of his head. The little man's dark eyes shone with unshed tears, but he clicked his tongue and turned the chair away. His scissors snipped the uneven area smooth.

"I have heard that some escaped. But the Ukrainians are no friends of ours. They see a Jew and they see money. The only reason they don't kill us outright is that the Germans won't give them any money for dead Jews. The rest . . . those that weren't killed by the Germans and Ukrainians on the first day were rounded up a few days later and taken outside of town. The men were forced to dig huge pits. Some realized what they were for and tried to escape or resist. They were killed." His voice held no emotion. In the hand-mirror propped on his knees, Bachner could see the old man's mouth working as he struggled to keep his wrinkled face from melting with grief.

"Then everyone," he continued, "from the oldest grandmother to the youngest babe was told to strip naked. They were lined up in groups, shot and kicked into the pit. Then the next group and the same thing. Some died not from the wounds but from being smothered by the bodies and the dirt the Nazis pushed into the pit when they were done."

"Did you see this? Are you sure?" asked Bachner.

"With my own eyes, I did not see this. It was told to me by another worker here. He came from a village to the east that was taken a few days after Berdichev. They would have shot him, but he is a blacksmith. Since they had no blacksmith, they brought him here."

The barber looked nervously toward the door and lowered his voice. Leaning toward Bachner he whispered. "The blacksmith told me that the night of the executions a woman came to their shtetl. She had only been wounded. Somehow she had crawled from the grave. She walked, naked and bleeding, to her parents' home in the shtetl."

The old man gripped the back of Bachner's chair with an iron fury, as if wishing he held some Nazi's neck between his gnarled fingers. The tip of his scissors nicked the back of Bachner's neck, and he froze, wondering if the barber remembered that the man in his chair was a Jew, not a German.

"She tried to warn them, but it was too late. The Nazis came the next day. This man, the blacksmith, he went to the site, he saw it with his own eyes. He said the ground was moving as the bodies settled, that you could still hear groans from those who had not yet died."

By the time the man finished his story, Bachner was speechless. This was far worse than he had feared. The ghetto in Warsaw was inhumane, terrible, appalling, but this—this was monstrous beyond belief. The barber relaxed his grip on the chair and removed the towel from around Bachner's neck. With a small soft broom, he brushed away the few hairs that remained on Bachner's collar, then stepped back, standing silently behind him.

"Is there anything I can do?" Bachner asked and immediately felt foolish for asking. What could he possibly do to help this man, what comfort could one give in the face of such tragedy?

"You can survive. You can make sure that the world knows what happened to the Jews of Berdichev. Now you know what these beasts are capable of. They won't be satisfied until every Jew is dead. You must warn them in Warsaw."

Even though the Jews were not supposed to be paid for their work, Bachner slipped some rubles to the barber. It might help him some way. The man nodded silently and looked at Bachner with both grief and satisfaction. Grief at having to tell about such things, but satisfied that he had survived long enough to tell someone, and satisfaction in knowing that some Jews were still surviving. "*Chazak Veamatz*, be brave and strong," the man said before he turned away.

*   *   *

The fate of the Jews of Berdichev was duplicated with horrific frequency throughout the occupied Soviet Union in the wake of the Nazi invasion. Prior to the invasion, it seemed that the Germans planned to confine the Jews to ghetto enclaves, extracting as much work from them as possible before they succumbed to hunger and disease. Although tens of thousands of Jews had been killed in Poland and other occupied countries, the systematic mass murder of Jews did not begin until after the June 1941 invasion. The rapid engulfment of the Baltics, Byelorussia and the Ukraine provided the Nazis with new opportunities to solve "the Jewish question." The region was remote and had a local anti-Semitic population willing to actively assist in executions that could be carried out under the cover of a rapidly advancing army.

In May 1941, a month before the invasion, SS Einsatzgruppen commanders attended a special session to prepare them to liquidate all potential enemies of the Reich. They were told that "Communist functionaries and activists, Jews, Gypsies . . . must be regarded as persons, who by their very existence, endanger the security of troops and are therefore to be executed without further ado." The need to steel oneself to carry out executions of women and children as enemies of the Reich was especially emphasized. Most of the Einsatzgruppen commanders were not obsessive fanatics, but middle-class businessmen and professionals, who had seen SS membership as a ticket to social and financial success in Nazi Germany. They frowned upon wild, disorderly pogroms, preferring organized and systematic executions like the one described by the barber.

Although not part of the Wehrmacht, or German armed forces, the Einsatzgruppen operated with the military's consent and assistance. The army provided rations, lodging and fuel to the extermination squads and also took part in the executions to get the job done quickly. The invasion and the wave of mass killing swept over the Soviet Union so swiftly that resistance was nearly impossible. Some did escape to the forests to join partisan groups, but the local population was reluctant to assist Jews even when they were not openly hostile to them.

The number of Jews killed in the first five weeks of Operation Barbarossa exceeded the number of Jews killed during the previous eight years of Nazi rule. In Vilna, Lithuania, five thousand in twelve days; in Kishinev, ten thousand in fourteen days; in Minsk, two thousand in one day; and in the village of Jedwabne, all sixteen hundred Jewish inhabitants were rounded up and driven into a barn, which was then set on fire.

By the end of September, over half a million Jews had been executed, one and a half million had fled to the east and two million remained. The spasm of slaughter slowed as the civilian administrators moved into the occupied areas and began to see the Jews as a source of slave labor rather than as a target for outright extermination. As in Poland, ghettos were set up in the larger cities and towns, and the Jews were forced to work under conditions designed to kill off as many as possible.

Despite the formation of ghettos in the occupied USSR, mass killings continued. However, there was individual and collective resistance. Einsatzkommandos, with typically twisted logic, claimed that increasing Jewish resistance retroactively justified the actions that had precipitated the resistance in the first place. All resistance was met with massive reprisals. When a German policeman was shot near Minsk, forty-five hundred Jews were executed in retaliation. And yet, collective and individual resistance continued. Those being executed would seize German weapons and kill as many as they could before being shot. Some even killed their tormentors with their bare hands. But the Jews were unarmed, facing impossible odds, and so the daily killing, the shots, the rivers of blood and the cries of the victims went on and on. The Germans would begin shooting in the morning, break for a hearty meal while their victims waited, and then resume killing until dusk.

Of all the killing sites used by the Nazis, one stands out: a ravine known as Babi Yar outside the Ukrainian city of Kiev. The Germans took Kiev on September 19, and a little more than a week later notices were posted throughout the city ordering all Jews to assemble for resettlement. The tens of thousands who followed the order were led to Babi Yar and told to undress. Then they were marched two by two in columns of one hundred along one edge of the ravine where they faced Einsatzgruppen armed with machine guns on the opposite side. They were mowed down by machine gun fire and fell into the pit, only to be replaced with another column of one hundred. During a thirty-six hour period on September 29 and 30, 1941, thirty-four thousand people were liquidated. Ukrainian workers then covered the victims with the sandy soil and left them. Like the woman in the barber's tale, some were not killed outright and managed to crawl from the pit and escaped to tell others of the obscenity of Babi Yar.

Despite their training and indoctrination, the executioners were not immune from the effects of their actions. Heavy drinking was common, as were nervous breakdowns. But for the most part the actions of the killing squads were questioned on the basis of *how* the executions were being carried out, not *why* they were being carried out. The Nazis knew that there had to be a better, cleaner, less messy way to dispose of the Jews. With single-minded efficiency, they set out to find it.

Willi Bachner knew nothing about the events in Kiev. He was still attempting to deal with what he had learned about Berdichev. He felt even more isolated than he had before, and although he longed to go back and talk with the few Jews who remained in the Berdichev ghetto, he dared not. There were too many people who depended upon him, not just his own family but the Jews, like Stamberger and Schwalbe, who were working for the Kellner firm under false identities.

He tried to focus on the job at hand, enduring Oberleutnant Gregor's daily *bonhomie*, his robust slaps on the back and endless bantering about the good old days. By December, the job was nearing completion and word came from Kellner in Warsaw that a new contract had been signed for the firm. They would still be subcontracting for Organization Todt under the direction of the Wehrmacht. The Kiev railroad station had been heavily damaged during the battle for the city. The entire complex—terminals, tracks, barracks and support facilities—were to be rebuilt. Work would start after the first of the year; Bachner was to have two weeks' leave in Warsaw.

*   *   *

Upon his return to Warsaw on the first night of Hanukkah, in December 1941, Bachner found that the situation in the ghetto had continued to worsen in his absence. Though he would have thought it hardly possible, the starving children were thinner and weaker, the goods being sold shabbier, the clothes more ragged. The whole atmosphere of resigned pessimism was summed up by the sight of the dead bodies of frozen children covered with Judenrat posters bearing the legend, "Our Children Must Live—A Child is the Holiest Thing."

One now left the ghetto only at his or her peril. On October 5, Governor Frank ordered the execution of any Jew caught on the Aryan side without permission. On the day Bachner returned, the ghetto was full of the story of the execution of fifteen people found guilty of this new crime. They had been shot by Polish police in the courtyard of Pawiak Prison, while a mass of people waited outside, weeping at the cries of the victims, some of whom were children.

The situation was so desperate in the ghetto that Jews continued to try to escape. Supplemental rations for "peoples' kitchens" had been suspended in October. The official ration upon which the Jews were supposed to exist was 230 calories per day, or 2 kilograms of bread per week, but there were no rations: the Germans had suspended all shipment of food packages into the ghetto. The savings from the cut in rations went to repair the ghetto walls, to keep the Jews confined in their prison. Death gnawed slowly away at the community. The thought of food, now nearly impossible to find, taunted the starving Jews. The scarcer it became, the more obsessed they became with it, an obsession that refused to sleep.

Along with hunger came its companion, disease. Of all the maladies caused by the crowded, unsanitary conditions and the debilitation of the ghetto populace, the worst was typhus. A microorganism spread by the lice which plagued nearly everyone in the ghetto, typhus raged uncontrolled there. Victims experienced headache, fever and chills, followed a few days later by a characteristic rash. Drugs to treat the disease were almost impossible to obtain in the ghetto, and for many, the disease progressed until death occurred, usually two weeks after the onset of symptoms. Czerniakow reported in his diary that during the two-month period of October–November 1940, when the formation of the ghetto was announced, there were thirty-nine reported cases of typhus. A year later, these same two months saw 5594 new cases.

The Germans set out to deal with the epidemic by cordoning off streets and forcing inhabitants into delousing baths, but rather than a solution this proved to be just another torment for the Jews of Warsaw. Those rounded up for delousing often had to spend the day outdoors exposed to the elements without food or water. The delousing techniques were ineffective and people were as likely to catch the disease in the process as they were to be rid of lice. In addition, thieves ransacked the apartments left empty and people returning from the ordeal found that whatever meager belongings they possessed were gone.

In October, the Nazis again used the High Holy Days to announce a shrinking of the ghetto. Once again the Bachner family found themselves just outside the new boundary. The whole of Sienna Street would no longer be in the ghetto. Too many of the buildings, which took up the width of the block, were being used to smuggle goods into, and people out of, the ghetto. A wall would be built down the middle of Sienna Street. Unfortunately, the Bachner's apartment was on the wrong side of that wall. In Willi's absence, his family had relied upon their friend, the diamond merchant Ostrowski, to help them find new lodgings. Along with Ostrowski, they moved one block north to Sliska Street, and several steps down in accommodations.

Bachner found his way to 18 Sliska and awkwardly hurried up the four flights of stairs, his pockets stuffed with food and presents. He found the new apartment shabby and cramped, but the welcome as warm as ever. Despite Willi's gifts and the traditional *latkes* Helena and Cesia had prepared from the potatoes that Heniek had managed to collect, the family was unable to escape the somber mood that dominated their lives. Cesia's father had recently died of typhus, and her two-year-old nephew had succumbed to pneumonia just a few days before. In light of this, she and her mother found it impossible to go through even the motions of a Hanukkah celebration.

In low tones, in a corner of the cramped main room of the apartment, Bachner shared what he had learned in Berdichev with Heniek and his father. As he glanced over at Cesia and his mother washing dishes, and at Bruno reading the book Bachner had brought back from the Ukraine, he found himself incapable of telling his family what he knew and what that knowledge implied of the fate of the two Bachner sisters. Telling them would not change things; it would only make their sad lives more unbearable.

That night, for the first time in months, he lay next to his wife. The frustration of being unable, because of the crowded apartment, to celebrate his homecoming as husband and wife should, left Wilhelm tossing fitfully on the uncomfortable, sagging mattress.

He found himself wishing that he could discuss his worries with his wife. He loved Cesia with a tenderness that seemed to fill every cell in his body whenever her eyes met his, but . . . if only he didn't have to pretend to be strong all the time. He longed to share his true feelings with her. He wanted to tell her how the tension of pretending, day in and day out, wore on his nerves; how he sometimes thought it would be better to just give in, to let despair wash over him like a wave swallowing a drowning man.

If only Anna were here. He thought once again of his sister, recalling the evenings at home during those harsh winter nights in Bielsko. Snow blanketed the town as the family huddled around the pot-bellied stove in the middle of the room. His father read the paper; his mother knit winter stockings, while Hilde and Bruno helped her roll up the skeins of yarn. He and Anna sat at the table, working on their homework, but always talking—about school, friends, problems, everything. If Anna were here, he could share his fears with her. She would nod her understanding, then tell him to square his shoulders, to be strong—to be a Bachner.

On this snowy night in 1941, after two years of German occupation, the recollection of Bielsko stung like sleet on bare skin, so fresh that the memory of the smell of potatoes roasting in the ashes of the fire made Willi's mouth water. With a sigh, he turned and looked at his wife.

"Sleep in peace, my sweet," he whispered, kissing her head before turning his face into the pillow. He would continue to be strong for her, no matter what it cost him. He must.

*   *   *

Bachner was reluctant to leave his family in the current situation, but knew that their best hope of survival necessitated a steady income, and the only way to assure that income was to continue to work for Kellner even if it meant returning to the Ukraine. Papa Bachner assured him that the Pole Kazaniecki had been faithfully bringing them money and maintaining communication with

Schwalbe and Stamberger in the Kellner office. For now, it was the best they could do. The risks of leaving the ghetto and being caught were too high.

They no longer had any illusions about what they were up against. Even the entry of the United States into the war, after the Japanese attack on Pearl Harbor, failed to lift their hopes. Indeed the US declaration had a paradoxical effect: all American aid to the Jews of Warsaw was terminated when the Americans pulled out of the city. It was clear to all but the most naive that an Anglo-American invasion was not likely to occur any time soon. England had held off the Germans in the Battle of Britain but was unable to go on the offensive even with the backing of the United States.

As Willi prepared to leave for Kiev, Heinrich sardonically shared a joke making the rounds in the ghetto. It was said that Churchill asked the Rabbi of Ger how the Germans could be defeated. "There are two ways," the Rabbi responded, "one natural, and one supernatural."

"What is the natural?" asked the Prime Minister.

The Rabbi responded, "A million angels with flaming swords descend from heaven and slay the Germans."

"If that's the natural, what's the supernatural?" inquired Churchill.

"A million English parachute troops land in Poland," replied the Rabbi.

5 HARBOR OF SORROWS

HOW LONG SHALL I HARBOR SORROW IN MY SOUL,
GRIEF IN MY HEART DAY AFTER DAY?
HOW LONG WILL MY ENEMY TRIUMPH OVER ME?
LOOK, ANSWER ME, O LORD, MY GOD.
                              PSALM 13:3

The train carrying the Kellner construction crew pulled into the Kiev railroad station a few nights before New Year's Eve, 1942. Bachner and his Polish workers emerged from the relative warmth of their straw-lined cattle cars into the bitter January cold of the Ukraine. Although some were prepared for the weather, most of the Poles who had signed up to work in the Ukraine did so out of need. They moved about miserably in their inadequate clothing, casting envious glances at the fur hats and thick coats of those around them. The snow that had formed a wall along the tracks across the flat steppe from Warsaw to Kiev was piled in dirty heaps around the platform. Although it was close to midnight, the railroad station was alive with activity: German and Italian soldiers, Ukrainian militiamen, well-clothed German and shabby Ukrainian civilians moved about, trying to stay warm as best they could.

The station building could offer little refuge from the cold because most of the roof was missing. The German attack in September had managed to destroy what little czarist opulence had remained after two decades of Soviet rule. The mass of passengers made their way amid piles of rubble, downed girders, burnt timbers and a cloud of dust that seemed to hang frozen in the cold night air.

Bachner told his workers to stay together and wait for him as he tried to negotiate his way through the chaos of the station and find the Reichsbahn office to arrange for accommodations. He was directed to temporary barracks near the station. After a few more hours of seeing that all his exhausted workers were accounted for, Bachner settled himself onto an uncomfortable bunk, covered himself with a threadbare blanket and fell into a fitful sleep.

The ride from Warsaw had taken three days due to damaged tracks and the higher priority given trains bringing troops to the front. It had not been a comfortable ride. The 150 workers had been crammed into five cattle cars lined with straw. The cars were not heated and the only light was a smoking kerosene lamp suspended from the center of each car. Stops were infrequent and the food consisted of dark bread and weak tea. For the Germans on the train, it was a different story. They rode in comfortable heated carriage cars and ate hearty meals in warm canteens at each stop. Some of the Germans were military, but most on the train from Warsaw were civilians: bureaucrats who would serve in the civilian administration of the Ukraine, Nazi party functionaries or just those flocking to the new German "colony" of the Ukraine to take advantage of the economic opportunities available there. The Ukraine provided an opportunity for those who had been less than successful in Germany, both in supplying the German army in the east and in extracting the resources of the Ukraine for the Reich.

The civilian administrators were a sorry lot. As Germany had taken over country after country from 1939 on, a civilian administration was set up in each occupied area. The USSR was the last country to be occupied, and those who were chosen to administer it were those not already assigned; they were the dregs of the Reich ministries. The bureaucrats of those ministries saw the Ukraine as a dumping ground for the irritating, the meddlesome and the incompetent in their midst. Because of their pomposity and their yellow-brown uniforms, these minions of the Ostministerium, Ministry of the East, were called *Goldfasanen*, golden pheasants.

Germany had drawn a line from Archangel, near the Arctic Circle, to the mouth of the Volga River in the south, and declared it to be a German colony. The Russians were to be contained in Siberia; the Slavs who remained would serve their Aryan masters. The Jews and other undesirables were to be exterminated. By January of 1942, hundreds of thousands had already met this fate. The German philosophy could be summed up as "First: conquer, second: rule, third: exploit." Russia's destiny was to feed Europe and nothing more. The German State Secretary said, "We wish not to convert the Russians to National Socialism, but to make them into our tools."

But until the Russians had been molded into proper tools for the Reich, the Germans would need to import skilled labor, such as that provided by the Kellner firm. The need for railroad infrastructure was particularly acute. Hitler and his generals had miscalculated the importance of the railroad in the USSR. The Soviet tracks were of a different gauge, which necessitated replacement if supplies and fresh troops were to reach the eastern front. The advance of the German army had ground to a halt as winter set in, but before the advance was slowed it had moved to the outskirts of Leningrad and Moscow, and was held at Rostov and Kharkov in the Crimea. The Soviets had destroyed all usable rail lines as they retreated; transportation by truck was difficult in the winter snow and ice and would become impossible when the spring thaw turned the roads to rivers of mud.

What had first seemed like an easy victory was daily becoming more difficult. By the end of 1941, a quarter of all the German forces on the eastern front had been killed and the Wehrmacht was calling for 2.5 million replacement troops. After their rapid victories in the west, the Germans had convinced themselves that the war in the east would be just as swift. They had not planned on massive reinforcements, and they had not planned on having to wage war in the middle of the Russian winter.

All construction supplies needed to be brought from the west, as did construction supervisors. Unable to obtain an adequate labor force from the Reich or central government, the Germans had to rely more and more on indigenous labor. Construction crews in the

Ukraine typically had a German supervisor, skilled Polish workers, and unskilled Poles, Ukrainians, Latvians and Lithuanians. The people of the occupied USSR willingly accepted this work for a very simple reason: working for the Germans entitled one to food rations not available to the general public. Even prior to the invasion of the USSR, the Germans had realized that the success of the eastern campaign required that German forces be fed at Russian expense, even though "tens of millions of men [would] undoubtedly starve to death" as a result. Those not employed by the Germans struggled to maintain an adequate diet. An added incentive was the fact that those not employed by the Reich in the east were likely to be sent to work for the Reich in the west. Just as Bachner and his crew were beginning their work on the Kiev station, the order had been given to "recruit" nearly a million Ostarbeiter, or eastern workers, for work in Germany.

*   *   *

When Bachner and his Polish workers showed up at the Reichsbahn construction office the next morning, he found about fifty Ukrainian laborers waiting for him. Their first job was to build new barracks for themselves and the hundreds of other workers who would be rebuilding the Kiev station. After they spent an uncomfortable night in the drafty temporary barracks, this was a job they were more than willing to accept. Although Bachner did not speak Ukrainian well, the language was close enough to Polish for him to make himself understood. With the assistance of some bilingual workers among the group, any problems of communication were easily overcome, and within a few hours the crew was making speedy progress.

The Kellner firm was given a small office in the damaged station. A Ukrainian woman, who spoke a little Polish, was provided by the Reichsbahn for clerical duties. Among these duties was the preparation of Arbeitskarte, work cards for foreign and indigenous workers. The secretary prepared the cards from lists of workers and then gave them to Bachner for his signature. Bachner had the cards authenticated with the eagle and swastika stamp of the

German authorities. The cards were then used by the workers to obtain both wages and rations.

The expendability of the indigenous people was made clear to Bachner a few weeks after their arrival. It was one of those bitterly cold winter days, with a monotonous grey sky, when a biting wind presaged the snow that would soon arrive. Some of the workers were clearing debris on the roof of the main station. Taking a break from their labors, they placed a barrel on some bricks and, filling it with wood scraps, made a small fire to warm themselves and heat tea. Bachner was talking to other workers about fifty yards away when he heard a shout, a burst of machine gun fire and the screams of men. Turning, he found four men on the ground and an SS stormtrooper dumping snow on the fire. He walked over, identified himself and demanded to know why the men had been shot.

"We shoot saboteurs. They were trying to burn the building down," one of the SS men replied, indignant that his actions should be questioned.

"They were just trying to warm themselves." protested Bachner, "They posed no threat to the building."

"Maybe not," said the other with a grin, "but consider it a warning to these animals against any future sabotage."

He slapped the arm of his companion at his jest and the two walked away laughing.

Bachner ordered some of his workers to take the bodies away for burial. But when frantic wives and children came to the station to find their tardy husbands and fathers, he found that he could not tell them the truth. Not only had they lost their men, they had also lost the food rations that made the difference between survival and starvation. They looked so miserable, standing in the thickly falling snow, bundled in their scarves with their children clutching their hands. Bachner was filled with a longing for his own family and an end to the shared misery the Germans were causing across the Continent.

"I'm very sorry . . ." he told them, then stopped, unable to go on. On an impulse he continued, "Your husbands were sent to Germany as laborers today. I'm afraid they were given no time to return home and tell you. But don't worry, they will be fine and as employees of the Reich, their families will still be eligible for rations. Just continue to come and receive your coupon books. I'm sure you will hear from your husbands soon."

Was his white lie more cruel than the truth? Was he acting to spare himself or to help them? He wasn't sure, but after sending the women on their way he turned and met the sad but sympathetic smile of Katerina, the Ukrainian secretary. Her eyes signaled a silent thanks, saying that she knew now he was different, not like the Germans or their lackeys. He bade her goodnight and trudged home through the snow.

*   *   *

The number of workers employed by the Kellner firm continued to grow and soon additional clerical help was required. Keeping the small station office to oversee the firm's work, the Kellner firm moved its bookkeeping office to large quarters on Sagsaganska Street, in a building that had previously housed the Kiev office of the Russian Red Cross. The German civil authorities provided housing for all Reich employees by simply commandeering the houses of Ukrainians. Bachner was assigned a comfortable house, complete with a Ukrainian housekeeper who was, not incidentally, its rightful owner. That the woman was willing, was again explained by the rations that came with her duties as housekeeper. She found this nice young Pole to be an easy boss and both parties were quite satisfied with the arrangement.

By March, Bachner was directly supervising close to 500 workers engaged in several separate projects as part of the rebuilding of the station and the outlying buildings. About a third were at work on a two-story building that was to house Reichsbahn administrative offices.

On a sunny morning, when the spring sunshine had begun to melt the grimy snow that was still piled up around the station, the SS served up another reminder of the dangers of working for the Reich. Just as the workers broke for lunch, shouts were heard from the lower level. Several workers ran up the stairs, followed by four Ukrainian militia men and a cadaverous SS officer. The workers scattered to the edges of the room, as though the bare walls might provide some protection.

"Where is Johannes Kellner?" the officer demanded, his words echoing in the large open space.

Bachner rolled up the blueprints he had been examining, and walked over to the officer as workers stood frozen. "Herr Kellner is not in Kiev, Herr Colonel. I am Wilhelm Bachner, Herr Architekt Kellner's Bauleiter. Can I be of assistance?"

"You are German?"

"No, Mein Herr, I am Polish," replied Bachner.

"Well, that explains it, doesn't it?" The officer sneered.

"Explains what?" asked Bachner. "I'm afraid I don't understand."

"Well, let me enlighten you, my little Polish friend! Allow me to help you understand. Last night a train carrying troops and supplies to the front was blown up by Bolshevik partisans at Borispol. We rounded up all the Bolsheviks we could find and guess what we found? Hmm? Come on now, make a guess."

From the officer's carefree tone of voice, one might think he was speaking to a friend about an amusing incident, but the malice was clear in his eyes, just as it was in the faces of the glowering militiamen.

Bachner's heart pounded so loudly in his ears that he thought the German must surely hear it. He swallowed to clear his dry throat and tried to sound merely puzzled rather than terrified.

"I have no idea, Herr Colonel."

The false cheerfulness disappeared as the officer stepped forward so that his face was only inches from Bachner's and screamed, "We found five of your men!"

He turned suddenly to the Ukrainian militiamen. "Get this vermin lined up, now!"

The Ukrainians shouted at the workers, who hurriedly assembled in two lines under the ready guns of the guards. Nearly 150 workers filled the cavernous room in two ragged lines. Bachner gratefully realized that all his workers were not present, that those who had been in the smaller side rooms had managed to climb out the windows and escape. "But Colonel, I don't understand," Bachner protested. "We have no business in Borispol."

"No business but attacking German soldiers. Now where is Kellner?"

Bachner rubbed his hand over his face, took a deep breath and tried to maintain his composure. "Colonel, Herr Kellner is at this very moment on his way from Warsaw. He will be arriving this evening. But I must assure you that the Kellner firm had no part in this tragic incident. We are simple workers. It—"

"Shut up!" screamed the colonel, his thin face purple and contorted with rage, his lips coated with spittle. He continued to stare at Bachner as he gave directions to the militiamen. "Have every tenth man step forward."

For a few seconds, no one moved and the silence seemed to close in on everyone in the room. Then the German shouted again. "*Verdammtes gesindel*, are you all deaf? Every tenth man! Forward now!"

The workers who spoke German stepped forward and the others were yanked or prodded forward by the muzzles of the Ukrainians' machine guns. Still, no one said a word as they waited for the German to make his move.

"So, how many of you are Bolsheviks? How many of you are Jewish, Bolshevik, enemies of the Reich?"

Another visceral wave of fear swept over Bachner and he felt a trickle of sweat run down the small of his back.

No one said anything. The workers didn't need to know German to realize they were in a very dangerous situation.

The SS officer walked back and forth in front of the workers, slapping his swagger stick against his boots. His anger dissipated, he seemed to relax as he said to one militiaman, "Take them downstairs, five at a time and deal with them."

One Polish worker, who understood German, cried out and was rewarded by being the first pulled out of line. He was joined by four others and led down the open staircase to the lower level.

Bachner stood helpless, clutching the crumpled roll of blueprints in his hand, looking at the ground, no longer able to bear looking the German in the eye.

From downstairs they heard one of the men sob, pleading in Ukrainian. The others remained silent; then a blast of machine gun fire echoed up the stairs, followed by the dull thud of heavy objects hitting the floor.

One of the remaining fifteen workers made a dash for a window, but only got about halfway before he was cut down by a burst of bullets from one of the militia. Their compatriots came down the stairs and took up the next five, then the next, as the SS officer continued to stand in front of Bachner, enjoying seeing him wince with every new burst of gunfire.

Finally, it was over. The whole thing had taken less than half an hour.

"Now, *mein Polnisches schwein,*" said the officer turning to Bachner, "now I will deal with you."

"You will do no such thing!" came an answer from the stairway.

The SS officer wheeled in surprise. There climbing up the remaining stairs, was Herr Falke, the head of Reichsbahn Direktion Ost in Kiev. "What is the meaning of this outrage? How dare you come in and shoot my workers?" Standing next to Falke were several members of the Civil Administration in their mustard-brown uniforms.

The SS officer shouted back just as indignantly. "These men are saboteurs! They are responsible for a partisan attack!"

"Don't be ridiculous," countered Falke. "They are construction workers, working on an important project for the Reich. Which, I might add, you are interfering with. Now I want you out of here now! And take your Slav thugs with you!"

After glaring at Falke for a few seconds, the colonel smiled and said to his militia. "Well, you heard what the Goldfasanen said. It would appear our work here is finished." He turned to Bachner. Their eyes locked. The colonel pointed his leather-fringed stick at the engineer, then nodded, as if to say that they would meet again.

Then he twirled on the ball of his foot; his boots clicked on the wooden floor as he marched out the door.

Falke walked over to Bachner and asked, "What was that all about?"

"Some Ukrainians carrying work papers from our firm were found near Borispol in a partisan roundup," Bachner replied. "You have my assurances, Herr Oberbaurat, there must be some mistake. I had nothing to do with this."

"Yes, well, we shall see when Herr Architekt Kellner arrives. In the meantime, send someone to those men's families and tell them to collect their bodies, I will not tolerate my building being turned into a charnel house. And get back to work."

As he walked out, Bachner heard him speaking to his companions. "Those SS bastards think they are running this war single-handed. Well we will just see about that."

Bachner fought down the wave of nausea that always seemed to strike him when he narrowly escaped discovery and turned to his assistant, a Pole who spoke Ukrainian.

"Go send someone to inform the families. If you need me, I will be in the office."

He walked out of the building, head bowed into the cold wind. He had no illusions about the Reichsbahn official's actions. What he had just witnessed was not a German coming to the defense of foreign workers, but a battle over turf, pure and simple. The Germans in Ukraine were not just fighting the Soviets, they were fighting among themselves. Himmler's SS, wishing to control the Ukraine, was in constant conflict with the Civil Administration of Reichskommissar Eric Koch, a fervent Nazi party member and protégé of Hermann Göring and Martin Bormann. The SS also fought for supremacy with the Wehrmacht forces of Field Marshall Keitel. Martin Bormann and the Nazi party officials sought to play off adversaries for their own advantage. Falke cared nothing for the welfare of his workers except as it affected output, but he cared very much about having the SS execute them without his permission, and was no doubt protesting the outrage at that very moment.

Kellner arrived that evening and was very distressed to hear about the day's events. He accepted Bachner's assurances of innocence but was not pleased to be greeted by the prospect of trouble with the SS.

As for Bachner, he held no illusions that he had seen the last of the SS Colonel. It was all he could do to get through the remainder of the day, welcoming his employer and finally making his way home with a crushing headache, sick at heart. He had never felt so helpless. When the Nazis herded those sad men down the stairs to their deaths, he realized he had been lulled into complacency over the last few months. Allowing himself the luxury of enjoying the satisfaction of beginning a new project and seeing it through, he had fallen into a predictable daily pattern. Today's events brought his deadly charade back into focus. The SS colonel and his militiamen provided a graphic reminder of the consequences of lowering his guard for even a moment. Retribution in the Reich was swift, final and arbitrary.

Early the next morning he answered a knock at his door and was greeted with the sight of two SS sergeants.

"We are looking for Bauleiter Bachner," one of them announced.

"I am Bauleiter Bachner. Please come in out of the cold. How can I help you?" he asked, keeping his face impassive.

"Is this your signature?" one asked, presenting Bachner with an Arbeitskarte. It was for the Kellner firm, and was issued to a Pyotyr Kravchuk for work at the Kiev Baustelle, or construction site. At the bottom, as plain as could be, was his signature: *Wilhelm Bachner.*

"Yes, it is. But I can't say that I know this worker."

"We will see about that. Get dressed. You are coming with us."

"Of course. I understand." Bachner nodded briskly. "We must clear up this confusion once and for all. Now if you will just excuse me, I will get dressed." He turned toward the bedroom.

"You are *not* excused," said the one who had showed him the card. "We have orders to keep you in sight at all times."

Bachner nodded his acquiescence. The colonel of yesterday was not about to lose his prey two days in a row. The younger sergeant followed him back to his bedroom, then to the bathroom, where he stood silently staring at Bachner as he used the toilet, combed his hair and straightened his tie. His face in the mirror had hardened like marble. Not even a vein twitched to reveal the turmoil that churned in his stomach.

"Well," Bachner announced, shrugging into his coat as he came into the front hall, "let's be off. We can't keep your colonel waiting."

Neither of the SS men said a word to Bachner or to each other as they drove to SS headquarters on Khryshatek Road, near the center of Kiev. The area had been the site for the Ukrainian State Parliament, the Communist headquarters and other government buildings. When the Russians retreated, the Germans took over the magnificent centrally located buildings. The Russians waited ten days for the Germans to settle in and then set off explosives, planted before the retreat east, heavily damaging the buildings and causing many German casualties. It was on the pretense of retaliation for Jewish acts of sabotage that the 34,000 Jewish inhabitants of Kiev were executed at Babi Yar.

Bachner, of course, knew none of this; he could only assume from what he had seen in Kiev that the Jews of that ancient city had met a fate similar to those of Berdichev.

Once inside SS headquarters, Bachner found himself once again facing the colonel. The name plate on the door had identified his nemesis as Colonel Rudolph Mueller. Mueller sat at a large desk in a well-lighted office that offered a fine view of the domes of the Cathedral of St Sophia, and beyond it, glimpses of the Dnieper River. Behind him hung the standard portrait of the Führer, chest-high, mustache bristling as his eyes stared at a vision only he could see— a vision of a world "cleansed" of Jews. A world without Wilhelm Bachner.

"Well, if it isn't my favorite little Pole."

Bachner's head snapped toward the voice. He focused his eyes on the colonel, trying to block the portrait of Hitler from his mind.

"How nice to see you again." The voice dripped molasses, but the smile was a knife poised to slice beneath Bachner's skin, revealing the Jew beneath the Germanic exterior.

"Herr Colonel, I am just as anxious as you to get this mix-up corrected," said Bachner. His voice filled the office, deep and sure, never betraying the tremors that ran along every muscle in his body.

"Oh, I'm sure you are," Mueller said. His smile sharpened. "I'm sure you are. Shall we start with the question of how five saboteurs came to be carrying Arbeitskarte with your signature on them?"

Bachner looked up at the ceiling as if he had to answer this question at least fifty times a day, then gave a deep sigh and looked the colonel straight in the eye.

"Look, there are over five hundred workers under my direct supervision. I sign the work cards that my secretary makes up from the rosters provided by the Reichsbahn Construction office. These rosters are constantly shifting. Just last week nearly a hundred of my Ukrainian workers were sent back to Germany to work in the factories there. I can hardly be expected to know all my workers by name or to investigate their background for security risks."

The words came out of Bachner's mouth with sincerity and not a trace of hesitation—not surprising, considering the fact that Bachner had spent most of the night tossing and turning, rehearsing what he would say during this interview. He stared back at the thin, sallow face of his black-clad adversary and added a bit haughtily, "The work we do is extremely important. I have better things to do than to spend my time interrogating Ukrainian peasants. If you have any problem with the workers provided to me, take it up with the civil authorities. I don't choose the Ukrainians, they do."

"This secretary you said typed up the work cards, who is she?"

"Again, Herr Colonel, she is a Ukrainian provided me by the civil authorities. I know nothing of her beyond her name and that she does an adequate job."

Mueller turned to the stormtrooper standing guard by the door and said, "Go to the Kellner office and bring me this woman. If this Kellner is there, bring him too. You," he said to Bachner, "may go wait out in the hall."

Bachner was shown to an uncomfortable chair along the wall and placed under the wary eye of a nervous stormtrooper who looked no more than nineteen years old.

About three-quarters of an hour later, the trooper returned, dragging Katerina to Mueller's office door. When she saw Bachner sitting outside the office, she stumbled. Before she turned her head away, he glimpsed the panic in her eyes.

Bachner's jaw clamped down, making his teeth throb as he fought to sit silently through the next few minutes. He heard Mueller's voice through the walls, muffled, snarling. The secretary lacked Bachner's skill in dealing with the SS. They were like wolves: the scent of fear drove them to greater bloodlust. Katerina was not used to standing up to Germans. Like many partisans in the Ukraine, her passionate commitment coupled with inadequate training left her vulnerable to interrogations.

They shouted questions at her. Her answers were hesitant, hurried along by the blows of the stormtroopers. Between her sharp intakes of breath and gasping sobs, Bachner heard her take complete responsibility for the false work papers. She had prepared them for the partisans and given them to Bachner for his signature. He had no knowledge of her actions.

Indeed he had not. Foolishly, he had been so concerned with his own charade, he had never thought that others around him might be acting out roles of their own. What would he have done if he had known? Would he have helped her if she asked him? Guilt washed over him; he had to admit that he probably would have been unwilling to take any additional risks. Was he as bad as the Ukrainian informants? Concerned only with his own family, like a mule wearing blinders, he had kept his attention straight ahead, ignoring others who dropped along the way, trampled beneath the grinding wheels of the German war machine.

The entire interrogation took less than five minutes. They dragged Katerina away; her hair hung over her face, but he could see blood flowing from a gash in her lip. Mueller left Bachner sitting in the busy outer office of SS headquarters, waiting. He could hear the clock ticking, papers shuffling as workers went about their jobs, but the sounds barely penetrated the jumbled haze clouding his mind.

About half an hour later, the other stormtrooper returned, escorting the head of the Kellner firm. Kellner had made his fear of the SS quite clear to Bachner during the Nieczajuk episode in Warsaw, but the full extent of that fear was now evident. He trembled so violently, he looked as if he had palsy, making his limp all the more noticeable. His face was the color of wet ash and his upper lip glistened with sweat. His furtive glancing stare held the accusation that all his discomfort was Bachner's fault. But he had no time to voice his thoughts; he was swept past Bachner into Mueller's office.

Mueller's voice carried easily through the transom over his door. "So, Herr Architekt Johannes Kellner. We meet at last." Gone was the brute who had interrogated the Ukrainian. Mueller's voice once again dripped with the supercilious condescension he reserved for German speakers.

"When did you hire Wilhelm Bachner? What do you know about him?"

"I hired him in Warsaw. He came with excellent credentials from the University of Brno, a fine German university. I assure you, Herr Colonel, Engineer Bachner had nothing to do with this unfortunate incident with false work cards."

"How can you be so sure?" asked Mueller suspiciously. "You know these Poles, they can't be trusted. They are just waiting for a chance to get back at us. How dare you put such a man in a position of authority?"

"But Herr Colonel," countered Kellner indignantly, "he was vouched for by a Luftwaffe Oberleutnant."

Bachner heard nothing for a few seconds. He silently congratulated Kellner on playing the Hans Gregor card at just the right moment.

"Who is this Oberleutnant?" Mueller asked.

"Oberleutnant Hans Gregor. You see, we had a contract in Berdichev to rebuild the airport. The Luftwaffe liaison with our firm was Gregor. Well, it so happened that he went to school with Bachner. He assured me of his reliability."

Again there was silence as Mueller considered this unexpected turn of events. "Go call Berdichev!" he snapped to the trooper. "Find this Hans Gregor and see what he knows about this."

The trooper came out of the room; his boots clicked against the floorboards as he hurried to obey the colonel's barked order. A second trooper escorted Kellner out of the office, telling him to sit next to Bachner.

The engineer glanced at his employer, then looked down at his hands resting on his knees. "I can't tell you how sorry I am about this, Herr Kellner," he apologized. "I had no idea that anything like this was going on." He looked up. The architect's usually immaculately-groomed hair poked up like dry straw around his ears.

Kellner sighed and looked at the floor. "I know that, Herr Engineer. But one can get into trouble with the SS even when one is innocent. You know that as well as I. I haven't forgotten how you helped when that fool Nieczajuk was seized as a Jew." Kellner might be a coward, but he was a decent coward, and he respected Bachner for his ability to stand up to the SS.

"When all this is over—that is, *if* and when this is over— why don't you plan to return with me to Warsaw for a few days? Your family is still there?"

Kellner had never shown the slightest interest in Bachner's private life, but now seemed genuinely solicitous.

"Yes, Herr Kellner. My wife is staying with my parents and my youngest brother in Warsaw." True enough, if not in the section of town that Kellner would have guessed.

"It will give this work card business a chance to settle down, and you a chance to see your family. Fauss has completed the project in Rovno. There's no reason why he couldn't take over here for a few days."

"Thank you, Herr Architekt. That is most kind of you. But it's really not necessary," said Bachner quietly. Fauss was a German Bauleiter for the Kellner firm, a vain and cruel man. Bachner did not feel comfortable with him stepping in to take over his work. What if Kellner decided he was a better supervisor?

"I insist," said Kellner. "You have earned some time off."

"Well, if you insist," agreed a reluctant Bachner. "But only for a few days. I am needed here. My workers know me. They work best when I am here."

Then they sat, waiting. As if it were ordinary, mundane, the day-to-day business of oppression went on around them with bureaucratic fervor. Phones rang; clerks typed. The façade of normality almost covered up the guttural orders, the plaintive pleas as the door to Colonel Mueller's office slammed behind each new Ukrainian suspect. Through it all, Bachner weighed the chances that Gregor would remember him after several months. Could they count on his enthusiastic goodwill to cover the months and miles between them? Would the tenuousness of his connection to Bachner become evident on questioning? The answer came mid-afternoon.

The stormtrooper left his desk and returned to Mueller's office. Once again, the conversation in the office flowed over the transom to Bachner's ears.

"Oberleutnant Hans Gregor is no longer in Berdichev. He has been transferred to Breslau."

"Well, then call Breslau, you fool!" barked Mueller.

"I did, Herr Colonel. Gregor is on a mission and will not be available for several days."

"*Verdammt!*" Mueller spat out. "Well, we'll just have to wait, won't we?"

For a moment, Bachner heard only the nervous shuffle of boots on floorboards.

Then Mueller's voice demanded, "Well, what's wrong?"

"It's the Reichsbahn Direktor Falke, Mein Herr. He keeps calling, asking when we are going to release his supervisor. He says the work cannot go on without the Polish engineer." His voice rose in pitch to a nasal whine. "He is threatening to call Berlin."

Mueller's sigh was audible to the eavesdroppers outside. It had been a long, fruitless day for the colonel, Bachner realized. He bent his head, hoping his dapper moustache would hide the smile that crept across his face. Unless you counted the Ukrainian woman, Katarina, who was hardly worth counting to an SS colonel, Mueller had wasted his day. Bachner hoped, for the woman's sake, that the colonel would soon find himself roasting over the fire of Berlin's displeasure.

"Very well, tell them they can go." Mueller raised his voice as though aware that they could hear them. "But let them know I shall be watching them closely in the future. There had better not be any more wandering work cards!"

*   *   *

Bachner returned to Warsaw, exhausted and ambivalent. He missed his family terribly, but he missed the old life they had shared just as much. Seeing them in the ghetto was a constant reminder of how much they had lost. It was hard to believe that things could have deteriorated further in the Warsaw ghetto, having been so unbelievably dismal during Bachner's December visit. But the streets were more crowded and the people less animated. The populace shuffled along, trying to hold on to survival, but lacking the strength to do it. Typhus was so rampant and sanitary conditions so poor, that confinement to a hospital was almost a sure death sentence. Children were dying of starvation in the orphanages. Corpses continued to litter the alleyways next to piles of garbage and excrement.

Disturbing, conflicting rumors filled the ghetto. Bachner was not the only one to bring back stories of extermination in the east. These stories eventually made their way to the streets where they mingled with fantastic tales of Soviet advances on the eastern front. Thirty thousand had been deported from Lwów. The Soviets had liberated Vilna. Liquidation squads were outside the ghetto waiting orders to enter. The Germans were evacuating Kiev. The Americans were landing in France. No one knew who to believe or what to make of it all, which contributed to the constant nagging anxiety.

The Judenrat was by now a largely discredited organization. Czerniakow continued to press his case to the Germans for more food and better conditions, but many of the others on the council were simply taking advantage of their position to obtain that which was denied to the other ghetto inhabitants. In February, Czerniakow had installed stained glass windows in the Council chambers, and concerts and plays continued to be sponsored by the council and cultural organizations. The ghetto black marketeers operated night-clubs, frequented by the few remaining affluent Jews and "tourists" from the Aryan side.

Bachner found his family to be managing well by ghetto standards, thanks to the large portion of his salary that was channeled from Stamberger to the Pole Kazaniecki, and from there into the ghetto to Bachner's father. Yet their spirits seemed to be starving, even if their bodies were not. The few days he spent with them shortly before the feast of Passover left a bittersweet taste in his mouth. He was plagued by guilt over his absence, over his failure to share their daily suffering. Rationally, he told himself, this was nonsense. Their only lifeline was the salary he earned outside the ghetto. But after what he had seen of the Jews in the east, he realized that soon he might have to risk removing them from the ghetto. He listened to them and watched them with a critical eye during those few days, wondering who would be able to "pass." Bruno and Heniek looked more like Poles than Jews and both spoke German flawlessly. But Bruno was now so thin and frail, having been sick for most of the winter, that the aura of the ghetto hung upon him, showed in his dull, listless eyes. Cesia could pass, given a change of hair color, and if she didn't talk too much. Unlike her husband, she had grown up in Warsaw speaking Yiddish at home and Polish at school. She knew some German, but like many Yiddish speakers, she frequently mixed in Yiddish words, a dead giveaway.

As for his father and mother, he had to admit that the chances were slim, especially for his mother. Should he risk taking some out now? What would happen to his parents if he took the others out? If they were discovered on the Aryan side, the penalty was death. How could he explain to Kellner the need to bring his family to Kiev?

Bachner paced the floor, his thoughts whirling as he tried to decide what to do. He stared out the window at the rubble-strewn streets of the ghetto. Across the way, sheltered from the biting wind by a broken door propped against the side of a building, an old man knelt with a shawl over his bony shoulders, praying. Would his faithful entreaty rise above the barbed-wire ghetto walls? Emotion clouded his reason, a dark cloud that would not lift to reveal the light of certainty he usually felt when choosing his direction. How could he make a cold, analytical decision when the lives of his family members were at stake? Yet he had to. His decisiveness had brought them through these long months safely. His instincts had been right all along. Now, much as he would have loved to pack Cesia's trunk and move her to Kiev, he knew that the time was not yet right. Given the money he provided and the contacts his family had through Lonia Ostrowski and Kazaniecki, they were safest right where they were.

The two Jews he had placed in the Kellner office, Adolf Stamberger (now Andrzej Staniecki) and his son-in-law, Julek Schwalbe (Juljusz Stroynowski), were also safe for the present. Being married to a Gentile Pole and looking very Polish himself, Stamberger felt confident about his ability to pass. His tall blond son-in-law, who had married his daughter Ruth, was also adept at posing as a Gentile. Both men had taken the extreme measure of having an operation which pulled the skin back over the penis to make them appear uncircumcised, enabling them to pass this ultimate test of non-Jewishness.

On the evening before his return to Kiev, Bachner returned from the ghetto to the Kellner office, where he planned to spend the night. Ruth and Julek Schwalbe now occupied the small apartment adjacent to the office and had offered him their couch. The farewell had not gone well, his mother and Cesia sobbing, and Heinrich merely glum and depressed. Again, the feelings of guilt threatened to overpower him. Could he really justify leaving them to such misery?

He sat alone in the darkened, silent apartment, thoroughly depressed. His reverie was interrupted by the return of the Schwalbes from their evening out. Ruth, a pianist, had been accompanying a friend at an impromptu recital. They came into the apartment in high spirits, but immediately became quiet when they saw Bachner sitting in the dark.

"Hello, Willi," said Ruth. "Let me introduce you to our friend, Gerda."

The woman strode confidently across the room and held out her hand. As Wilhelm shook her hand, she leaned closer and her blue eyes widened.

"Willi? Willi Bachner? Is that you?"

Bachner's forehead furrowed and an uncertain smile curved upward from beneath his trim moustache. He shrugged. "I'm sorry, I—"

"It's Gerda. Gerda Reichenbaum from Bielsko," she prompted. She sat down beside him, pulling off her gloves. "You probably don't remember me. I was school friends with your sister, Hilde."

Willi raised one dark brow.

"My sister Halina was a friend of Anna's," Gerda continued; then she smiled, a broad smile that showed off her even white teeth and lighted up her whole face.

Willi remembered that smile. "Of course, Gerda," he replied, reaching for her hand again. "You must forgive me. You were just a child when I saw you last. What brings you to Warsaw? And on the outside, if I might add?"

Gerda squeezed his hand, then relaxed against the couch cushions. A soft sigh whispered between her full lips as she smoothed her gloves across her knees.

"It's a long story. I came to Warsaw just before the war broke out. I was staying with my voice teacher whose husband was a diplomat." She waved a hand. "He had diplomatic immunity until a few months ago. When he lost it, I moved in with friends. A small apartment." Gerda pursed her lips. "So, I am not Gerda Reichenbaum any more. I am Gertrude Ferencz."

"Why Hungarian?" asked Bachner.

"My Polish, it is so bad." Gerda's hair rippled as she tossed back her head. "Whenever I open my mouth, people know I grew up speaking German. How did you ever learn to speak it so well?"

Willi chuckled. "You girls in Bielsko lived a sheltered life. You and my sisters didn't have to fight all those Polish bullies in the school yard if you sounded too German."

Gerda laughed and said, "I guess you're right. Anyway, I couldn't say I was German. Then they would want to research my background to declare me Volksdeutscher, so Hungarian seemed the perfect choice."

"And you've had no trouble?" Bachner referred to the daily difficulty of "passing."

"Of course not," she replied with the confidence of the young. "Look at me, I'm blonde, blue-eyed. Who would suspect me? But what about you?" She lifted her gloves and crossed her knees, tucking her trim black cotton skirt beneath them. "I just never made the connection when Juljusz and Ruth talked about you. How is your family?"

The now commonplace ritual of accounting for various family members followed—a sober incantation of who was still alive, who was in what ghetto. Gradually the conversation faltered as the air filled with ghosts. After a few moments of grey silence, Gerda rose and pulled on her gloves. The smile which had jogged Willi's memory of the carefree girl no longer softened her pale young face. Impulsively, she hugged Willi, resting her head for a moment against his shoulder. Then she stepped back.

"Good luck, Willi," she said, staring at the faded wood floor beneath her feet. Unable to meet his eyes, she shook her head, turned to the door and departed.

Bachner shared a final glass of vodka with his hosts and went to bed. He shrugged out of his clothes, feeling drained. As he stretched his weary body across the borrowed mattress, the alcohol burned like the embers of a dying fire in his belly. He tossed from side to side until numbness spread in red-washed waves through his veins, lulling him, at last, to sleep.

In the morning, both Schwalbe and his father-in-law tried to glean whatever information Bachner might have about acquaintances and conditions "inside." They had never lived in the ghetto, and they too were feeling no small amount of guilt over their relative comfort in the face of the misery on the other side of the walls.

Bachner had little information to offer them; he had spent nearly all of his time within the barbed-wire-topped walls with his own family. Still, he had plenty to tell them about conditions in the east. As he boarded a train for Kiev, Bachner realized that, far from rejuvenating him, the brief trip to Warsaw had only deepened his gloom.

Weariness had seeped into the marrow of his bones, leaving him aching for the life envisioned by that confident young man who had come to Warsaw two years ago. His future had glowed in his mind then, a blueprint for a precisely engineered future. Over two years now, he mused, two years of abuse at the hands of an enemy for whom he had held no enmity, two years of being the target for a hatred he could not fathom.

If only it could end. If only somehow this seemingly unstoppable Nazi deluge could be dammed. If only he could return to just being a good husband, dutiful son and good employee. He sighed, staring at the passing landscape of eastern Poland. Spring was beginning to win the battle with winter, the promise of hope, of new life and renewal. But in the world of men, the world of war, hope was still buried under the chill of the "Master Race."

When the train to Kiev stopped in Lwów the next morning, Bachner got out of the third-class car to stretch his legs. Groups of workers were completing work like what was being done in Kiev, clearing away rubble from damaged buildings. But these were not Ukrainians or Poles, Bachner realized. They were Jews. The men were emaciated and filthy, barely able to respond to the Ukrainian guards' constant admonitions to work faster. On each of their backs was a broad stripe of red paint, to prevent them from slipping into the crowds at the station. They sluggishly picked at the rubble with shovels, the stronger ones hauling away debris in wheelbarrows.

One of the workers caught his eye, and with a hint of a smile touched his cloth cap as if in a greeting. At first, Bachner didn't recognize him. His head was shaven, like those of the others. The neat mustache was lost amid several days worth of stubble, and the round face had become lean and haggard. But the eyes retained their sense of mischief, and Bachner realized he had just been recognized by his favorite uncle, Heinrich Fabiszkiewicz. Uncle Fabish, as he was known to the family, had been a successful contractor in Bielsko. How strange a coincidence that Bachner should run into him here.

He couldn't risk contacting Fabish directly so he sauntered over to one of the Ukrainian guards sitting on a pile of lumber, his rifle across his lap. Offering the man a cigarette, Bachner asked where the workers were from.

"Janowska," came the reply. "Walking corpses, that's what they are. These," he nodded toward the others, "these are the strong ones. You should see what's inside the camp."

Bachner nodded disinterestedly and wandered away. But a plan was already forming in his head. The gloom and despair that had gripped him on the train were gone, replaced with a determination and sense of purpose. He would have to get his uncle out of Janowska, and he didn't have much time.

WILLI BACHNER
IN 1942

CESIA IN 1942

WILLI AND CESIA BACHNER IN CALIFORNIA IN 1977

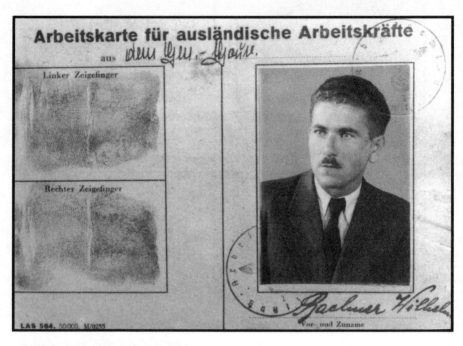

"WORK PERMIT FOR FOREIGNERS" FOR WILHELM BACHNER (ABOVE)
AND CESIA BACHNER (CZESLAWA DAMBROWSKA) (BELOW)

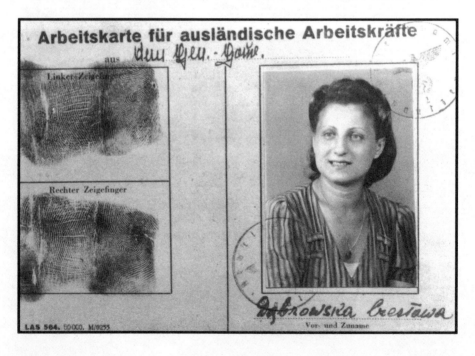

WILLI'S FATHER,
HEINRICH BACHNER
IN 1945

WILLI'S MOTHER,
HELENA BACHNER
IN 1941

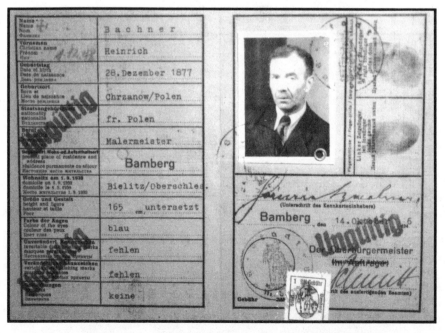

HEINRICH BACHNER'S IDENTIFICATION.

IDENTIFICATION CARD FOR JADWIGA HUDZIK (JADWIGA FINDER) (ABOVE), AND HER WORK PERMIT AS A COOK (BELOW).

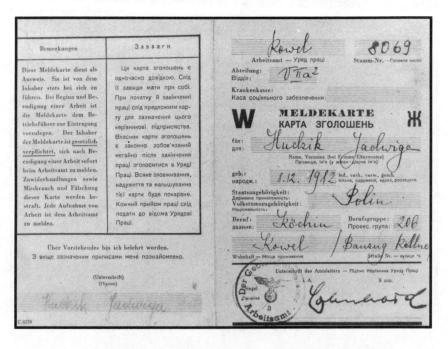

THE INSIGNIA FOR ALL THE PEOPLE WORKING ON THE RAILROAD. THE "R" STANDS FOR REICHSBAHN. THIS ALLOWED BACHNER TO BUY FOOD AND OTHER PRIVILEGES.

GERDA
FERENTZ-BUCHEN

Sensation of the 1953 show, lovely Gerda Ferentz-Buchen, coloratura soprano will again grace Khaki and Corn stage. With National Opera Baritone, Nissum Cunio, she will sing the Duet from Don Giovani by Mozart. Gerda has appeared on the Continent in many productions, and over the air in Oslo, Norway.

GERDA REICHENBAUM DURING HER ACTIVE SINGING CAREER (LEFT) AND IN JULY 1993 (ABOVE)

WILLI BACHNER AND
HIS SISTER HILDE IN 1958

WILLI'S YOUNGEST
SISTER ANNA IN 1935

WILLI'S BROTHER
BRUNO IN 1940

CESIA, WILLI, HILDE AND HEINRICH IN 1947

HANIA TEIFELD
IN 1942 (LEFT) AND
GENIA TEIFELD IN
1945 (BELOW)

"PAPA" BACHNER'S SMALL PRAYER BOOK (ABOVE), AND ITS FRONT PAGE (RIGHT), WHICH SAYS "PRAYER BOOK" IN POLISH: *MODLITEWNIK*

סדור

שַׁעֲרֵי תְפִלָּה

נוסח ספרד

סדר התפלות לכל השנה,

בְּאותיות יותר גדולות משאר

סדורים כאלו, וכולו מנוקד.

וְעַכּ דִיּנִים הַנחוצים.

בהוצאת במ״ה של

אברהם כהנא

ווארשא, נאל׳ עזוקי 39

רתרצ״ד — 1934

Modlitewnik

Printed in Poland

Locations of the Kellner Firm: 1940 to 1943

1. Warsaw, Poland: Aug. 1939 to Jan. 1941
2. Bialystok, Poland: Jan. to June 1941
3. Berdichev, Ukrainian S.S.R.: Aug. to Dec. 1941
4. Kiev, Ukrainian S.S.R.: Dec. 1941 to Sept. 1943
5. Kovel, Ukrainian S.S.R.: Nov. 1943 to Jan. 1944
6. Minsk, Byelorussian S.S.R.: Jan. to April 1944

Other Kellner Worksites 1941 to 1943
Boguslav, Ukrainian S.S.R.
Spola, Ukrainian S.S.R.
Novograd Volynsky, Ukrainian S.S.R.
Dnepropetrovsk, Ukrainian S.S.R.
Zitomir, Ukrainian S.S.R.
Vinnizta, Ukrainian S.S.R.

Locations of the Kellner Firm
January 1944 to May 1945

1. Bromberg, Poland: May to October 1944
<u>October to December 1944</u>
2. Gdynia, Annexed Poland
3. Stettin (Sczcecin), Annexed Poland
4. Eberswald, Germany
5. Wittichenau, Germany
6. Cottbus, Germany
7. Bautzen, Germany
8. Berlin, Germany: 24 hour stopover, Jan. 1944
9. Erfurt, Germany: January to March 1945
10. Gera, Germany: March 1945
11. Plauen, Germany: April to May 1945

SWEDEN

Baltic Sea

Gdynia
Gdansk
Stettin
Eberswalde
Bromberg
Bialystok
Berlin
Treblinka
GERMANY
Cottbus
Warsaw
Erfurt
Wittichenau
Dresden
Bautzen
Lodz
POLAND
Frankfurt
Gera
Plauen
Plaszow
Prague
Auschwitz
Krakow
CZECHOSLOVAKIA
Bielsko
Brno
Munich
Vienna
AUSTRIA
Budapest
ITALY
HUNGARY

6 Deliverance and Destruction

Rescue me out of the mire;
  May I not sink.
Let not the flood waters overwhelm me,
  nor the abyss swallow me up,
  nor the pit close its mouth over me.
                          Psalm 59:15-16

The gates of Janowska loomed ahead of him like some Dantesque portal to Hell, and Bachner momentarily lost some of the resolve that he had felt at the train station. He knew that being sent to Janowska was the equivalent of a death sentence, and that he was his uncle's only hope of survival. But this was madness. How could he have ever considered boldly marching into a Nazi labor camp and demanding the release of one of the inmates? On the other hand, he had the paperwork to back him up, a requisition from the Kellner firm for the release of the carpenter Fabiszkiewicz for important work in Kiev.

German efficiency, he thought. I must become the essence of the efficient engineer, disdainful of anyone who would impede the most efficient way of completing a crucial task. He had dressed for the part, wearing his black leather coat, knee-high boots and his best trousers. He walked up to the two guards at the gate and announced that he would like to speak with the commandant.

The guards told him that the commandant was hardly available to anyone who came calling, and ordered him to state his business.

"I have come to pick up one of the inmates of this camp for important work in Kiev," he announced forcefully, hoping that by acting as though what he was doing was legal and proper, he could somehow make it easier. "I wish to see Oberstürmführer Gebauer."

One of the guards left to check with the camp office. Bachner was not allowed in through the gates, but that was just as well. He had the feeling that if he entered the camp, he might never leave, that something about the awful place would reveal his Jewishness to all around him. But one did not need to enter the gates to see just how bad the conditions were. Bachner realized the workers he had seen at the station were, in fact, the strongest and healthiest at the camp. Those who remained moved listlessly around the camp yard, moving rocks from one side of the camp to the other or digging ditches to drain away the muddy water that collected in foul pools.

The laborers worked under the multiple eyes of the SS, Ukrainians and some Russian POWs, who acted as camp kapo, enforcers of discipline for the Germans. There were guard towers with searchlights at regular intervals along the perimeter. The inmates were identified not only by their physical appearance, but by the red stripe painted on their backs and the dish and spoon that was held to their waist by a cord and slapped against their thin legs as they shuffled along.

Off to one side, on a slight elevation, was a jumbled pile of what Bachner at first took to be old rags, but when he looked more closely, he saw movement. Bachner recoiled; his hands clenched, his nails biting into his palms as he realized with horror that the mass of ragged cloth held dead and dying men. Those who had recently died and those whose condition indicated that they soon would die were thrown in careless heaps like soiled laundry waiting to be washed. Bachner averted his gaze, his face frozen, cold as marble, lest he betray any hint of emotion to the guard.

As Bachner stood silently, trying to keep his simmering anger from melting his mask of indifference, the other guard returned with an SS Officer. "I am Stürmführer Wilhaus. What is this about taking one of our workers?"

"Herr Wilhaus," began Bachner, forcing a confident, somewhat conspiratorial smile to crack the marble façade. "I am Wilhelm Bachner. I am an architect rebuilding the Kiev railroad station for the Reichsbahn. Today, while at the station, I recognized one of your inmates. He is a master carpenter from my home town Bielitz. As a matter of fact, he worked for our family firm. Such a man is wasted working here. He can serve the Reich far better in my employ."

Wilhaus stared at Bachner incredulously. "So you think I should just give him to you? Are you crazy? We are not a hiring hall for anyone who comes here."

"I assure you, I have all the proper authorization for a transfer," Bachner said, pulling from an inner coat pocket the mass of paperwork he had prepared in advance.

"But the man is a Jew! You can't take a Jew to Kiev."

"Look," said Bachner wearily, "I don't care if he's a Red Indian. I have important work to do in Kiev. Do you have any idea how hard it is to find skilled workers there? This Jew can serve the Reich far better in Kiev."

Wilhaus still seemed more astounded than angry. Bachner tightened his lips and clasped his hands behind his back, forcing himself to maintain eye contact. This was probably a new situation for the SS officer. Bachner doubted that anyone had ever dared to march into his camp and demand the release of a Jew. He watched the play of emotions on the officer's face—disbelief, confusion, uncertainty—as he went through the rapid calculations that underlings go through when faced with something new.

As the seconds passed, Bachner's fingers began to clasp and unclasp behind his back. Would his bravado not be enough to win his uncle's freedom? From the deep creases crisscrossing his forehead, Wilhaus appeared to be a man practiced in the art of imagining the worst. If he weighed the decision carefully, the SS officer could only conclude that the release of a Jew would be liable to bring the wrath of his superiors down upon him, while the dismissal of this unknown Reichsbahn architect would have few, if any, repercussions. It was a simple choice.

"There will be no transfer of workers from this camp. Good day, Herr Architekt," he said with finality, then turned and walked away, leaving Bachner with the two smirking guards. Bachner gave what he hoped was the exasperated sigh of a harried supervisor and turned back to the waiting car. As he walked toward it, his legs felt like two sacks of wet cement. The picture of his uncle lying amid that pile of discarded human rags filled his mind, and he ducked into the car, trembling. As he drove away, he could not take his eyes off the rear-view mirror. The gates of Janowska closed behind him. Uncle Fabish would remain in this Nazi hell-camp unless he could think of a better plan. How could he obtain his release? How . . ? That, he could not answer.

The Warsaw -Kiev train had already left, so Bachner had to wait until the next morning to return to the old Ukrainian capital. He had failed to gain the release of Uncle Fabish, but he was by no means ready to give up. Upon returning to Kiev, he formulated a plan for an even more audacious rescue.

He had made the acquaintance of one of the many Ukrainians who sold food and clothing on the black market. The underground market was not new, having existed under the Communists. The German invasion and rationing only provided more business opportunities. Bachner made inquiries about hiring a discreet driver in Lwów, good pay, no questions asked. His acquaintance was more than happy to assist him and gave him the name and address of just such a man.

Accounting for another trip west was simple. The Kellner firm had an office in Lwów. Bachner invented a reason to return there—a conference with another Kellner Bauleiter—and told his own foreman that he would return late the following evening. Timing was everything, he realized, and he pored over the railroad schedules, praying that it would all fit together.

The next morning he boarded a train back to Lwów. He spent the afternoon meeting with the other supervisor, pretending to be fascinated with his managerial technique and admiring the efficiency of his worksite. That night, he made contact with the driver who had been recommended to him and the additional man that his plan would require. They were more than willing to put one over on the SS and the price Bachner was willing to pay certainly helped to make the risk tolerable. He gave the driver 100 marks, half of the agreed price, and promised him the rest when the task was complete.

It was riskier than anything he had done, because he had to rely on strangers who might betray him at any time, but he saw no other way. It would be only a few weeks before his uncle would begin to resemble the walking corpses of the Janowska camp, if he lasted even that long.

The next day was cold and drizzly. Bachner inquired at the station about the train schedule and was assured that they were all on time; no delays were foreseen. He rendezvoused with the Ukrainians, and they made their way to the outskirts of the rail yard where the Janowska inmates were at work clearing rubble. One of the Ukrainians went over to his fellow countryman who stood guard over the workers. Cigarettes appeared and an animated conversation followed. Bachner's accomplice waxed eloquent about the war, the Jews, women, vodka, etc. The guard, grateful for this small diversion on such a miserable morning, responded in kind.

None of this was lost on Fabiszkiewicz, Bachner noted. The old man watched the exchange for a few moments, then glanced toward his nephew sitting in a car adjacent to the track. Willi nodded, and Fabiszkiewicz gradually made his way over to the car. At a signal from Bachner, the gregarious Ukrainian diverted the guard's attention to the construction nearby. Seeing his opportunity, Fabiszkiewicz moved toward the car. Bachner opened the rear door from the inside. His uncle dove in and crouched on the floor.

With a quick glance around to see if anyone had raised a cry of alarm, the driver calmly pulled away while his friend continued to find the Janowska guard a fascinating conversational partner.

"Greetings, Willi," said Fabiszkiewicz from the floor in the back. "You certainly took your time returning. But I had faith that my favorite nephew wouldn't forget me. Did they notice my departure?"

"No, no. They are far too busy inhaling cigarette smoke and patting each other on the back. As far as I can tell." Bachner reached

behind the seat to grasp his uncle's hand. "You are safe, Uncle."
Squeezing his eyes shut momentarily, he willed himself to hold back
the tears.

Would they even notice that one of the inmates was gone?
Probably not. The inmates' appearance made it impossible to blend
in with the crowd and the idea that someone from the outside would
arrange an escape probably struck the over-confident Nazis as so
ludicrous that twenty to thirty workers had only one guard. His
uncle's absence would not be noticed until appell, the roll call that
would take place when the inmates returned to camp.

"Might I inquire as to where we are going on our little drive?
And how it is that you find yourself wandering around the Lwów
central station?" asked Fabiszkiewicz. Even his weariness could not
entirely suppress his characteristic teasing.

"We're going to Kiev, Uncle. In a few minutes we will be
boarding a train. I know you have lots of questions, but I can't answer them now. Just do exactly what you are told. Be ready to move
and move quickly."

The car made it back to the central area of the station and
pulled alongside a train. Bachner handed an envelope with the second half of the payment to the Ukrainian and got out of the car. He
walked up to the Reichsbahn worker near the end of the train, showed
him his Kellner identity card and asked about the departure time.

"Anytime you are ready, Herr Engineer," he was told.

He went to one of the rear cars and opened the door. It was
full of supplies going to the Kellner construction company in Kiev.
Nodding toward the car, he turned to the official and began to go
over the manifest with him. The driver of the car opened the back
door and out came Uncle Fabish. Bachner wished he had eyes in the
back of his head, to make sure his uncle had made it, but he had to
make do with the sound of the Ukrainian driving off.

After telling the official he still wanted to check out the shipment and preferred to ride in the car, he gave a wave and shut the
door. Placing his finger over his lips, he cautioned his uncle to remain silent as the last few tense minutes passed. Then with a whistle,
the train slowly began to move. Bachner walked over and silently

embraced his uncle, no longer making any attempt to stop his tears. He had done it! He had saved one of his own!

Once the train was up to speed, they knew they were safe until it stopped once again. The cattle cars which were used to transport supplies had no access except the side door. Bachner took bread and sausage from his bag and a flask of tea. His uncle began to eat ravenously while he told Willi all that had happened to him since they had last seen each other in early 1939. Like Heniek, Uncle Fabish had been deported from Bielsko (they always called the town by its Polish name when no Germans were present). But unlike Heniek, he had succeeded in making it over the border into the USSR.

He had been in Lwów at the time of the Nazi invasion and had escaped the first wave of exterminations carried out by the Ukrainian nationalists on behalf of their German sponsors. He worked in the Lwów ghetto for a time. But a few weeks ago, Aktions, or raids, had stepped up in frequency. Whole buildings were emptied out. Those Jews deemed unfit for work were frequently shot on the spot. Those with a few more weeks of work left in them were sent to Janowska. There they labored, until one day they moved too slowly and their guards clubbed them down or pumped bullets into their gaunt bodies.

Tentatively, Fabish asked about his wife, Anni. Had Bachner heard from her? Bachner told him that his parents had seen her last in early 1940, when Bielsko reverted to its German name of Bielitz. As in other areas of "Greater Germany," Jews were forbidden to reside there and had to relocate to the portions of Poland under the German occupational forces of the Generalgouvernement. In return, he asked if perhaps his uncle had seen Hilde or Anna when he came to Lwów. His uncle expressed surprise that his two nieces had been there, and said that he had not made it to Lwów until the summer of 1940. But no, he had not seen either of the girls.

The trip to Kiev took all day, from Lwów to Dubno, from Dubno to Sepetovka, from there to Zitomir, and finally, in late evening, to the central station in Kiev. Bachner had left his uncle alone in the cattle car at Dubno, being unable to justify remaining there for the whole trip. When the train arrived at its final destination, Bachner walked to the Kellner car. Kellner workers were waiting there to unload the supplies. Inside Fabiszkiewicz had changed into the clothes Bachner had brought for him. He slipped in with the dozen men unloading the car and, following Bachner's careful instructions, slipped away from the group once he was outside.

When the unloading was complete, Bachner bade his workers good night and told them he would see them in the morning. He began to walk to his house, located near the station. His uncle followed and fell into step with him as they neared Bachner's residence.

"Welcome to Kiev, Uncle." Bachner grinned.

"How can I ever thank you, Willi?" Fabiszkiewicz's wrinkled face crumpled until deep grooves sagged beneath his hunger-sunken eyes. All traces of his earlier good humor disappeared. "I had just about given up," he whispered.

Wilhelm grasped his frail uncle in arms that shook with relief. "You are safe, now, Uncle. You and I, we are too stubborn to submit without a fight, eh? We are Jews. We survived the pharaohs, we survived the Romans, we will survive the Germans as well."

Fabish wiped his eyes with the back of a blue-veined hand. "You know? You may be right. We may just beat those Nazi bastards yet."

Wilhelm kept all traces of doubt from his voice. His uncle needed to believe they would make it; that their family would live through this insanity. As he placed his arm around his uncle, sharp-edged shoulder blades, bared by months of starvation, dug into Willi. He guided his uncle toward what would be his new home. One more refugee to hide within the ranks of Reichsbahn workers. Thanks to God for one more life saved. For now.

It took a few weeks for Uncle Fabish to regain his strength. The housekeeper was told he was a new member of the firm. They kept a set of blueprints at the house, which Fabish pored over, making numerous corrections when the Ukrainian woman was present. Bachner gave him a Kellner Arbeitskarte which identified him as a Kellner foreman. Fabiszkiewicz was a Polish name, so an alias was unnecessary. By early May of 1942, Fabiszkiewicz was supervising, haranguing and treating the Kellner crew to the good-natured abuse he always gave his workers.

The Kellner workers were only too glad to see the return of their Bauleiter. Fauss, as Bachner knew, was not an easy man to work for. Both the workers and Bachner were happy to see the German set off to a new Kellner construction site.

*   *   *

The spring thaw was well on its way when Bachner returned in mid-April. Rail transportation was largely the only way to travel; the dirt roads would be impassable until the ground dried. Even Hitler's unstoppable war slowed as the earth was transformed from solid to liquid. The Soviet offensive, begun in December to turn back the advancing German armies, ground to a halt. The Germans reformed and stabilized their positions. The German advance had been halted, but by attacking on three simultaneous fronts without adequate logistical support, the Red Army had sustained heavy casualties. Stalin's grand designs to retake lost territory were once again foiled by his underestimation of the enemy, his failure to concentrate his forces and his continuing refusal to believe any intelligence information that ran counter to his preconceived notions.

As for the Jews of Europe and the occupied Soviet territory, their treatment at the hands of their oppressors took a new turn in 1942. On January 20, 1942, senior officials of the Reich met in Wannsee, a suburb of Berlin, to address the "Final Solution to the Jewish Problem." Forced immigration was seen as impractical, as was continuing to feed the Jewish populations in the ghetto. It was decided that the Jewish population of western Europe would be exported to labor camps in the east, where they would work until their deaths. The last protocol called for the establishment of Vernichtungslager, extermination camps, where those unable to work would be eliminated. The entire project was put in the hands of Heinrich Himmler, the head of the SS. Unlike earlier anti-Semitism, the Final Solution was not a hate-filled emotional pogrom, but a cold, efficient, bureaucratic policy of extermination. It was the logical

successor to the "clean bureaucratic violence" that had been practiced in the ghettos by allowing "useless mouths" to succumb to
starvation and disease. But in a never-ending quest for efficiency,
the Nazis found such methods, as well as those of the chaotic extermination of the Jewish population in the occupied USSR, unaccept-
able.

The solution had been tested in September at the Auschwitz
concentration camp. Six hundred Soviet POWs and three hundred
Jews were placed in a cellar which was flooded with a gas called
Cyclon B, prussic acid in crystalline form. All died quickly and the
experiment was declared a success.

On December 7, 1941, the same day that the Japanese attack
brought the United States into the war, the extermination camp at
Chelmno, near the Polish city of Lodz, opened. Jews and Gypsies
from the surrounding area were told they were being sent to camps
in the east. Loaded into vans which had been rigged to pump ex-
haust fumes into the back, they suffocated slowly, gasping for mercy.
The Germans drove on, until the last desperate plea was silenced.

The drivers then ordered Jewish workers to empty the truck
so they could return for more victims. Once the bodies were returned to the camp, the inmates, responding to the barked commands
of their guards, stripped them of clothing and valuables before burying them. After this gruesome task was completed, the Jewish inmates who had been forced to assist their oppressors joined the other
victims in the burial pits.

In the second week of March 1942, around the time that
Bachner returned to Warsaw, a second extermination camp opened
at Belzec, north of Lwów. The first deportees sent there were over a
thousand persons from the ghetto at Theresienstadt. A third camp,
Sobibor, opened in May. By summer the three camps were extermi-
nating thousands daily. Construction neared completion at two more
camps, Treblinka, near Warsaw, and Birkenau, a part of the Auschwitz camp complex, in southwestern Poland, north of Bielsko, near
Krakow. All the camps were located on rail lines in remote areas.

Vague rumors of the camps soon began to filter into the ghettos, brought by those who escaped or smuggled out scrawled de-

scriptions. The Nazis, determined to keep up the deception of "re-settlement," went so far as to send false postcards back to the ghettos describing life in the camps. Rumors of death competed with rumors that all Jews would be settled in Arabia, that all Jews would be allowed to return home after a German victory. With so little to bolster hope, it was not surprising that many clung blindly to the Nazi fabrication.

*   *   *

Back in Kiev, work continued on the central station. Bachner was glad for the company of his uncle, which made his existence far less lonely. The news about the war was greeted with enthusiasm by the Germans and with despair from the occupied peoples. The Allies had met setbacks in North Africa and the Baltics. There was no sign that the Anglo-American forces were ready to invade the Continent. In the east, the Soviet front held in the north and center, but the German spring offensive had seized the Crimean region. Hitler's forces now pushed toward the Volga River and the strategic city of Stalingrad.

On occasion, Bachner and his uncle would go to visit some of the sights in Kiev: the Byzantine Cathedral of St Sophia, the museums and other sites which filled the ancient city. It was a world turned upside down. On the surface, parks bloomed with flowers, insisting on bringing spring to the city. Beautiful buildings stood grandly amidst the rubble of neighbors lost to the Nazi bombing.

Yet, even as he stopped to sniff the cinnamon sweetness of a blood-red rose, Wilhelm could not forget that death and danger lay beneath the thin crust of normality, ready to shoot through the cracks in the sidewalk, looming just around the next corner. The return of flowers could not lift the oppressive pall of war that lay over Kiev.

Bachner tried to keep up with what was happening in Warsaw by casually questioning newly-arrived personnel, as did his uncle, but the news was spotty and only served to increase his anxiety as rumors of the camps began to reach the Polish populace. Organized executions of up to sixty people a night were carried out in the ghetto. Rumors of impending deportations circulated constantly, competing with rumors that the Warsaw ghetto would remain.

The latter belief was reinforced by the arrival of many Jews from western Europe. Warsaw was to be a major Jewish center for Europe, it was said. The new arrivals thought this was what the Germans meant by "resettlement in the east." People said the war would be over soon. They allowed themselves a small amount of optimism, but there was little objective evidence that any hope was justified. Besides the daily executions, starvation and disease continued to decimate the ghetto population. In May 1942, 3,636 Warsaw Jews died of starvation.

Reports continued to make their way into Warsaw, and from Warsaw to Kiev, about mass shootings, deportations and extermination centers. Bachner's anxiety rose, but there was no way he could return to Warsaw so soon after his last leave. If he returned now, he might not be able to do it when he really needed to. He was reassured somewhat by a letter he received from Schwalbe, slipped in with some Kellner paperwork. It was cryptic enough that any stranger would have found it innocuous, but Schwalbe managed to let Bachner know that his family now had special permits, stating that they worked at a German factory. This, the work once again of the influential Lonia Ostrowski, not only helped make ends meet, but provided extra protection against being sent to the labor camps.

Bachner would have been even more anxious had he known that a new death camp was being prepared for the Jews of central Poland, including the 350,000 Jews remaining in the Warsaw ghetto. The Jews of Warsaw were already familiar with Treblinka. Jews had been sent to the labor camp since it opened in December of 1941. What they did not know was that Treblinka was spawning an awful twin. No longer just a labor camp, Treblinka was to be the latest death camp.

*   *   *

By late June, it seemed less a question of *if* than of *when* the deportations would begin. The panic increased when, on June 26, the Jews of Poland heard the BBC report on the extermination of Jews in Poland. There was no longer any reason to doubt what the Germans had planned. Still, wishful thinking persisted. Nowhere was this myopia more evident that in the diary entries of the head of the Judenrat, Adam Czerniakow. He wrote of concerts, visiting children's playgrounds, obtaining extra supplies of flour from the Germans and petty bureaucratic annoyances. Almost daily, he quizzed the Germans on rumors of deportations. After being reassured that the rumors were false, he traveled through the ghetto trying to reassure the population. Despite his forced optimism, when questioned, the Judenrat leader nervously admitted that he could not explain why forty railcars stood waiting in the rail yard at the north end of the ghetto.

*   *   *

On Friday, July 26, a Kellner supply transport arrived at the Kiev railroad station. Bachner was on hand to oversee the distribution of lumber, tools and miscellaneous construction materials to the various worksites in the station complex. He was surprised to see the tall, thin figure of Julek Schwalbe emerge from the rail car and stride toward him. Seized by a sudden sense of panic, Bachner started toward Schwalbe. His heart pumped faster as he pushed past a worker, so intent on carrying a heavy pack filled with tools, he did not notice the smaller man.

"Excuse me, Panie Bachner," the worker apologized, but Bachner waved him aside.

"It was my fault," he admitted. He continued across the yard, trying not to let his pace reveal his fear. Julek's appearance could only mean something bad. Schwalbe was not one to come to Kiev on a whim. He felt secure in Warsaw with his Polish wife and his job at the Kellner office. Though totally assimilated and very Polish in appearance, he never took unnecessary risks. His serious demeanor confirmed Bachner's anxieties.

"Julek, what is it?" Bachner inquired anxiously.

Schwalbe started to speak, but Bachner interrupted him, pointing his chin toward the milling workers.

"Not here," he said.

He gave a few instructions to one of the Polish foremen, and led Schwalbe to the one-room office of the Kellner firm in the main building of the station. He told the Ukrainian office worker to take a break and having closed the door behind her, turned to Schwalbe, anticipating the worst.

"It's started," Schwalbe said. He turned away, looking out the window as he told Bachner the news. "Deportations from the ghetto. They took six thousand on Monday."

"My family! Are they gone?"

"No. They are safe for now. But for how long?" He shrugged, turning to face his friend. "I can't say. Kazaniecki is in daily contact with Ostrowski, your father and his girlfriend's brother, Teifeld. They are taking those without work permits. Seizing people on the streets."

"Where . . . ?"

"No one knows for sure. Rumor says Treblinka."

"The labor camp?" Bachner asked in agitation tinged with hope. Even the labor camp was better than some of the rumors he had been hearing.

"Willi," said Schwalbe, "I just don't know. But we knew you would want to know. Luckily, the transport was scheduled and Kellner was back in Dresden. I'm catching the return train tomorrow, will you be coming back with me?"

"Of course. We'll have to move quickly. Do you have the documents ready?"

"Documents are no problem. Getting them out of the ghetto is a problem. Now that they have sprung the trap, the Germans have sealed the ghetto tighter than ever. It can be done, but it's going to be expensive."

"Don't worry about expense, you and your father-in-law can hide the expense if need be. Can we count on Kazaniecki?" asked Bachner.

"I trust him completely," replied Schwalbe. "He really loves Teifeld's sister. He will do anything for Hania, and any friend of hers is a friend of his. He is already working on contacts to help."

Just then, Fabish burst through the door. "Willi!" he shouted. "I just heard—" He stopped in mid-sentence, noticing Schwalbe for the first time.

"It's all right, uncle. This is Julek Schwalbe, alias Juljusz Stroynowski."

"Our Jewish bookkeeper?" asked Fabish warily. Then he continued tensely, "Do you know what I just heard from one of the new workers?"

"I can guess. The deportations?" said Bachner.

"So you know. What are you going to do?" asked his uncle.

"We will have to bring them here, Warsaw is no longer safe for Jews. What about you, Julek?"

"I will stay in Warsaw. I feel safer there. Besides, you will still need someone at the office. My father-in-law and I can be of more help there."

Bachner agreed. "Uncle Fabish, I'm going to leave you in charge. I don't know how long this will take. Do you think you can handle it?"

"No problem, nephew. Just get them out." He gripped Bachner's shoulders with work-strengthened hands. "Bring them here safe, and in one piece."

"If you have any problems, you can contact Engineer Nieczajuk. He is the Kellner supervisor in Zitomir. He doesn't know our secret, but he owes me a favor. Just tell him I sent you."

When the secretary returned, she found the three men engaged in earnest conversation. Bachner told her that he had urgent business in Warsaw and that Fabiszkiewicz would be in charge until his return. He went through the rest of the day in a daze and slept very little that night. The train to Warsaw left early the next afternoon and because of the ever-present delays, it was an exhausted Bachner who emerged into the Warsaw station on Sunday morning, July 28, 1942.

Kellner was still out of Warsaw. His work in the Ukraine had been so profitable that the firm was expanding its operations. He was now in Norway, bidding on a contract for a hydroelectric dam for the occupying Germans and their puppet government under Vidkun Quisling. He would not be returning to Warsaw for at least three more weeks.

When Bachner and Schwalbe returned to the office, which also served as the living quarters for Julek and his wife Ruth, they found Gerda Reichenbaum sitting with Ruth. Gerda's face was streaked with tears; she seemed to have lost her characteristic confidence.

"Gerda," inquired Schwalbe, "what is it? What has happened?"

"It's Dita," she replied, fresh tears filling her eyes. "They— they were found out. A szmalcownik found out about her and her husband. She gave him all her mother's jewels but he wants 10,000 zlotys or he will turn them in to the Gestapo."

The szmalcowniki were Poles who made their living hunting down Jews for rewards from the Gestapo, or to extort money from the victims—frequently both. Gerda had been living with her friend Edith and her husband: Jews who, like her, were passing as Gentiles.

"How did you get away?" asked Bachner.

"That Dita," said Gerda forlornly, "she is so quick, she never panics. When the scum came to the door, she went right to my room, opened the door and whispered 'Leave.'" Gerda dabbed a white kerchief at her tear-filled eyes. "I went out the window and down the escape. Then I called her from across the street. 'No,' she said, 'I am much too busy, I can't see you today.' I knew something was wrong, so I waited until she came out of the building and followed her down the street.

"She told me she had given the szmalcownik everything she had, but still he held her husband. The swine had sent her out to get money. Julek," she reached for Schwalbe's hand, "I know she is not your friend, but she is mine. They gave me a place to stay when I had nowhere to go. Can you lend me the money?"

"Gerda." He sighed, shaking his head. "I'd like to but . . . we have to get Willi's family out of the ghetto. And the Teifelds. The

Ostrowskis. I just don't know where the extra money will come from."

"We'll get you the money, Gerda," interrupted Bachner, "but you can't return there." He got 10,000 zlotys from a desk and put it in an envelope. "Give this to your friend, get your things if you can, but don't take any unnecessary chances. Come back here. You can help us. We have a lot to do."

Within a few hours Gerda was back safe. Her friend and her husband were also safe for the time being, having found shelter with a mutual friend. The incident had a profound effect on Gerda, however. Until that time she had moved about Warsaw freely, working as a beautician or a secretary during the day, and pursuing her true love—music—in the evening. She had allowed herself to live almost normally. Now, with the deportations and the loss of her safe housing, she told Bachner that she felt adrift. Concerned, he suggested that she come along when he took his family to Kiev. It was an offer she eagerly accepted.

The next day, July 29, 1942, the planning for the escape began in earnest. Bachner was frustrated to learn that a wait was unavoidable; security was just too tight in the ghetto now. Those susceptible to bribery refused to cooperate until the Germans relaxed the iron grip that had seized the ghetto in the first few panicked days of deportations. On the first day of deportations, the ghetto walls had been surrounded by Ukrainian and Latvian soldiers in SS uniforms at 25-yard intervals. Security had loosened somewhat as the week progressed, but leaving and entering the ghetto was still impossible.

Their contact was by phone: although most of the ghetto was cut off from outside contact, some phone lines had been clandestinely maintained. Most of the remaining lines had been stolen earlier from unsuspecting ghetto inhabitants. For a bribe, telephone workers would rewire a line from an old number to a new location. Bachner used a black marketeer's phone to communicate with his father and Lonia Ostrowski. Anything could be purchased in the ghetto for a fee now—anything, that is, except freedom.

Of all Bachner's acquaintances, Tadeusz (Tadek) Kazaniecki, although he could no longer move in and out of the ghetto, knew the most about what went on there. Tadeusz was an unlikely choice for underground activities. From an upper-middle-class Gentile family in northern Poland, Kazaniecki had gone to school in Warsaw, then returned to his native Gombin to work as a banker. There, he renewed his acquaintance with an old school friend and prosperous jeweler, Abraham Teifeld. Through Abraham, he met Hania, Teifeld's sister.

Kazaniecki knew his family would never accept a Jewish daughter-in-law, just as the orphaned Hania knew her brother would not really approve of her marrying a Gentile. That did not stop the tall, blond, handsome Tadek from falling in love with the petite, blue-eyed Hania.

When the war broke out, the Teifelds' store was seized by the Germans. Kazaniecki announced to Hania that he would save her and her family. He returned to Warsaw and stayed with the family he had lived with when he went to school there. The Teifelds—Abraham, Hania and three other sisters—soon followed.

Bachner, Schwalbe and Kazaniecki decided that family and friends would be removed from the ghetto a few at a time, then sent to Kiev on several transports scheduled for the second half of August. Willi would go on the first transport to be there to help all new arrivals. They would bring Bachner's parents, brother Bruno and wife Cesia, Heniek and Gerda. The Teifelds and Ostrowskis planned to stay in the Gentile section of Warsaw.

The old and the young were most at risk, especially the young. The Germans seemed intent on removing all children from the ghetto. Fifteen-year-old Bruno, therefore, would come out first; very small in stature like his father and brother, he had grown pale and emaciated after two years in the ghetto. He now looked much younger than he was. Slipping Bruno into a work detail would not be feasible, so Bachner came up with a riskier plan.

A courthouse straddled the ghetto. It had two entrances: one on the ghetto side which was closely monitored and another outside the ghetto where Gentile Poles could freely enter and leave. For a hefty bribe, Bachner managed to arrange for Bruno to be called to the courthouse on the morning of August 6, as a witness for a trial.

Another bribe went to a Gentile Pole who would meet the boy and bring him out the Aryan entrance.

That morning Bruno and Heniek did not go to work, but remained at the apartment on Sliska Street to wait until the eleven o'clock rendezvous at the courthouse. On the other side, Bachner waited anxiously at the Kellner office. Eleven o'clock came and went, eleven-thirty, then noon. Still there was no word. Bachner paced back and forth, watched anxiously by the others. Finally, at one in the afternoon, the phone rang. It was the Pole.

"There's a problem," Bachner heard him say, his heart sinking. "I waited until now just to make sure. There was an Aktion today in the Little Ghetto. Your brother never showed up here."

"Where are they taking them? Do you know?"

"Where they take them all. To the assembly point, the Umschlagplatz," the caller replied, referring to the rail yard at the north end of the ghetto where the Jews were loaded onto railcars for transport to the camps. "I'm sorry, Panie Bachner, but there's nothing I can do."

Bachner hung up and turned to the others. "It's Bruno and Heniek, they're being taken to the Umschlagplatz." His flat tone gave little sign of the panic he felt.

Kazaniecki got up and hurried toward the door. "I have a contact, a German officer. We'll get him to go there and see if he can find them." The door slammed behind him and Bachner returned to his pacing.

The afternoon dragged on. There was little anyone could do but wait. Bachner could only imagine what must be going on in the streets of the ghetto. Bruno was only fifteen, Heniek twenty. Would they have any chance of escape?

At nearly four o'clock, Kazaniecki returned to the Kellner office. He shook his head at the others. "I waited outside the walls. The German was there for almost an hour, but he said it was impossible. There were ten thousand people there." He put a hand on Bachner's shoulder. "There is still some hope. The German said that some with work papers were returned to the ghetto."

And so, the wait continued. Hoping against hope, Bachner and the others sat in the Kellner office as dusk overtook the August day. At seven or eight, the phone rang. Bachner answered. It was his father, calling from the ghetto. Heniek had returned to the apartment, but Bruno, the youngest Bachner child, was gone. Wilhelm held the cold phone to his ear as Papa Bachner told his eldest son the story of his brother's disappearance.

That morning the two young men had waited in the deserted apartment. Bruno put on his best clothes, which were at least two sizes too small. He had not worn them for over a year. The day was warm and sunny. But at around eight, about an hour after the others had left for work, the sound of trucks and screaming had come in through the open window.

"Aktion! Aktion!" The loudspeakers told everyone to leave the buildings and assemble on the street. Bruno and Heniek froze. They were trapped. Unlike some families, they had no hiding place in their apartment. They had not thought they needed one because they had work permits. As they sat staring at each other, they began to hear screams and gunfire from across the street. The Ukrainian henchmen were going from room to room in the buildings, making sure no one escaped. If they did not assemble willingly, they would be shot.

"Heniek," said Bruno, "we'd better do as they say."

His older cousin, seeing no alternative, grabbed some bread, wrapped it in a napkin and handed it to Bruno.

"Here, take this. You've had no breakfast and who knows when we'll be able to eat again." Bruno shouldered the small backpack he had filled with his belongings in preparation for his escape from the ghetto. The two young men sadly went downstairs and joined the throng in the street.

Nearly a thousand old people, children and women milled around in panic. They were surrounded by a few SS officers, hundreds of Latvian and Ukrainian guards and a contingent of Jewish ghetto policemen. Heniek looked up and down the street; for as far as he could see, it was the same. It looked as though the entire Little Ghetto was assembled on Sliska Street.

To his right were the children from Janusz Korczak's orphanage. Many were crying, but most were trying to follow Korczak's instructions to line up and stay calm. They stood there, emaciated limbs sticking out of their blue uniforms.

Every few minutes, the rat-a-tat of gunfire burst through the noise of frightened whispers and crying children, as the militia searched the buildings for any who had tried to hide, or dealt with someone on the street who tried to dart into a building or alleyway. Heniek walked up to a Jewish policeman who stood armed with a truncheon.

"Where are they taking us?" he asked.

"Where do you think? To the Umschlagplatz," he replied flatly. "The Judenrat has been ordered to deliver six thousand Jews every day."

"And Czerniakow agreed?" asked Bruno.

"Czerniakow?" the policeman snorted. "Czerniakow is dead. He committed suicide the minute he found out the Germans had lied to him about the deportations."

"How can you do this?" Heniek asked. "How can you help send your own people to Treblinka?"

The policeman became defensive, looked around and said under his breath, "Look, it's you or me, my friend. I have a wife and two children. So what should I do, fight the Nazis and get myself and them killed?" With that, he shoved Heniek back into the ragged line of Sliska Street inhabitants.

"But we have work permits!" Heniek protested.

"Don't talk to me about it. Tell it to them at the Umschlagplatz."

They stood for at least another hour as the August sun cleared the buildings to the east and began to warm those who waited for orders. Finally, the group began to move, down Sliska to Twarda, then up to the overpass on Chlodna that connected the Little Ghetto to the main one. They looked down over the finger of Aryan territory that separated the two Jewish quarters and at the few Gentiles and guards who watched them trudge over the wooden bridge, a human river of misery and fear.

Looking back, Heniek could see Korczak at the head of his orphans, a small girl in his arms, and a boy of about eight clutching his hand. An older boy carried the orphanage's banner, green with the Star of David, just as others had done when the orphanage had been forced to move into the ghetto.

Should he run for it? Heniek wondered. What were the chances that he could escape the machine guns of the militiamen? Probably pretty slim. Just then, Bruno reached out and grasped Heniek's hand; he looked to his cousin for reassurance. It was a gesture one would expect from a small child, not a boy of fifteen. Heniek wanted to reassure him that it would be all right, that they would both be home before supper, but he knew it was not all right. He knew that those who went to the railroad cars did not come back.

The trip to the Umschlagplatz took hours. Before they had left the Little Ghetto, the people of Sliska Street had been joined by those from Panska, Prosta, Marianska and others. Thousands of Jews had been forced into ragged lines. At times, all forward motion stopped, but for most of the interminable morning, the line crept like a worm, inching toward the edge of a chasm. The sun grew hotter as the day progressed. Bruno and Heniek ate some of the stale bread they had brought, but they were plagued by a terrible thirst they had no hope of quenching.

It was late in the afternoon before they reached the northern end of the ghetto. The crowd moved even more slowly as it funnelled through the gate to the Umschlagplatz. There, SS officers checked over the work papers of those fortunate enough to have them. Occasionally, a relatively strong-looking man would be pulled out of the line that shuffled toward the rail cars.

Bruno looked up at Heniek, his eyes brimming with tears. "I really don't care anymore." He sighed. "But what will Mamma say?" As Heniek and Bruno went through this gauntlet, the officer glanced at their papers, then at both of them. He looked at Heniek and jerked his head to the left. Heniek was pulled from the line and joined the small group of men just inside the gate. The officer looked at Bruno, and once more at his work papers. He snorted in disgust and threw the papers down upon the growing pile that lay at his feet. One of the militiamen nearby shoved the small boy into the crowd making its way to the railcars.

Heniek looked on helplessly. Neither he nor Bruno shouted or protested. It would do no good. The yard was filled with shouts. Machine-gun fire swiftly answered any who resisted in the slightest fashion. Guards dragged bodies from the ground where they fell, placing them in a heap next to the wall to prevent them from interfering with the steady flow of the living into the railcars. Bruno looked back at his cousin briefly, then was lost from sight.

Bachner's hand held the phone receiver still throughout his father's story until he asked one last question.

"Kazaniecki bribed a man, a German officer, to look for them. Did they see him?"

"No," Papa Bachner said, his voice a whisper of despair.

Wilhelm's hand trembled; his fingers clamped like a vise around the hard plastic, aching as he listened to the tragic news that neither Heniek nor Bruno had noticed the German officer moving through the chaos calling their names. His calls were lost among the shouts, cries, curses and gunfire of the Umschlagplatz. Lost along with Bruno, amidst the mindless terror of the Third Reich.

Bachner slowly hung up the phone. Without looking at the others, he walked into the office he had been using. Shutting the door against the silent stares of Tadek, Ruth, Gerda and Julek, Wilhelm turned to face the desk. He kept his own desk in the Kiev office as tidy as his appearance. Rows of pens lay neatly marshalled, fencing in carefully separated stacks of forms and folders.

Papers were strewn across the desk in front of him. Earlier, he had tried to work, to fill out the papers his family members would need if they were to escape the ghetto. As the hours passed, he had struggled to block out the despair that crept from his gut into his throat. When he had filled in Bruno's name in bold black strokes across a Reichsbahn work permit, he had frozen, pen poised above the half-finished document. With a curse, he had wadded the paper and tossed it toward the trash.

Now Willi knelt to pick up the crumpled piece of paper. Still kneeling, he smoothed it flat across his knee, staring through his tears at his brother's name. *Bruno Bachner.*

His stomach cramped and he leaned forward, pressing his fists into his midsection. He felt as if iron fingers gripped his intestines. Of all those he hoped to save, why Bruno?

"He is only fifteen!" Bachner shouted. "Fifteen, do you hear?"

Clenching his fist with the paper clutched in it, he fought against the wail rising from his lungs, fought to maintain the cool arrogance that had muffled his mind like a down comforter, keeping the Nazi terror from fully entering his consciousness. He failed. No amount of German-schooled certainty could contain the cry of animal anguish that broke through the silence, spilling despair into every corner of the carefully maintained Kellner office.

7 HOPE IN THE EAST

WHEN WICKED MEN GAIN PRE-EMINENCE,
    OTHER MEN HIDE.
AT THEIR FALL, THE JUST FLOURISH.
                    PROVERBS 28:28

Friday, August 7, 1942, passed in almost complete silence. All pretext of work ceased at the Kellner office. For most of the day, Bachner was alone, the Schwalbes and Gerda having gone to Stamberger's house. Tadek Kazaniecki stopped by briefly, but after trying unsuccessfully to alleviate Bachner's grief, he too left.

Waves of guilt and self-recrimination swept over Bachner as he lay on the bed in the dim office. The August heat became more and more oppressive as he tossed and turned. His family had been spared up to now. Granted, no one was sure that Anna and Hilde were alive in Russia, but he chose to believe that they were, that they had moved east in time, had avoided the flood of death that swept behind the Nazi invasion. But now, Bruno—only fifteen years old, with his whole life ahead of him.

Bachner shifted on the uncomfortable bed. Perhaps the boy could survive the camp. Perhaps he could try to get his brother out. Bachner cursed, shoving his pillow against the back of his neck. The foolish hope he held close to his heart could not be stretched that far. His brother was probably already dead. He had heard the rumors; after his experience in the east, he believed them. The Nazis had replaced the disorganized slaughter of the Ukraine with the bureaucratic efficiency of the Vernichtungslager, the death camps.

His mind continued to spin out "whys" and "if onlys" until any other course of action than the one he had taken seemed preferable. He had thought he could fool the entire German Reich, he told himself bitterly. Did he think that he was any more blessed by God than the hundreds of thousands who had already died? Of course not. He had been lucky, and now his luck had turned.

He knew what he should be doing. He should be inside the ghetto, sharing the pain of his parents, comforting the wife that he felt he hardly knew—being a Jew, not pretending to be one of the oppressors—not contaminating himself with this ongoing contact with the monstrous master race.

Should he stand with the scores of voiceless, silent victims who accepted death with dignity, accomplishing nothing with the sacrifice of their lives? What did the Germans care about Jews dying with dignity? Did it soften their hearts to see sons and daughters refuse to abandon elderly parents? Did it make them see the humanity of the Jews when parents struggled until the end to protect their children from the inevitable?

No, how could they see humanity in others when their own humanity had been buried beneath the bodies of thousands of Jews—smothered in ditches, choked in gas chambers, gunned down in the streets of village after village. Any compassion the Nazis had ever known had been drowned in the blood of an entire race of people. They felt no empathy for their victims.

The only way to defeat them was to live, to live in spite of their efforts. To survive, despite their lust to exterminate. He must continue to resist: for Bruno, for every Jew sacrificed on the altar of Hitler's madness, he would recommit himself to the task of removing the remainder of his family from the ghetto. Their survival would be the best revenge. But how? The cordon around the ghetto had loosened only because the initial manpower demands were too huge to sustain. Guards were no longer stationed every twenty yards, but security at the gates was still doubled. The smugglers who usually could be bribed to take someone out were refusing until ghetto security was eased.

On Saturday, he met again with Julek and Tadek. Everything was ready. Papers had been prepared for Bachner's wife and parents, Heniek, Hania Teifeld and her family and the Ostrowskis. A series of transports of equipment to Kiev would begin the next week. The escapees would go in different groups. Bachner would go with the first transport; Kazaniecki, now a bona fide employee of the Kellner firm, would supervise the second; and Schwalbe, the third. Bachner's accommodations in Kiev would be a safe house for the new arrivals as they came in, at least until other arrangements could be made.

As they sat checking and re-checking the documents, a call came in. It was his father.

"Willi, you must come. It's your mother."

Bachner drew in a sharp breath, "Another Aktion?"

"No, no," his father replied. "Not that. She has given up, Willi. She will not eat. She will not talk. She does not look at me when I try to talk to her. We took her to the factory this morning, but she does nothing but sit and stare. If you come, maybe she will break out of it."

"But Papa," said Bachner gently, "getting in and out of the ghetto is not as easy as it used to be."

"Just try, Willi. That's all I ask. Just try. We will be at the Többens factory on Leszno and Zelazna all day. Please come."

Bachner hung up the phone and turned to the inquisitive Kazaniecki. "It's my mother. She is very depressed about Bruno. My father insists I come to see her."

"It's risky," said Tadek. "You might get in and not get out."

"Well, then," replied Bachner with a hint of humor, "you will just have to add Wilhelm Bachner to the list of people you need to rescue from the ghetto."

He turned to Gerda, who was typing up Kellner manifests for the upcoming transports, "Gerda, make me out a very official requisition form for the firm of Walther Többens for wool coats for the Kellner Baustelle in Kiev."

"Wool coats in August? Do you think that will work?" asked Tadek.

Bachner turned and said, "Come now, Tadek, you must think like a German. I will tell them I do not need them until October, but that I want to order early to assure that I have them in time."

"Well, all I can say is you have more nerve, or what do you say in Yiddish . . . chutzpa, than anyone I know . . . except Hania, that is," he added with a laugh.

"I'll need all the chutzpa I can muster," said Bachner caustically.

Despite the heat, he wore his leather coat and boots. It seemed that every inhabitant of the occupied areas had been conditioned to cower in the presence of black leather. When black boots stamped impatiently, documents tended to be given a cursory glance and their bearer was wished a good day and passed on his way. Such was Bachner's reception at the Leszno Street gate, which opened directly across from the entrance to the German-owned Többens clothing factory. Once inside the gate, however, he found his way blocked by a group of Jewish workers trudging along in a long line under the watchful eyes of Ukrainian guards. He waited as the men shuffled along in a seemingly endless stream. Suddenly, impatient and unable to wait any longer, he shouted, "Halt!"

The nearest guard looked up in surprise and without even turning to look at him, the Jews opened a space for him to proceed through. With a self-castigating curse, Bachner walked through the parted line of his people and proceeded across the street to the factory. Glancing back, he saw the river of Jewish men close ranks and resume their lethargic pace.

He presented his requisitions at the Többens office with typical efficiency. He was assured that there would be no problem filling his order, a fact he sincerely doubted, but accepted good-naturedly. He wished the clerk good day and left the office but not the building. If anyone questioned him, he would show them his receipt and say he had gotten lost.

In the main work area, there was little danger of his being noticed. The huge drab grey room was filled with drab grey people.

Only about a third of them were working, some sorting used clothing, others mending, still others making new garments from blankets and other recycled material. Along the walls on either side and especially in the back of the room hundreds of people sat, stood or lay on the floor. Supervisors at the Többens plant had discovered a new source of income, selling work passes to people even when there was no room or materials for them to work with. It was here that Bachner found his wife and parents. His father thanked him for coming. Cesia held back uncertainly until he came over and embraced her. He then turned to his mother.

Helena Bachner was there, but not there. No sign of recognition sparkled in her eyes when her son knelt down and took her hands in his. As he spoke soothingly to her, telling her that it would be all right, that soon he would take her out of the ghetto, she continued to stare off into the distance. Her once thick, dark hair formed a wispy grey halo around her head; her hollow cheeks had lost their rosy color. The loss of her younger son seemed to be the final blow; she looked as if she could take no more. Willi squeezed her limp hand; her body just had not yet joined her vanquished soul.

"Has she eaten anything?" he asked his father.

"I spoon-fed her some broth this morning," Heinrich replied. "But it's not enough, Willi. She won't survive unless she eats."

"I sat up with her all last night," said Cesia wearily. "I don't think she even slept. Once she called out Bruno's name. But other than that she has not spoken since Thursday night."

"Well, do what you can. Try to get her to eat and drink something." He hesitated, then took his wife's hand and looked down at the floor. "Cesia, I'm sorry I haven't been here for you. I know I haven't been much of a husband."

"But Willi," she protested, her voice warm, urgent, "without you we would be dead. The money you send keeps us alive, not just us but Heniek, and my mother too. I know you are trying your best."

He looked up and stared silently at her as she waited for him to say something more. Her face blurred as his eyes welled with tears. Suddenly he embraced her with a ferocity that surprised them both, holding her against his chest until he could scarcely breathe.

"Soon, Cesia, very soon, I will take you away from here. I have such a beautiful house waiting for you in Kiev. It has a yellow kitchen, a huge stove. Even a piano. We've never had a chance to be happy, Cesia, but I promise you we will be happy, very soon."

He kissed her forehead and broke away, turning to his father. "I'm sorry, Papa. I wish I could do more." He lowered his voice so no one else would overhear. "All I can say is hold on. I'm not sure when, but sometime in the next week. Ostrowski will let you know. How is Heniek?"

"Heniek is fine," Heinrich replied. "Still a little shook up, but who wouldn't be after a trip to the Umschlagplatz? He is still working at the laundry. Now he spends the nights there too. He says it's safer. But he is coming for dinner tonight. I will pass on your message."

Bachner nodded. With one final embrace, he turned and slipped out of the factory, crossed the street and exited the ghetto.

*   *   *

That next evening, Papa Bachner once again called the Kellner office with grim news. That morning, just as they were getting ready to eat, people had started screaming in the street below, "Aktion! Aktion!" The screaming spread through the street until it filled the air above and below them, accompanied by the frantic thudding of panicked feet. Papa Bachner and Heniek had looked at each other; then the elder man shouted for Heniek to run, to try to get back to the factory before the street was blocked off. They never saw Helena get up. It was the first time she had moved of her own volition since she learned that her son had been deported. She was already on the small balcony outside the apartment before they noticed her. She had not paused or hesitated, but pitched headfirst over the railing as Papa Bachner and Heniek had stood horrified, unable to move.

The two men rushed to peer over the railing. Helena's small form lay crumpled on the pavement, four stories below, ignored by the people who continued to run past her in every direction.

Papa Bachner ran from the apartment, stumbling down the stairs two and three steps at a time with Heniek on his heels. One of the other tenants called from a landing as they passed him, "It's all right. It was a false alarm, there is no raid. Hey! Didn't you hear me? There is no Aktion."

Heniek and his uncle did not stop until they reached Helena. They found her lying face down, her head in the street and her body over the curb. Papa Bachner lifted her wrist, felt along the broken bone for a pulse. He pressed an ear against her back, listening, hoping. He felt only stillness, heard only silence. Heniek put a hand on his shoulder.

"Come, Uncle. We must get her off the street."

They carried Helena up to the apartment and lay her on the bed. Heniek apologized repeatedly for needing to leave for work.

"Go." Papa Bachner waved him toward the door. "You cannot risk being late and losing your job. There is nothing to be done here." He turned back to his wife. "Go," he repeated softly.

He had stayed with his wife until the Chevra-Kadisha, the collectors of the dead, came to take her away. His voice on the phone sounded hollow, more ancient than the faded prayer book he kept in his coat pocket. Wilhelm wondered if his father would find a prayer to ease this pain. His father explained that he had tried to phone earlier, but the blackmarketeer, whose phone he paid to use, had not let him call until now.

"If she only could have held out for a few more days, Willi. She would have been safe," he lamented.

Willi felt the muscles in his throat tightening, hardening against the words he wanted to shout. *No! If only I had acted months ago, she would be safe. Bruno would be alive. I risked your lives because I was secure, far away in Kiev. I left you all here in the ghetto to die.*

But he said only, "Papa, I'm so sorry."

"Well, perhaps God knows best. She would have had a hard time pretending to be anything but what she was. She just couldn't take it any more. Her baby gone, her two daughters, God knows where, and you . . . never knowing if you were coming back. Having to lose you again each time you left."

Bachner clasped the phone to his ear, trying to think of something to say, trying not to let the weight of his guilt overwhelm him. After a long pause, he asked his father, "What will you do now, Papa?"

"Well, I think I will go stay with Cesia and her mother. There is a rumor that the small ghetto will be liquidated completely in a few days. I don't know if it's true, but I think I'll be safer in the large ghetto. Besides, with Heniek sleeping at the laundry, I'd be the only one here." With uncharacteristic candor, he added, "I don't want to stay here, Willi. There are too many bad memories."

Bachner rang off, warning his father to keep Lonia Ostrowski aware of his whereabouts in case the time came to leave the ghetto. The pressure to remove them at all costs was mounting. Kazaniecki still felt it was too risky, and reminded Bachner that if one of the party was caught, he or she might implicate everyone left in the ghetto and their whole operation out of the Kellner office.

But a few days later, on Friday, August 14, it was Kazaniecki who pushed for a rescue as soon as possible. Tadek came to the Kellner office that morning, pale and agitated, "You're right Willi, we can't wait any longer. We'll just have to increase the bribes until the smugglers agree to take them out."

"What made you change your mind?" asked Bachner.

"Yesterday afternoon, there was a raid at the Többens factory."

Bachner stood, grasping the edge of his desk.

Tadek held up a hand. "Don't worry. They're all safe. I talked to Teifeld this morning."

"Well, what happened?" interrupted Schwalbe. "They were supposed to be safe there. Lord knows those work cards cost enough."

"The Germans finally realized that not everyone was in the plant to work. They came and began pulling out those they thought were just hiding, including Hania."

"But you said they were all safe." Bachner walked around his desk to face Kazaniecki.

Kazaniecki held up a hand and continued, "Let me finish. You don't know Hania. Get her mad and she can be something else. She marched up to a German officer, all five-foot-one of her, and said *'Mein Herr, Sie haben ein Irrtum.'* Can you believe it? She told the Gestapo he was mistaken. She looked up at him and complained, saying she was a good worker, that she had worked there for a long time." Tadek shook his head, chuckling. "He called her a liar, but he pushed her back in line with the other workers."

"I can believe it," said Bachner. "Hania's instincts were perfect. Sometimes getting mad at them is the best way. They don't expect it. I've used that trick myself a few times."

"There she was," continued Kazaniecki, "bodies on the ground, anyone resisting getting shot. And she gives a German officer a piece of her mind." He clicked his tongue.

"Tadek, I am looking forward to meeting your Hania," said Bachner. "We can use someone like her in Kiev."

"Well, I can tell you, after this, I am looking forward to getting out of Warsaw myself. Her brother says we can't wait any more, no place is safe. Stay at home, you get taken; go to work, you get taken." He shook his head and sighed. "So what do you say? Shall we go ahead?"

"Yes. We planned to move next week anyway." Bachner stepped back behind his desk and riffled through some papers until he found the one he wanted. He ran his finger along the schedule. "The first transport leaves on Tuesday. I'll be on that one with my father and Cesia. You will come on the next transport a week from Tuesday. Do you have some place where Hania can hide until then?"

"Don't worry. It's all arranged. Abraham wants his sisters out as soon as possible. Genia will leave after Hania."

"Good. Now," he pointed at Julek, "Schwalbe will go on the final transport on Friday, the 28th. Heniek will be on that one, along with Julek's brother and Ruth's uncle. Are they ready to go, Julek?"

"More than ready." Schwalbe nodded. "They are tired of hiding." Richard Schwalbe and Moritz Stamberger, unlike Julek and his father-in-law Adolf, could not "pass" easily and had been in hiding on the Gentile side of Warsaw for months.

"Tadek," continued Bachner, "we will need some help getting Heniek a place to hide outside the ghetto and someone to get him to the train station. I don't like to make the circle any wider, but we have to trust someone."

"I have someone in mind," said Kazaniecki. "He is an old friend from school. I roomed with his family. We are like brothers."

"Brothers are well and good," cautioned Bachner, "but can you trust him?"

"He already knows about Hania. We will be staying at his parent's house. But I've thought of an incentive. Give him a job in Kiev. He's a good worker."

"Let's see if he can get Heniek there safely. If he can, you can tell him we will give him a job."

*   *   *

As luck would have it, the raids slowed somewhat after August 15. On August 11, the order was given to empty the Little Ghetto by 2:00 p.m. Papa Bachner had left none too soon, which had given him time to remove the few things he wanted to take with him. He and Cesia waited at her mother's apartment for word to come of their exodus from the ghetto.

Cesia had tried repeatedly to talk her mother into leaving the ghetto, but the woman would have none of it. She had been born and raised in the Jewish quarter of Warsaw. She knew she could not pass and would only endanger the others.

Worry gnawed at them all. Each hour felt like a day, each day like a week. As the sun rose on the cloudless morning of August 18, the pressure of the still, unmoving air made it hard to breathe. The night had not removed all the heat that lingered from the day before.

Papa Bachner and Cesia had been told to wear several layers of clothing, for they would not be able to carry any luggage with them. He squeezed Cesia's hand and laughed.

"It's just like Willi to pick the hottest day of the year and then tell us to wear layers of clothes."

They were leaving with separate work details, so Papa Bachner bowed deeply to Mrs Diamant, thanking her for her hospitality. He embraced Cesia, wished her good luck and told her they would drink a toast to freedom that evening. Then he was gone.

Cesia's mother came with her to the place where she was to join the work detail. Lonia Ostrowski was there with Abraham Teifeld and a small dark-haired woman with thick glasses. There was no time for introductions.

Cesia turned to her mother. "Mama, I can't leave you here alone," she said, starting to cry.

Her mother gave her a hug and then held both her shoulders and looked her in the eye. "Cesia, I am old, my life is almost over. My husband is gone. My sons are gone. You are all I have left. Your life is with your husband now. Go. Live! It is what I want."

Cesia embraced her mother as both of them sobbed quietly. After a moment, Lonia Ostrowski, who had waited quietly as mother and daughter said their goodbyes, gently tapped Cesia on the shoulder.

"It is time, Cesia. You and Hania must go."

Cesia and the dark-haired woman, now identified as Hania Teifeld, shared no words as they walked across the street and slipped into the line of workers getting ready to leave the ghetto. The Polish foreman made eye contact briefly, then looked over and nodded at Ostrowski. He turned and started moving the group toward the gates. The Jewish policemen stopped him, looked at his papers, then counted the workers. The procedure was repeated by the Ukrainian guard outside the gate.

The two young women tried not to look around too much, even though it was their first trip outside those few square miles of misery in almost two years. Cesia glanced at the smaller woman as they neared the arranged location. Large bushes lined the street beside them. Hania took the lead, pulling her companion into the mass of twigs and leaves. If the foreman noticed, he gave no sign.

There they waited, hidden beneath the oppressive weight of greenery as the sun rose toward midday, growing hotter with each passing moment. By mid-morning, even the shade of the shrubbery could not protect them from the stifling heat. The smell of sweat, trapped in the layers of wool they wore, mixed with the earthy smell of the dry leaves that crackled underneath them. They went rigid, like rabbits caught in the sights of a hunter's rifle, whenever anyone passed by. They couldn't talk, fearing someone would hear them, so they sat, two strangers glancing furtively at each other and at the activity on the street beyond.

They froze once again as they saw a man's legs approaching. Then they heard him say softly, "Hania?"

Hania smiled and started to get up. Cesia grabbed her arm.

"It's fine," Hania reassured her. "It's Tadek, my friend."

"Come out," whispered Kazaniecki. "Just start walking normally."

Emerging from the bushes was the greatest risk they had yet taken. Once they were walking down the street with this handsome blond man, they would be unobtrusive, but should someone see them coming out of the bushes . . .

Hania stood. Taking Cesia's hand, she pulled her up and out into the bright sunlight.

Tadek hugged her with one arm and smiled at Cesia. "Come, Willi is waiting for you."

Nervously, they walked several blocks until they reached the Kellner office. Kazaniecki told Cesia to go in. He would take Hania to his own lodgings. "See you in Kiev, Panie Bachner."

Cesia timidly walked up the stone steps of the building, opened the door and peered inside.

"You must be Cesia," said the attractive blonde woman seated at the desk. "I'm Gerda. Willi!" she called to the next room.

Bachner came out, strode across the room and gathered his wife into his arms. She clung to him desperately, tears falling as if she had been fighting them all morning.

"It's all right now," he soothed. "You're safe. I won't let anything happen to you. But now we must give you a new look. I can get away with my dark hair," he said, rubbing his hand over his dark curls, "but you, you we will make a blonde. What do you think, Gerda? How will she look as a blonde?"

"Absolutely beautiful," said Gerda, smiling.

"And not only new hair," continued Bachner, "but a new name too. Miss Ferencz, let me introduce my good friend, Miss Czeslawa Dambrowska."

"Miss?" Cesia stepped back, staring at Willi. "Am I not to be your wife?"

"A wife might raise too many questions," said Bachner. "For now you will have to be my friend," he added with a wink. Her pale cheeks turned the shade of a ripe apple and Willi laughed, pulling her to him once more. He kissed the soft brown hair falling over her forehead. "Cesia, no matter what we must pretend to keep you safe, you will always be my wife where it matters. In my heart."

Gerda took Cesia to the living quarters adjacent to the office and began her transformation. Having worked as a beautician before the war, Gerda had put her skills to work many times, helping her friends look more Aryan. When Cesia emerged a few hours later, she had been transformed.

Her hair was peroxided and arranged in stylish curls, her eyebrows plucked to a narrow line. She wore a simple white blouse and wool skirt, but to her husband she looked elegant.

Papa Bachner, whom Willi had brought to the office a few hours earlier than Cesia, looked up from the newspaper he was reading and teased, "Well, well, who is this? Willi, does your wife know you are seeing a Polish girl?"

"Yes, Papa," said Bachner, never taking his eyes off his wife. "She knows that Czeslawa Dambrowska is the most beautiful girl in all of Poland.

"But she is missing something," he added with a smile as he went to his desk, removing a small box from the middle drawer. He opened it and took out a large silver cross. As he started to place it over her head, Cesia pulled away.

"Is that really necessary?" asked his father, voicing Cesia's thoughts.

"It is necessary," said Bachner, matter-of-factly. "Anything that helps us fool them is necessary. God knows what we believe in our hearts. Now, tomorrow we go to Kiev."

They drank the toast Heinrich had promised that morning, and after some more conversation, retired to spend their last night in Warsaw.

The next morning they made their way to the train station. After the previous day, Cesia and Papa Bachner were thankful for the luxury of suitcases and only one layer of clothing. Once at the station, Willi had to assume his supervisory charade, and so was unable to stay with them. He did manage, however, to stay in close proximity until their papers had been checked and they had entered the third-class car along with other workers being sent to the Ukraine. Shortly before the train left the Warsaw station, Bachner returned to the passenger car to join them. The hard wooden benches were uncomfortable, but the car was clean and, most important, it was taking them away from the ghetto.

By mid-morning, they arrived at their first stop: Lublin, in eastern Poland. Gerda said she would like to get up and stretch her legs. Willi gave her a look that told her to be careful, but Gerda just smiled. She was not used to being in hiding and seemed fearless when it came to being around Germans. He knew that she was not about to spend the entire day sitting on a hard wooden bench.

Outside the train, there was considerable activity in the station. Lublin was a major rail center, a routine stopping place for trains between the Reich and the eastern territories. Willi kept a close eye on Gerda as she walked down the station platform watching soldiers, civilians, children and the elderly.

As she neared the end of the station building, she lifted her head, as if she heard a sound. Later, when she returned to the train, she described the sound to Willi. She had heard a strident mewling, like puppies crying, a piercing wail that spoke of pain and separation. It came from a railcar standing alone on a side track. As she looked toward it, a sudden movement in the small window about five feet up the side of the car caught her eye. Every few seconds a white shape would briefly appear then vanish from view, while the multi-voiced wailing continued, unabated.

Gerda covered her mouth with her hand as she realized that they were children. Children no more than eight or ten years old.

Children with shaven heads who managed to gain a purchase on the window sill just long enough to glance outside before they fell back down. An entire railcar full of small frightened children, wondering where they were and what was going to happen to them. Jewish children, of that she had no doubt, evidence that deportations were occurring in more places than just Warsaw. Gerda turned her head away and gulped air to quell her heaving stomach. It was all the worse because she could do nothing. She could offer no comfort to those tiny doomed souls who wailed out their misery.

She returned to the railcar, pale and sweating, and could only shake her head at Willi's worried look. She was silent at first, as if trying to forget, to erase the horror from her mind. Then, in a harsh whisper, she described what she had seen. When she finished, the images of small shaven heads haunted her eyes. She turned to stare out the window, saying no more for the rest of the long, silent trip.

*   *   *

The children Gerda saw were most likely on their way to the Belzec extermination camp. Perhaps the train had been overloaded with its human cargo and had to leave a car behind for a later train. The trains came to Belzec with terrifying frequency in August, 1942.

During that month, 145,000 Jews were gassed at Belzec. Having exterminated most of the Jews from the Lublin area, the Nazis began deporting Jews from Lwów and the Ukraine. Incredibly, the number exterminated at Belzec was only half the total number of Jews killed in occupied Poland during the month of August. In Warsaw, more than 140,000 Jews were sent to their deaths at Treblinka, as well as close to 100,000 from the surrounding areas. At the newest camp, Auschwitz, 13,000 persons from the surrounding area met their deaths along with 22,000 from France and the Lowland countries. Children as young as three were sent to the camps without their parents. In one month, over 400,000 people were gassed.

*   *   *

The escapees arrived in Kiev late on the evening of August 19. They were met at the station by Uncle Fabish, who took them to the house on Yeveshenko Street while Willi oversaw the unloading of the transport items.

Fabish assured Willi that things had gone well during his absence, and that Nieczajuk had been most helpful. Willi told them all the story of how he had earned Nieczajuk's gratitude at the Gestapo office in Warsaw.

"Does he know you are Jewish?" his father asked.

"No, I don't think so," replied Bachner. "I have the feeling it wouldn't change our relationship. Seeing how afraid he is of the Gestapo, it's not information I would want to burden him with."

Gerda agreed, saying she had encountered several people in Warsaw she strongly suspected of being Jews, but she had never said anything. If they were ever caught they would be pressured to denounce others. "What I don't know, I cannot tell," she said with finality.

A few days later, Kazaniecki arrived with the next transport. He and Hania came to the small house on Yeveshenko Street. The housekeeper was told that these were all new employees of the firm. She was a little put out to find that they had brought their own cook with them.

"What could this tiny Polish girl know about cooking?" she asked, hands on her broad hips. "She doesn't look like she has eaten good food in her life."

Cesia lifted her chin and opened her mouth, but Bachner quickly stepped between the two women.

"I would greatly appreciate it if you would allow Miss Dambrowska to manage the kitchen," he said. "You can continue to do the housework, at the same salary, of course."

From the set of her lips and the question narrowing her eyes, Bachner knew that the Ukrainian woman suspected the "cook" was actually much more, just as he had hoped. He hoped that as long as the rations kept coming to her and her family, along with the salary he paid her, she would keep quiet about his new "cook." If she did not, she would do nothing more than spread the rumor that the engineer had finally taken a mistress, a rumor he counted on to protect his wife from closer scrutiny.

In the first week of September 1942, as the war entered its third year, Heniek finally arrived in Kiev. Willi met him at the station late one evening and brought him home to a hearty welcome at the little two-story house that was by now full of former Warsaw inhabitants. As he consumed vast quantities of food at the dinner they had prepared for his arrival, Heniek told the others about his escape from the ghetto.

He had paid a foreman 3,000 zlotys to let him leave the ghetto. After leaving the ghetto, he went with a group of workers to a factory. Outside the factory, he had been contacted by a woman who took him to an adjacent courtyard filled with huge pipes.

"She told me that I was to stay inside a pipe until someone came for me," Heniek said between mouthfuls of food. "She said she would bring me bread and water, but I had to pay her for it."

"Who was this woman?" inquired Bachner, nervous about the number of Poles in Warsaw who knew about their escape.

"I don't know." Heniek shrugged. "She never told me her name, but she charged me enough for my bread." He chuckled.

"She was working with the foreman," said Kazaniecki. "She was the one who got the message to my friend Mietek that Heniek was waiting for him."

"Who is this Mietek?" asked Heniek. "He barely said three words to me the whole time. I waited in that pipe for two whole days, you know. One night there was an air raid, bombs dropping on the street, anti-aircraft guns blazing away. Finally, here comes this guy, calls my name and takes me to his relative's house, all the while complaining about his hangover. Never talked to me, never asked me any questions. Just dropped me off at a house with people who put me in a room and told me to stay away from the windows. A week later he comes again, takes me to the train and puts me on with the other workers. Then he proceeds to empty a bottle of vodka and falls asleep for the rest of the trip."

Kazaniecki looked chagrined. "The last few years have not been kind to Mietek."

Troubled, Bachner frowned at Kazaniecki. "You entrusted my cousin's safety to a drunkard?"

Kazaniecki protested, "Mietek Wilaski is my best friend. He's no drunk. He just likes his vodka a little too well. He can be trusted, believe me. And look, didn't he bring Heniek here safe and sound?"

"Where is this Wilaski now?" Bachner inquired.

"He's in the barracks with the other Poles," said Kazaniecki. "Don't worry, Willi, it will be fine."

"I have to worry, Tadek." Bachner stood up and walked to the window. "I have to worry for all of us. One person can ruin everything. One mistake and we are all dead." He turned back to Tadek. "I worry about the Poles more than the Germans. I can fool the Germans, but the Poles I worry about."

"That's for sure," interjected Hania. "Those Poles, they can spot a Jew a mile away. I may have blonde hair, I may have my papers saying I'm Bronka Kazaniecka, but they look at me and say she could be Jewish.'"

"That happened to me once," said Gerda. "In Krakow. I got help from a German."

"A German helped you escape, a Pole?" asked Bachner incredulously.

Gerda nodded. "I was going to visit my mother in Tarnow. She was in the ghetto, but I could go in and visit her with my papers. I had to wait for a train in Krakow. I was sitting there when a young man came up and sat beside me. He kept trying to start up a conversation. I kept ignoring him. Then he said, 'You don't want to talk to me. You may have to talk to me.' He said it so sweetly, but we both knew what he meant. He knew I was Jewish and was threatening to turn me in.

"I got up and walked away. He followed me. I went out on the street; he was right behind me. I knew I was in big trouble. So what could I do? I went up to a German railroad official and said, 'Sir, that young man over there is bothering me and I don't know what he wants.' Then I tried to look as innocent as I could."

"You didn't!" Hania gasped.

"I did," said Gerda with a satisfied smile. "He asked me my name and I told him. I handed him my papers, then I had a stroke of luck. Earlier, a small boy had been selling holy cards on the platform. He was so insistent, I bought one just to get rid of him. Well, I just stuck it in the folder with my papers. When the German opened it up, out came Mary and Jesus. He asked me if I was Catholic. 'Of course,' said I. Then he went and talked to another official. The two of them went over and spoke to the young man. I don't know what they said, but his face went white and he left in a hurry. Then back to me comes the German, and he says, like my favorite old uncle, 'Don't worry, Fräulein, he won't bother you any more.'"

Everyone laughed except Bachner, who said, "Gerda, you should be more careful. Some day your luck will run out."

"Look who's talking!" said Uncle Fabish, and then proceeded to tell them the story of his daring escape from Janowska.

It went on until long after midnight. The tales of escape somehow helped to blunt the losses that all of them had suffered: those who had been left behind and those who were already dead.

It was impractical for all of them to remain at the small house. Bachner kept the downstairs as his apartment with a spare room for Kellner or others from the firm who might be in Warsaw. Heniek, Papa Bachner and Gerda roomed upstairs; Cesia moved upstairs whenever visitors came. Kazaniecki and Hania rented a small apartment nearby, as did Uncle Fabish.

Gerda immediately went to work in the Kellner office. Her knowledge of German and her typing skills, to say nothing of her reliability, were a great asset to Bachner in Kiev. When Kazaniecki and Hania arrived a few days later, Kazaniecki also began working in the office as a bookkeeper.

Heniek and Papa Bachner remained at the apartment. Bachner didn't trust his father's ability to "pass" and there was no job that he could do in the office. Heniek was strong, but his experiences in the ghetto, especially his near deportation, had been hard on the young man and Bachner thought he needed some time to recover.

On September 17, 1942, Willi Bachner celebrated his birthday. He was thirty years old, but told Cesia he felt as though he were a hundred.

The increased presence of Jews in Kiev was both a comfort and a worry for Bachner. It was wonderful to once more be around people with whom he could talk freely, to say nothing of the comfort of sharing a bed with his wife every night. On the other hand, each person was a potential source of identification if he or she should be caught and tortured. Each Jew was a possible target of suspicion from Gentile workers.

Willi was helped in his task of keeping them all safe by the expansion of the Kellner operations in the Ukraine. Work on the railroad station was winding down, but opportunity called in other locations in the Ukraine.

Kellner came to Kiev in late September, bringing along his Polish mistress. He expressed his pleasure with what he saw at the Kiev station. He also seemed pleased that his young engineer had gotten himself a mistress. Like many womanizers, Kellner probably found it reassuring that others shared his weakness for a pretty face. He explained to Willi that the group would soon be expanding their operations. Their contracts would remain with Reichsbahn Direktion Ost, but they would work at other rail junctions, Vinnizta, Dnepropetrovsk, and, as soon as possible, at Bobrinskaya, a town southeast of Kiev.

Bachner tried not to show his excitement. Bobrinskaya was the closest town to the village of Boguslav, the last known location of his sister Anna. If he had papers allowing him in Bobrinskaya, he would have the opportunity to look for her. Up until now he had no legitimate reason to go east of Kiev. If he could find his sister and her husband and bring them to Kiev . . . He knew the chances were slim, and that his sister would be far better off behind Soviet lines than in Nazi-occupied Ukraine, but he had to know.

Bachner went to Bobrinskaya in mid-October with a group of workers. Now that the main rail centers were repaired, the Reichsbahn was working on smaller strategic centers. The Kellner firm was to build barracks and offices. Bachner hired a Ukrainian driver to take him to Boguslav, because a narrow dirt road was the only way there. Willi was wearing a black Reichsbahn uniform; his pockets filled with cigarettes and chocolate.

As they bumped down the rutted dirt road, Bachner willed himself to relax and go over his story. The road led through spent wheat fields and birch forests that shimmered with leaves in autumn colors. He spoke very little to the dour Ukrainian driver, preferring instead to bask in the warmth of the sunny day.

When they arrived in the village, they caused quite a stir. It wasn't all that often that they got visitors, especially those wearing German uniforms. Like all Ukrainians, they were suffering the hardships of occupation by a force they had originally seen as liberators. Now, they slowly awakened from their revolutionary dream to the nightmare realization that even the detested Stalin was better than the Nazis. Despite their initial distaste, their curiosity got the better of them and Bachner soon had about fifty men and women, along with a gaggle of barefoot children, surrounding his wagon.

He spoke to them in a mixture of Polish and Ukrainian, "Good afternoon. I have come from Bobrinskaya, where I work for the Reichsbahn. But I am not German, I am Polish."

This brought a slight thaw to the cool reception, but the villagers remained wary.

"I am from Warsaw. Some Jews in Warsaw asked me, that is, they paid me to come to your village to ask about their daughter. Her name is Anna Bachner Hirschhorn. Do you know where she is?"

"There are no Jews in this village," said one man. He spat on the ground.

Bachner's heart sank, but he tried to look unconcerned. "Did she live here?"

"She lived here," a middle-aged woman's shrill voice rose above the chorus of denials. "That was her house, right over there."

Bachner got out of the cart and followed the woman over to a tiny wooden house with small windows. She knocked on the door and an old woman answered. Yes, Anna Hirschhorn had lived there with her husband. Bachner strained to understand the old woman.

Her husband was taken by the Red Army, just like all the young men in the village, but she stayed. When the Germans came they killed her, just like all the Jews."

"They didn't kill her," came a voice from the back of the crowd.

Bachner turned as another woman pushed forward. She said to Bachner, "They didn't kill her. The rest they took outside the town and shot them. We heard their screams all day long. But Anna they took with them. She spoke German, that Jewish girl, and they needed her to translate. I saw her with my own eyes." She looked around at the rest of the villagers, daring them to disagree. "There she was in the back of their truck. There she was, big with child, trying to stand up as they drove away."

"She was pregnant?" Bachner stepped toward the woman.

"What is it to you?" the woman asked, then peered at him. "You know, she said she had a brother in Warsaw. You look a little like her, around the eyes. You could be her brother."

"No, no." Bachner shook his head impatiently, backing away. "Her brother hired me, you foolish old woman. She was a Jew! I am a Pole." With that, Bachner opened up his pockets and passed out all the cigarettes he had. To the children he gave small pieces of chocolate, and whatever suspicions the villagers had they managed to suppress in the face of such luxuries. Bachner pressed for further details, but got none. Anna was last seen leaving the village in the back of a German truck; she had never returned.

The ride back to Bobrinskaya seemed endless. As the sunny afternoon transformed itself into a cold, gloomy dusk, Bachner's hopes of rescuing his sister grew cold as well. Helena Buchführer Bachner, Anna Bachner Hirschhorn, Bruno Bronislav Bachner: the first, dead by her own choice; the other two, lost to the Nazi death machine, presumed to have perished. His family circle shrank around him, like a birch forest surrounded by fire. Counting the two men in Warsaw, he had saved eight Jews so far. More would be coming soon. They would all be his family.

8 HIDDEN IN THE SHADOWS

KEEP ME AS THE APPLE OF YOUR EYE;
  HIDE ME IN THE SHADOW OF YOUR WINGS,
FROM THE WICKED WHO USE VIOLENCE AGAINST ME.
                    PSALM 17:8-9

Bachner returned to Kiev to find a veritable reunion in process at the safe house. Kazaniecki had just returned with a transport of supplies from Warsaw. He also had brought Lonia Ostrowski and his wife Kaethe, and Hania's sister, Genia. Despite his attempt, Tadek had been unable to convince Hania's brother, Abraham Teifeld, to leave his hiding place in Aryan Warsaw. One sister remained in the ghetto and he would not leave until he could get her out.

Tadek also brought with him the latest grim reports from Warsaw. His listeners found little comfort from his news. The transports from the Umschlagplatz continued. Every day, thousands more were sent to their deaths. Even the Jewish policemen, who had hoped to save themselves by assisting the Nazis with their work, had themselves been sent to the Umschlagplatz and loaded onto the trains. The few remaining had the magic work permits, but a growing number had simply burrowed down in abandoned buildings, trying to escape the daily Aktions.

"What I can't understand is, why don't they fight?" asked Kazaniecki incredulously. "They know what the Germans will do to them. Why do they go along meekly?"

"Don't be a fool, Tadek!" Willi said furiously. "What are they supposed to do? Attack the Reich with their bare hands? How dare you call us cowards!"

"But that's exactly what some of them are doing," said Lonia. "The young ones. The ones who think they might as well take a few Germans down with them. Not that they manage to succeed. I heard that they formed their own underground. The Zydowska Organizacja Bojowa, some Jewish fighting organization. Most of their leaders have been shot already. Still, you have to admire their courage."

Lonia paused, then added quietly, "For others it is not so easy to fight. They are trying their best to survive. Do you know what the Germans are doing now? They are running their bayonets through every knapsack at the selections. Parents have been drugging their children and placing them in knapsacks to try to get them through selection. There are hardly any children left in the ghetto. When the knapsacks show blood, they shoot the parents on the spot."

They all fell silent. Tadek looked chagrined at having called the courage of these people into question. Bachner realized that the younger man spoke more out of the need to explain inexplicable events like the systematic murder of millions of people. Calling up old stereotypes of Jewish cowardice prevented the mind from trying to grasp the horrible truth.

But Tadek had seen the ghetto for himself. He had heard the others' stories about Janusz Korczak, who turned down a chance to escape and accompanied his orphans to the trains. He knew of the parents who gave up their lives in attempts to save their children. Old concepts of bravery and cowardice no longer applied in the nightmare world of the ghetto, where months, even years of degradation, dehumanization and hardship had made the extension of life, for even a few hours, a worthwhile goal.

Moreover, he had seen the actions of Poles, Ukrainians, Russians and Latvians when they faced the forces of the Reich. When the populations of whole towns were rounded up and shot for suspected partisan sympathies, their behavior was no different from that of the Jews of Warsaw.

Resistance, however, was growing. The Zydowska Organizacja Bojowa had a disastrous beginning, losing many of its leaders and the few weapons that had been gathered. Learning that they would get little or no support from the Polish underground, members pulled back and began to gather resources within the ghetto. Escapees from the transports to Treblinka had made their way back to the ghetto to warn the others. There were no longer any illusions about their fate. The ghetto was being liquidated. In late August, Governor Frank had announced that food would no longer be provided to the ghetto. Those who remained would work until they were too weak, then they too would be deported.

"Oh, Gerda," said Tadek, as if feeling a need to change the subject, "how could I have forgotten?" Tadek riffled through his pockets, producing a wrinkled envelope. "Julek said to give this to you. Your music teacher's husband brought it to the office just before I left. She said it was sent to her from Tarnow."

The letter became the focus of everyone in the room. Gerda reached for it; her hand trembled as she slid a finger beneath the flap, slowly prying it open. She smoothed the single sheet across her lap, as if afraid of the words scrawled across it in bold black ink. As she read, her eyes filled with tears; she turned away so the others wouldn't see, clasping the page to her breast. The minutes ticked by in silence; everyone in the room seemed to be holding his breath. Regaining her composure at last, Gerda turned to Willi.

"It's from my sister. She says if I ever want to see any of them again, I must come now."

Bachner stood, pacing the floor as he tried to think. What could he do? He could not send Gerda back. "Maybe we can see if Julek can get them out, or maybe Tadek." He glanced at the men. "I hate to send you back there."

Kazaniecki looked at Willi, then at Hania's worried face. Bachner knew that Tadek would not relish another return to Warsaw so soon. Even though he was a Pole, the trips were not without risk, especially when transporting Jews in hiding. The young man frowned. Bachner could see that he desperately needed a rest.

Before Tadek could respond, Gerda stood up, clutching the letter.

"They're my family, and I must go get them. I should have done this before. How could I have come east without them?" She spread her hands wide, taking in the comfort of the safe house. "I have been eating well, working as though nothing in the world was wrong, while they have been in the ghetto, not knowing from day to day if they would live." She covered her face. Her shoulders shook.

"Gerda, it is much too dangerous. Let one of the men go," Bachner insisted.

"No." Gerda lifted her head, brushing away the tears that streaked her face. "I will go. I must."

Bachner recognized in Gerda the determination motivated by guilt that he had experienced so often. He nodded.

"You can go back tomorrow. I will get you your Marsch-befehl."

No one could travel in the Nazi-occupied areas without both identification and special travel papers—Marschbefehl—stating the reason for the journey and its duration. Bachner knew the risks that Gerda was facing, but he also knew, from personal experience, that saving one's family was worth any risk. If he had found courage like Gerda's sooner, Bruno might still be with them. He saw her off the next morning, issuing contradictory admonitions for caution and speed in returning to Kiev. Gerda smiled resolutely and assured him that she would be fine.

In the meantime, it became obvious that there were too many people for the house they had been occupying. Now that his wife was with him, Bachner found himself longing for privacy. He converted a room at the Kellner office on Sagsaganska Street into a small apartment for the two of them and gave their room at the house to the Ostrowskis.

There was little or no work for a diamond merchant in Nazi-occupied Kiev and the slight Ostrowski was ill-suited for manual labor. "He wouldn't know one end of a shovel from the other," remarked Heniek sarcastically.

Ostrowski's wife, Kaethe, was from a prominent Viennese family. She had somehow retained her imperious airs throughout her confinement in the ghetto. Bachner and the others often became impatient with her superior attitude. She wasted no opportunity to remind them that she was used to associating with a better class of people than current circumstances had forced upon her.

Papa Bachner, of an age and temperament that did not suffer snobbery gladly, seldom missed a chance to tease the elegant Kaethe. He once went so far in his teasing that she responded by slapping him across the face. Lonia Ostrowski, though he usually deferred to his wife's demands, was unfailingly polite and tried his best to smooth the way between Kaethe and the others.

Genia Teifeld, who, like her sister, spoke both German and Polish well, dyed her hair and became Janina Matjewska. Tadek found lodging for her with a Ukrainian couple. At first, like the Ostrowskis, Genia was on the Kellner payroll for the purpose of obtaining rations, and did no work. However, as she grew more comfortable in the city, she too began to help out at the Kellner office.

Work went on, but the former Warsaw residents waited anxiously for Gerda's return. She arrived late one afternoon, emerging from the second-class car with a bewildered and obviously frightened young woman. She swept the woman away to the safe house, with only a weary shake of her head and a brief word to Bachner, asking him to come by the safe house later.

When Bachner and Cesia came to the house that evening, Halina was asleep in the room reserved for Kellner when he visited Kiev. Gerda was telling Bachner's father, Heniek and the Ostrowskis about her experience as a rescuer.

"'Baruch!'" she said with exasperation. "Can you believe it? Some idiot in Tarnow had taken her money and given her false papers with a name just as Jewish as her own. Julek and I just about fainted when we saw it." She clapped her hands on each side of her face. "We decided to make her Czech, because her Polish is just as bad as mine. She is now Helena Lipek."

"Did you have any trouble?" asked Bachner.

"Not really," Gerda replied airily. She seemed like someone who had walked into the lion's den, dismissing it as little more than a stroll through the zoo. "Except..." She shook her head and laughed.

They stared, open-mouthed, baffled at what Gerda could possibly find amusing in such a dangerous situation.

"On the train, on my way to Warsaw," Gerda said between chuckles, "there was a young German officer on his way back from the front. He kept staring at me. I just knew he was looking at my nose. It's the one giveaway that I am Jewish. Well, I turn this way and that." She demonstrated, exaggerating her movements. "I look out the window. I pretend to sleep. But every time I glance over, he is staring at me."

"This is funny?" asked Papa Bachner, puzzled.

"Wait, let me finish. So I get up and who follows me out but this officer? By then my heart was pounding. I thought I was going to faint. I am standing in the corridor looking out the window and I hear him come up behind me again." Gerda started to giggle again.

"Well, don't keep us waiting," said the elder Bachner.

"He says to me . . ." Gerda dropped her voice an octave and imitated the officer's polished German, "Please excuse my staring, Fräulein, but I cannot keep my eyes off your aristocratic nose."

Again she began to laugh, while the others just stared, until Heinrich asked, "Well, what happened then?"

"What do you think? He tries to chat me up. You know. Where am I going? What am I going to do in Warsaw? He was probably hoping for a dinner date. A little diversion while stuck in Warsaw. I just wanted to get away from him. . . ." Gerda's voice trailed off as all trace of mirth suddenly drained from her face. "Even more so when I saw the corpses."

"What corpses?" asked Bachner.

"All along the track outside of Warsaw. Dead people. One every ten or twenty yards. Some had been dead for quite a while. They were swollen." Gerda's hands went to her face. "They had old shabby clothes. They might have been Jews." She paused in silence for a moment, then picked up her story.

"When I got to Warsaw, I went to see my teacher, Madame Kaszowska. She had a friend, another music teacher, who lived in Tarnow. The friend agreed to put on an arm band and go into the ghetto and get my family. Only my sister was left. My parents had already been deported. Halina had hidden under a staircase.

"Madame Kaszowska sent word to me that my sister was at her house, and I went there. We were hugging and crying and the woman who had brought her burst into tears. She said 'I feel so ashamed to take money for this, but I must have money to feed my children.' I told her I understood and paid her. Then, after I changed Halina's papers, 'Baruch'! Have you ever heard of anything so silly? We got to the station and here we are."

"How is she?" asked Bachner, with a nod to the bedroom.

"As well as you could expect." Gerda's shoulders sagged. "She's frightened, Willi. I practically had to drag her on to the train. I was glad there were so few people heading east; I don't think she would have passed if we were questioned. Her spirit is crushed." She stared at the braided rug covering the floor beneath her feet.

"Do you know how she learned what happened to her husband? She got up enough courage to go to the court and ask, after he was arrested last year. The man said '*Der Mann ist tot.*' He never even looked up. Halina just stood there.

"She stood there. As if—as if her body had turned to stone, until someone finally shoved her away." Gerda shook her head, "What did we ever do to deserve this? Three days she spent under the stairs, while everyone else in the building was taken away. I don't think she'll ever recover." Her eyes met Bachner's and he looked away, unable to bear the look of defeat in those usually confident blue eyes.

"It will take time," replied Bachner. He reached for Gerda's hand and squeezed it gently. "We will all help."

And help they did. Each of the new arrivals gradually emerged from the shroud of the ghetto into a semblance of normality in Kiev. The simple but ample food was an inconceivable luxury to stomachs shrunken by months of hunger; the opportunity to sleep in warm, uncrowded lodgings, a gift to be relished each night.

On October 11, as the war entered its third year, Kazaniecki threw a birthday party for Hania. All of the Bielsko and Warsaw Jews attended, except Willi and Cesia. October 11 was an important day for them—their third anniversary—and the first they would be able to spend alone. Cesia prepared a meal at their office quarters. It was then that she broke the news.

"Willi," she said hesitantly, as if struggling to find the words.

He looked at her, sensing her apprehension and embarrassment. "Cesia, what is it? Come on. You can tell me." He was struck once again by the fact that even after three years, they really didn't feel at ease with each other.

She didn't look at him, but stared at her hands. "Willi, I think I'm pregnant."

"Pregnant!" Bachner sprang to his feet. "God, that's all we need!" He stood in the middle of the room, his hands on either side of his head. "How could I have been so careless and stupid?" He looked back at her. Cesia's eyes misted with tears, her mouth set in a thin line of disappointment. Suddenly, he realized that his reaction was not what she had expected.

"Cesia," he said, softening his voice, "you can't be serious. We can't have a child now. We could have to run at any time. We could be forced into hiding. A baby is out of the question."

"I thought, maybe now, in Kiev . . ." Her voice caught and tears began to roll down her cheeks. She no longer looked at her husband but stared at the table. "What can I do?"

Bachner thought for a moment. "I will take you to a doctor here," he said at last. "This isn't Poland. It's the way Ukrainian women limit their families. It won't be any problem." Bachner sat down and embraced her. "There will be others, Cesia. When the war is over. We will have many children, I promise."

Cesia said nothing; she sat quietly as tears dripped onto her clasped hands.

*   *   *

A few days later, Bachner took Cesia to a Ukrainian doctor and told him she needed an abortion, choosing not to divulge their true relationship. Since they did not share the same name, he knew that they would be seen as lovers, not spouses. Abortion was a common procedure in the Soviet Union, where guarantees of reproductive freedom were part of the legacy of the Revolution. After examining Cesia, the doctor told Bachner to bring her to the hospital on a future date. Cesia clung to Willi in terror at the prospect of being alone in a strange hospital.

Bachner patted her arm and reassured her. He had expected her reaction. He explained to the doctor that as Poles, they were Catholics, and of course the doctor could understand what a delicate matter this was and how they would like the operation to be discreet, and perhaps for a little extra . . . ?

The doctor said he would be willing to do the procedure in Bachner's house. He told Bachner what he would need and instructed Cesia not to eat or drink anything after midnight the day before the procedure.

On the appointed day, everyone left the Kellner firm's house except Gerda, Hania and Willi. The doctor arrived to find Cesia ready. The dining room table had been covered with clean sheets as the doctor instructed. There was, of course, no anesthesia, and Cesia fought hard not to cry out with the pain, clutching the hand of her husband, who sat grimly throughout the procedure. The doctor was competent enough and had at least taken the precaution of boiling his instruments in water. The procedure was over quickly. Cesia was taken to the downstairs room where Gerda and Hania helped care for her. The doctor told Bachner to call him if Cesia developed a fever or had any abnormal bleeding, accepted Bachner's thanks and payment and left.

For the next several days, Cesia remained in bed, less physically ill than sick in spirit. Bachner found himself sharing her depression. Now that it was over, now that his son or daughter was not to be, he found himself wondering if he had acted too hastily. Maybe they could have managed. Maybe he should have left the decision up to his wife, but Gerda, always practical, reinforced his belief that Kiev in 1942 was neither the time nor the place to start a family. She reassured him that Cesia would get over it, that he had made the right decision.

*   *   *

Cesia returned to the couple's apartment at the Kellner office after a few days. She gradually put the abortion behind her as things once again settled into a routine. Willi and Cesia continued to live at the Kellner office. Papa Bachner and Heniek, Gerda, and Lonia and Kaethe Ostrowski filled the other Kellner house to the rafters. Hania and Tadek now lived in an apartment nearby. Gerda found lodging for her sister at the home of a Ukrainian mother and daughter and Hania did the same for her sister, Genia. Uncle Fabish had become involved with a Ukrainian woman and lived nearby.

New arrivals from Warsaw continued to come in. Adolf Stamberger, known as Andrzej Staniecki even before the war, had been raised in Bielsko. Jews from Bielsko knew of his alias and that he was married to a Gentile Pole. Five additional Bielsko Jews made their way through the Warsaw office of the Kellner firm: Edith Frischler, her sister Uta and brother-in-law Erich Pollak, Hugo Goldberg and Alfred Nichtenhauser. Bachner saw that all were provided with safe lodging and Kellner ration cards.

One evening, when Willi and Cesia went to visit the others, they found that Papa Bachner had also managed a rescue. A frightened-looking woman, who looked vaguely familiar to Bachner, sat with his father while a young man talked with Heniek.

"Willi," said his father. "This is Mrs Neuman from Bielsko and her son Georg."

Bachner said hello with an inquiring eye toward his father. After a few moments of pleasantries he took his father upstairs and asked him how they had come to be there.

"I found her on the street. She was running away. Such a look she gave me when I tapped her on the shoulder. She came to

Kiev last summer and was staying with a Ukrainian family. Somehow she was denounced and the Gestapo is after her."

Willi shook his head. "She can't stay here if they are looking for her. We'll have to find a place for her and her son to stay."

"Willi, be gentle with her. Already she has lost her husband and one son. She is from Bielsko. She is one of us."

"I know, Papa. I didn't say I wouldn't help. I'll find her some place to stay."

It was Gerda who first noticed a more notorious former inhabitant of Bielsko. She and Bachner were working in the small Kellner office within the train station. Glancing through the window at the crowd outside, she drew Wilhelm's attention with a hiss.

"Don't look, but someone out there is staring at you," she whispered.

"SS?" asked Bachner, still sorting nonchalantly through the papers on the desk.

"He's not in uniform, but he's German, at least his clothes look German. On the right, in a black overcoat with a white scarf."

Bachner took a deep breath and turned, glancing toward the spot Gerda had indicated. A tall, slim, elegantly dressed man lounged against the wall. He caught Bachner's eye and smiled, touched his hat and moved toward the office with athletic grace.

He came through the door and walked right over to Bachner.

"Well, Willi Bachner! It has been a long time. Imagine meeting you here!"

Gerda stood poised to run if necessary, but Bachner said, "Don't worry Gerda, we know each other. You're probably too young to remember Otto. Gerda, let me introduce you to Otto Feuereisen of Bielsko."

Gerda laughed with relief, "Willi, how could I be too young to remember the best soccer and polo player in Bielsko? I've heard stories about you since I was small. But how did you get to Kiev?"

"Same way as you," said Feuereisen, seating himself in an office chair and lighting a cigarette. "By being selective about what I reveal about my past." He opened his coat and tossed out an identity card, which identified Otto Feuereisen, native of Bielitz, as a Volksdeutscher.

"Isn't that a bit risky?" asked Bachner. "Don't they look into your background before they issue those?"

"My dear Willi," said Feuereisen while winking at Gerda, "it wasn't issued. I made it. What about you, with your good German name?"

"I didn't try it. My papers show me as Polish. Gerda is Hungarian. But you haven't answered our question. What are you doing in Kiev?"

"Business. Buying and selling. Salek and I. You remember Salek Meisner, the coach from the high school in Bielsko?" He waited for Bachner's answering nod. "Well, the two of us travel the length and breadth of the Greater Reich, buying a little here, selling it across the border there. We've done quite well."

"So I see," said Bachner guardedly. He remembered Otto Feuereisen very well. The immensely popular Jewish athlete was the hero of all the young Jewish boys in Bielsko, a soccer player who could hold his own against any Gentile player in the region. He caused young girls to swoon and their fathers to curse. He had supposedly left his ne'er-do-well ways behind him, but Bachner saw that he had reverted to them when the war provided an opportunity.

"Look, Otto. It's nice to see you, but I don't need any trouble around here." He lowered his voice and said under his breath, "I have over two dozen Jews here under false papers. If there is any hint of my involvement with the black market, that would be the end of us all."

"Come now, Willi. You can trust me," said Feuereisen in a wounded tone. "I am not just concerned with money. I am also a smuggler of others, like yourself. Former residents of Tarnow are my specialty. My own mother is here now in Kiev. I have plans to move people out through Odessa or Bucharest to Palestine. I plan to put my profits to good use. Well," he stood and bowed stiffly toward Bachner, "I can see you have work to do, so I will be off." He walked up to Gerda and took her hand. "I shall look forward to seeing you again soon." He touched her hand to his lips, then swept out of the office, disappearing into the crowd outside.

Bachner looked after him, shaking his head.

"What?" asked Gerda. "He seems nice enough."

"Oh, he's as nice as can be. But I don't trust him completely. Not that he would turn us in, mind you. But Otto has always been a little too willing to cut corners and pull strings. He may be smuggling Jews to Palestine, but I would bet he is making a profit while he's at it. Stay away from him, Gerda, he could be dangerous."

Gerda, however, was never one to be overly concerned with danger, even in Nazi-occupied Europe. In early December, Cesia told Willi that Gerda had been accepted into the Kiev Conservatory of Music where she had resumed her voice studies. "When will she take this seriously!" Willi fumed. "How could she do such a thing without consulting me?"

He went to bed that night, unable to sleep for worrying about the danger Gerda's behavior could cause them all.

"Fraülein Ferencz, would you come in here please?" he called from his office door the next morning.

"Yes, Herr Engineer," Gerda replied, grabbing her stenographer's pad.

Bachner closed the door to his office and said quietly, "What's this I hear about you going to the Conservatory?"

"Yes." Gerda smiled. "Isn't it wonderful? You should have seen them, Willi. Three ancient Russians with white beards sitting at a table listening to me audition, not saying a word . But I made it. I sang 'Voi, che sapete' from *The Marriage of Figaro*. I was so nervous, but I did it."

Willi sat down behind his desk, invoking the authority of his position as her employer. "Gerda, how could you do this? Don't you think you should have asked?"

Gerda raised her carefully sculpted brows. "Willi," she said, "you may be my employer, but you are not my father. I don't have to ask you about everything."

"But the danger! What if you are caught?"

"No one will ever get anything out of me. I will die before I tell them anything. Oh, Willi," she jumped to her feet and paced in front of the desk, "you have to understand. If I can't have my music, I might as well die. No matter where I have been in this war, I have not abandoned my music. I didn't do it in Warsaw and I won't do it now." She stopped before the desk, directly in front of him and leaned forward. "You worry too much," she said.

Willi felt suddenly old, weary. He ran a hand through his wavy hair, wondering how quickly it would turn grey with worry. "I have to worry for all of you, all the time," he said. "I lie in bed at night thinking what to do if someone is caught. What will I say, where will we go? I know your music is important to you. But until this is over, protecting each other, avoiding discovery, saving all our lives is the only truly important thing."

"Look," Gerda drew herself up to her full height. "I am not some country peasant. I speak German like a native. I have excellent papers. And, unlike you, there is nothing about me that betrays my identity."

"And if someone denounces you?"

"Then you will have been right and me wrong." She shrugged and sat back down, resting her elbows on her knees. "Nothing anyone could do to me would make me denounce the rest of you. I know what I am capable of, Willi."

Bachner continued to argue, but Gerda was adamant. She told Willi that withdrawing from the Conservatory would only raise questions. She assured him she would be very careful and turned and opened the door.

"Yes, Herr Engineer," she said as she left, for the benefit of the Ukrainian office girls. "I'll get this typed up right away."

∗   ∗   ∗

As the holidays approached, plans were made for a Christmas party for the office workers. All of the Jewish members of the firm were invited as well. Papa Bachner grumbled a little at celebrating a Christian holiday, but reluctantly went along since the party was to be held at the lodging house. Hania and Kazaniecki arrived with Tadek's friend Wilaski, who, true to form, showed signs of having begun to celebrate even before his arrival. Gerda played Christmas songs on the piano. Cesia piled the table with great quantities of roasted potatoes, steamed cabbage and beef sausage. She had even prepared a plate of deviled eggs from the fresh eggs Heniek had bought from some local peasants earlier in the day.

As the evening wore on, the Ukrainian employees departed, leaving the Bachners, Ostrowskis, Heniek, Gerda, Halina, Hania, Tadek and Wilaski, who was by now thoroughly drunk. Cesia went into the kitchen to replenish some food and the inebriated Pole followed her there. He blocked the door and began to tell her expansively how wonderful she was, such a great cook, and so pretty. When one of the others came in, knocking him off balance, Cesia darted out, her breath coming in short, shallow gasps as she sat down with the others.

Wilaski staggered through the door and came over and sat down close beside her. He leaned over and whispered into her ear, "It's no good to run away from me, Cesia. I know who you really are."

By now Cesia was in a panic. She got up and pulled away from Wilaski as he tried to grab her arm. She went over to Bachner and told him what had happened.

Bachner turned to Kazaniecki and said, "I think it's time you took your friend Mietek home."

Kazaniecki glanced over his shoulder at Wilaski, who now sat staring at them blearily. "Oh, no! Not again! Well, Hania, I guess the party is over for us."

He walked over to his friend and said good naturedly, "Come Mietek, it's time we went home."

"I don't want to go home," the drunken Pole replied belligerently. "I want to stay here. You can't tell me what to do. I want to stay here with the Zids. Tell me, Tadek. How come we're here on Christmas Eve with a room full of Jews?" He lurched to his feet, and stood, swaying. "You all think you're better than me, don't you? But you're not. Bloody Christ killers, that's what you are. I'll show you. I'll show you Jewish pigs you can't treat me like dirt. We'll see who's better when I get finished."

They all sat in stunned silence, except Kazaniecki, who put his arm around his friend. "That's enough, Mietek. Come now, Hania and I are going to take you home."

Wilaski's rage disappeared as drunken rages often do, "Good old Tadek. I know. Let's go get a drink. Just you and me."

"Sure," said Kazaniecki, moving him toward the door as Hania got their coats. He looked over his shoulder at the others. "Don't worry, he's just drunk. He won't say anything. He doesn't mean it, really. Vodka always seems to make Poles revert to the language of the schoolyard."

The door shut behind them. The others continued to sit in stunned silence, saying nothing. Outside, Wilaski began to sing a Polish Christmas song in a loud, braying voice.

"So, what do we do now?" asked Gerda.

"I don't know," said Bachner. "What can we do? Tadek thinks there's nothing to it. But I think it's clear that his friend resents us. It is only a matter of time before he tells someone when he's drunk. Oh, God." Willi stood and began pacing back and forth, shoving his hands in his back pockets. "This is the last thing we need!"

They discussed various scenarios in hushed tones. Was Tadek right? He had always had more faith in Wilaski than any of the others. What could they do to prevent Wilaski from walking up to any German on the street and denouncing them?

About five minutes later, a sudden sharp knock at the door froze Willi in mid-step. Already? Could the Germans be coming so soon? Bachner went to the door, opening it just a crack.

Their Ukrainian neighbor stood, shivering on the doorstep, still in his nightclothes with a coat and cap thrown over them. "I just thought you should know," he said. "A man who just left here was hit by a car right in front of my house. He's badly hurt. It was a German car. They didn't even stop."

Bachner stared at him incredulously.

The Ukrainian waited for a response, then said, "Well, are you going to do anything? It's not my fault. You're the one who let a guest go into the street drunk. I won't take care of him."

"Of course," said Bachner. Regaining his wits, he grabbed his own coat to follow the man out to the street. A few of the others joined them momentarily. As the man had said, Wilaski lay crumpled by the side of the icy street, face down in the fresh snow that covered the icy remainders of earlier snowfalls. Bachner turned him over and checked his wrist. Blood oozed from a laceration on his forehead.

"He's alive," said Bachner. "Come, we must get him back to the house." With some help from his father and cousin, Bachner managed to get Wilaski back to the house. They placed the still body on the sofa. Gerda and Heniek left to call an ambulance.

A short while later, Kazaniecki returned and asked if they knew where Wilaski was. He was shown the figure on the couch. Bachner explained what had happened. "But where were you?"

Kazaniecki sat down in shock. "I left him to take Hania home. He was making such a fuss. I thought I should get her home first. I came right back. This is terrible. It's my fault." He rested his head in his gloved hands. "I shouldn't have left him."

No one responded. No one dared admit that the death of Tadek's friend would be a relief. After what seemed an interminable time, during which nothing was heard except Wilaski's erratic, labored breathing, the ambulance came and took him away.

It was now almost three o'clock on Christmas morning. Bachner and Gerda decided that someone would have to go to the hospital to find out if Wilaski had regained consciousness. Kazaniecki continued to insist that there was no danger from his friend, that his denouncing them was just drunken babble. They all retired for a few hours of fitful sleep, wondering if at any time the fateful knock would come at the door.

The next morning, Gerda went off to the hospital to check on Wilaski. She returned a few hours later to report that the young Pole had serious abdominal and chest injuries and was not expected to live. He had not regained consciousness. Kazaniecki sat beside his friend until death finally came, late Christmas night.

They did not speak of it again with Kazaniecki, who was truly distraught at the loss of his longtime friend. But, among themselves, they said that God had once again saved them from the Nazis. Bachner decided that he would avoid letting any other Gentiles know their secret. As Gerda had said, you cannot tell what you do not know.

*   *   *

Problems continued around Bachner as the others insisted on taking unnecessary risks. Julek's brother, Richard, was fond of going to the Kiev marketplace. Heniek and Papa Bachner both liked to take walks in the evening. Gerda enjoyed a full social life centered around her music. She often visited Otto Feuereisen. She told Bachner about the New Year's party she had attended.

Bachner again cautioned her about associating with black marketeers, but Gerda had a much higher opinion of Feuereisen.

"Willi, you don't understand. He is helping lots of people escape. His sister lives in Bucharest. Otto brings Jews from the ghettos here. He gets them travel papers to Rumania. From there, they go to Odessa, then on to Palestine. He has offered to help Halina and me get there."

Willi opened his mouth to speak, but Gerda waved a hand. "It is much too risky an offer. Still, it is a generous one. You should give Otto more credit for the work he is doing."

"Gerda, you do what you think is right, but please be careful." He picked up one of the pens from his desk, disturbing the tidy row. "Otto moves around too much. He's too cozy with the other black marketeers. One day he'll make a mistake." He shook the pen at Gerda. "I don't want you there when that happens."

"You're right on one point," said Gerda. "He does have some scary friends. On New Year's, I met this huge bear of a man. His name is Yuri Strelzov. He's from Lwów. Says he knows Otto from his soccer days." Gerda's blue eyes clouded. "There's something about him . . . the way he looks at you." She shivered.

"Does he know you are Jewish?" asked Bachner.

"I don't think so, unless Otto told him. But he knows that Otto is. He wants Otto to get him out of the Ukraine. Otto has given him money too, I know that."

Bachner shook his head in frustration at his young friend. "You know how I feel, Gerda. For the love of God, be careful."

Despite his best efforts, Bachner was unable to get those under his protection to take things as seriously as he would have wished. One night when he was away at a Baustelle in Zitomir, even Cesia decided to take a chance.

For weeks Gerda and her sister Halina, who were in touch with musical events in Kiev, had been talking about a ballet that was coming to the Kiev Opera House. If Willi had known that their plans involved taking his wife to the opera house, he would have put a swift end to them, but he did not learn of Cesia's misadventure until he returned from the Baustelle.

"*Copellia*," Gerda had assured Cesia, "is the most wonderful story of a beautiful dancing doll. Why don't we all go? We can dress up and spend a night at the opera."

Cesia, Hania and Genia were caught up in Gerda's enthusiasm, and the prospect of a night out was just too much to resist. When the night came, they fixed each other's hair, put on their best clothes and presented themselves on the steps of the opera house. There they found themselves surrounded by Germans, who, with the exception of a few Ukrainian collaborators, were the only patrons of the arts in Nazi-occupied Kiev.

They took their places in the upper balcony of the elaborate opera house and sat down to enjoy the ballet. The first act was magical. As the lights went down and the orchestra began the overture, it was almost possible to imagine that life was normal. But reality returned at intermission when they went out with the crowd to the lobby. In the crush of the crowd—smoking, drinking champagne and tea—the excitement wore off and fear set in. Hania, Genia and Cesia, finding themselves the target of much male Teutonic attention, began to panic.

"They're staring at us," whispered Hania to Gerda as a young blonde Wehrmacht officer smiled and nodded at her appreciatively.

Gerda laughed. "Of course they are. That's what they do during intermission. There are more men here than women, you know. Look," she added, smiling and barely moving her mouth, "there's nothing to worry about. These are Germans. The only way they can tell you're a Jew is if a Pole or Ukrainian tells them so. Relax, don't look so nervous."

But unlike the Reichenbaum sisters, Cesia and the Teifeld sisters were not used to being in crowds of the enemy. The rest of the ballet, along with the hurried trip through the lobby when it ended and the silent ride home, offered little pleasure.

When Bachner and Kazaniecki found out what Cesia and Hania had been up to in their absence, they cursed their stupidity for leaving the women alone. Kazaniecki, who was extremely protective of Hania, couldn't decide if he was more angry or relieved.

"Are you out of your mind?" Tadek confronted his petite, distraught girlfriend. "I leave you for a few nights and what do you do? You go to the opera with half of the Wehrmacht! Can I not trust you for a minute?"

Hania offered little excuse for her actions. For her, the whole thing had been a mistake which she promised Kazaniecki she would never repeat.

For Cesia, Willi's unspoken disapproval seemed enough. Later, alone in their room, he wrapped her in his arms.

"Cesia, my dear." He kissed her wet cheek. "You must promise me that you will never, ever do such a thing again. Yes?"

Cesia buried her face in his shoulder.

"You need not worry about me," she reassured him. "One night at the ballet was more than enough."

* * *

During the month of February, members of the Kellner crew busily completed their work at the Kiev railroad station. The firm had begun to establish satellite offices in the surrounding area—in Zitomir, Dnepropetrovsk—and to the west, in Novograd Volynsky, which the Germans had renamed Zwiahel. They began to notice a change in the atmosphere of the Kiev station.

Since autumn, casualties from the battle of Stalingrad had moved through the station on their way back to Germany. The battle for this strategic city on the Volga River had begun the previous summer. The Germans had captured the territory to the north and south, but throughout the ensuing months they were unable to take the city. Stalin had given the order to hold the city at all costs. The beleaguered and ill-supplied Soviet forces held out against repeated attacks by the German Sixth Army.

In November, the Soviets launched a three-front counter-offensive called Uranus. Hitler, unable to conceive of defeat by the "inferior" Slavs, told the Sixth Army Commander, von Paulus, to stand fast. In the meantime, Soviet forces encircled the Germans.

Worn down by both the Russian winter and the lack of supplies or relief, General von Paulus surrendered the decimated Sixth Army at Stalingrad on January 31, 1943. The German onslaught had finally been stopped. By the beginning of 1943, the Germans had lost over 13 million men, over 10 million on the eastern front. From that point on, until the end of the war, the eastern campaign was one long withdrawal back toward Berlin.

It was the first stage of this retreat that the Kellner workers began to see in Kiev. The import of Stalingrad was felt throughout the occupied USSR. The retreat exacerbated the ongoing rivalry among the military, the SS and the civilian government. The whole totalitarian edifice began to unravel into what one Nazi official later called "authoritarian anarchy—an orgy of mutual throat-cutting."

If it was not entirely clear to the Germans the way the war in the east was going, it was quite clear to their Italian allies. Italian troops began to appear in Kiev in the spring, with one thought on their minds: to get out of Russia and return to Italy. The Germans blamed their defeat in the east on Italian cowardice, that being much more acceptable than the Führer's incompetence. Frequent fights broke out between German and Italian soldiers. The preference given to Germans for food rations forced the Italians to get by with less and less.

The Italians responded by going to the bazaar and selling their weapons for food. Gerda, who had become friendly with an Italian, kept the others apprised of this conflict. When word came that the Italians were being sent back to their native country, this young man offered to smuggle Gerda and Halina along on the troop transport. Gerda politely declined, fearing the unknown dangers of Italy more than she did the known ones in Kiev.

Bachner spent a great deal of time shuttling by train or car to the various Kellner sites. He began to place some of the Jews in work crews at the smaller sites, but these placements were not without risk.

Uta Frischler Pollak had obtained employment as a typist in Dnepropetrovsk. The Germans were always looking for clerical help who were fluent in German. Bachner placed Uta's husband, Paul, at the Baustelle in that same city. Tragically, when questioned by a German at the door one day while visiting his wife at work, Paul panicked, giving himself away. Paul, Uta and their infant son disappeared without a trace.

The Jews in hiding, now over thirty individuals, constantly sought reassurance from Bachner. "This goy is looking at me suspiciously," someone would say, and Bachner would have to transfer either the Jew or the suspicious worker. He realized that those in hiding had a great need to talk to him, but he also had to be careful that his attention to these workers did not arouse suspicion. Bachner found himself nearing exhaustion as he tried to complete his normal engineering duties, while serving as confidant and savior to so many people.

Returning to the Kellner office after one such trip, he found the place in a panic.

"It's the SS!" Kazaniecki rushed to his side. "They came here looking for you. They said you are to report to their headquarters."

Those two initials could always turn Bachner's insides to ice. "Did they give you any idea what it was about?" he asked.

"No." Tadek shook his head. "They just marched in, demanding to know where Engineer Bachner was. We told them you were in Zitomir and wouldn't be back until this evening." He put his hand on Bachner's shoulder, trying to steer him toward the door.

"Look, Willi, go. Hide. Do whatever you have to. I'll hold them off here as long as I can. We can start moving everyone out. I can take most of them back to Warsaw. Between Julek, Adolf and myself, we can find hiding places."

Bachner held up a hand. "Hold it, Tadek. Let's not move too soon. If I run, they will know something is wrong. Then what will happen to everybody? We can't possibly get them all back to Warsaw."

"But the SS! What could it possibly mean but that someone has denounced you?" asked Tadek, impatient that his friend refused to see the danger.

"Tadek, do I have to remind you? This is not the first time I have had a chat with the SS. I managed then and I can manage now. Remember what I said, they don't expect you to stand up to them. It throws them off balance."

He turned to leave, saying over his shoulder calmly, "If I'm not back by morning, start moving everybody out."

Bachner made his way once again to the imposing edifice on Khryshatek Road. Once again, taking a deep breath and silently saying a fortifying prayer, he entered the building. Approaching the desk he said, "I am Herr Engineer Bachner, I was asked to report here."

The German looked up at him and down at the paperwork on his desk. "Bachner . . . Bachner. Ah, yes . . . Well, this is a surprise. It's not often that people come for our little visits so promptly. Wait here." Summoning an aide he said, "Go tell the colonel that the engineer he was looking for is here."

9 THE WORK OF THEIR OWN HANDS

THE NATIONS ARE SUNK IN THE PIT THEY HAVE MADE;
  IN THE SNARE THEY SET, THEIR FOOT IS CAUGHT.
IN PASSING SENTENCE, THE LORD IS MANIFEST;
  THE WICKED ARE TRAPPED BY THE WORK OF THEIR
  OWN HANDS.

PSALM 9:16-17

Bachner waited in the main hall way of SS headquarters, trying to look as though a trip to the SS was a routine event for him. After a few minutes, an aide came down the stairs and asked Bachner to follow him. They made their way up the stairs, past the office where Bachner had had his confrontation with Mueller just about a year before. The sign on the door informed Bachner that Mueller had been replaced by another officer. How strange, he thought, that I should be in the same position while the Germans are the ones whose circumstances change.

They made their way through the crowded main office to a room with a sign on the door, Oberstabsfeldwebel: Chief Warrant Officer. Bachner felt the tension drain from his body. Interrogations were not conducted by warrant officers.

After knocking, the aide announced Bachner and departed. The German officer rose, smiling, and offered Bachner a chair.

"Herr Bachner, I have a favor to ask of you. We will be honored with the visit of one of the highest ranking officers in the SS next week. Of course, we want everything to go well. But after eighteen months in Kiev, our offices here are looking, well, quite frankly, shabby." He gestured around the room. The state of disrepair was plain to the most casual observer.

"You have been highly recommended to me by a friend from the Reichsbahn. He says you do excellent work, and, unlike most of your countrymen, can actually be trusted to act in an honorable fashion."

"I am pleased, Mein Herr, that the Reichsbahn thinks I am doing an adequate job," said Bachner, inclining his head modestly.

"Yes. Well, that brings me back to my problem. We need someone to come in and refurbish our office. You know, fix a broken window here, patch up a roof there. Apply a fresh coat of paint."

"But of course, Mein Herr," replied Bachner. "I would consider it an honor. I shall put my best men on it immediately. How long do you have until the inspection?"

"Until next Tuesday. Can you do it?"

"I see no problem. Do you have time to show me what you think needs to be done? It will give me an idea of how many men I will need."

"Excellent. Rudi was right. You are an unusual Pole. How is it that you speak German so well?"

As they made their way through the office, Bachner gave his standard explanation for his fluent German. The officer clucked appreciatively at the mention of Deutsche Technische Hochschule at Brno, and prattled on about the difficulty of finding good construction workers in the Ukraine.

Bachner nodded and agreed at the appropriate times, but all the while he was thinking about how his luck had held once again. If someone in the group had revealed their true identity, it would have been his last trip to Khryshatek Road. If he had followed Kazaniecki's advice, they would have given themselves away. He thanked God once again for helping him to make the right decision, all the while realizing that his luck would not hold forever.

The proposed job was really quite simple. Bachner told the officer that he felt that with enough men, it could be completed in one day. With a promise to return with a crew the next morning, he departed.

Bachner returned to the Kellner office and told the story of his "interrogation" to the incredulous group.

"Willi, I don't know how you do it," said Kazaniecki, wiping his sweat-soaked brow with a handkerchief. "You have better luck than anyone I have ever known."

"So far, Tadek," replied Bachner. "So far."

The next day, Bachner selected about a dozen of his more efficient Polish and Ukrainian workers. He did not include any of the hidden Jews. There was no sense in tempting fate. He brought his crew to the SS offices where the warrant officer waited. After giving them orders in a display of his best German officiousness, he introduced the Polish foreman, and said that he would return that evening to collect his workers.

Returning as promised, he found that the work had been completed and the offices were gleaming under a new coat of white paint. His workers were lined up waiting for him. The foreman looked somewhat distressed, however. He hurried toward his boss, but before he could speak, the warrant officer intercepted Bachner.

"Engineer Bachner, it is good to see you. I am quite pleased with the work of your crew. There was just one small problem."

Bachner glanced at the foreman who nodded; shifting nervously from foot to foot, he confirmed that there was indeed a problem.

"What is that, Mein Herr?" replied Bachner, hoping his voice did not betray his growing anxiety.

"One of your workers, a Ukrainian," he added, spitting out the word distastefully, "found some vodka in one of the offices and proceeded to get drunk. Not only drunkenness, but also theft. This is very serious."

He held up his hand to stave off Bachner's response. "Now, I don't blame you, Engineer. You cannot control the behavior of these animals. But I am deducting that worker's wage from your payment. And he will remain here for the SS to deal with."

To dispose of, you mean, thought Bachner. He mustered up all the anger he could manage and said tersely, "I apologize for this despicable incident. But I must see this worker."

Pulling himself up straight he continued. "Indeed, Mein Herr, I must *insist* on seeing this idiot. The honor of the Kellner firm is at stake."

"Very well," said the officer, obviously amused at the antics of the little Polish engineer.

Bachner told the foreman to take the workers back to the Kellner barracks. Then he followed the German to an interrogation room at the back of the building. The offending worker sat in a straight-backed chair, his head buried in his hands. One of his countrymen, wearing a Ukrainian militia uniform, stood close by at attention, a rifle draped across his chest.

The worker glanced at Bachner, then at the German. With a groan, he returned his gaze to the polished wood floor at his feet. He appeared to be at that point of inebriation when the last vestiges of euphoria have fled: the stomach begins to churn, the head to pound, as the body starts to protest its ill treatment.

Bachner stood before the man and, in Polish, ordered him to stand. The man ignored him, continuing to stare sullenly at the floor.

Bachner shouted at him, "I said *get up!*" He grabbed the worker by the collar, pulling him to his feet. The Ukrainian was fifty pounds heavier and a good six inches taller than Bachner, but his boss's actions were such a surprise that he obeyed.

"Is this the thanks I get from you? I give you a good job, treat you fairly, make sure you have enough to eat. And this is how you repay me?"

Bachner drew back and slapped the man twice, with as much force as he could manage.

"You have shamed the firm and you have shamed me. Yet, I can see that you are incapable of shame." Bachner noted the German's amusement in the corner of his eye. He continued to berate the man, punctuating his tirade with shoves and slaps. The worker wavered, weakly fending off the blows.

Bachner turned to the German. "Again, Mein Herr, I apologize for this disgrace," he said through clenched teeth, his chest rising and falling from the exertion of his attack on the worker. "But you must release this man to me. It is a question of honor. My own, and that of the Kellner firm. Believe me, Herr Kellner and I shall deal with him in the strictest fashion."

The officer looked at Bachner, then at the Ukrainian and the militiaman who had watched the whole display, eyes wide as he observed Bachner's fury. Did it really matter to him? Bachner wondered. Was the warrant officer one of those people who enjoyed inflicting pain? Or was the SS simply a job, a position in an out-of-the-way city in the Ukraine where he could avoid the fanaticism of his fellow officers? No one was likely to challenge the Oberstabs-feldwebel's decision to release the man to the Pole's custody. Bachner held his breath and waited.

"By all means, Herr Engineer," he replied at last, with a chuckle. "Take this unfortunate excuse for a man away from here."

Bachner allowed himself to breathe, apologized once more and departed, dragging the worker by the collar. A few blocks from the barracks, the worker turned and vomited into some bushes. He faced Bachner, fully expecting more abuse, but found that all trace of anger had left the engineer.

Bachner held out a white handkerchief.

"Here," he said gently. "Wipe yourself off. That was a really stupid thing you did back there. I almost didn't get you out."

"Yes, Panie Bachner," the man replied. The belligerent scowl left his face as he slowly became aware that he owed his life to this Pole. "Thank you, Panie." He bowed shakily toward his savior. "I won't forget what you did."

The Ukrainian not only didn't forget what Bachner had done, he made sure that no one else forgot it either. Bachner noticed that he was being treated with increased deference by his workers. Everyone seemed to know that the Polish engineer had saved a Ukrainian from the SS.

The respect and cooperation of the workers was not missed by Johannes Kellner when he came to Kiev in early March of 1943 to oversee the expansion of the firm into the satellite offices. Kellner brought his Polish mistress with him on this trip, a thin, frail, blonde woman, to whom he was very devoted. Gerda, who shared the same house with the young woman, described her as quiet and shy. Gerda strongly suspected that the young woman's pallor and emaciation were due to tuberculosis. She was often racked with fits of coughing that left her breathless.

Kellner asked his chief engineer to return with him to Warsaw to help prepare the annual report for the firm. For Bachner, Warsaw meant only bad memories: Bruno's disappearance, his mother's suicide. He had no desire to return there, but having no good excuse, he complied with his employer's wishes.

When they arrived in Warsaw, they found the city in an uproar.

"The ghetto is in revolt! The Jews are fighting back!" Whether the speaker was German or Polish, the air of surprise was the same.

German mortars, bent upon leveling the ghetto and crushing the revolt, kept up a steady barrage, while German troops made house-to-house sweeps, trying to eliminate sniper and grenade attacks directed at German troops entering the ghetto. On Easter morning in Warsaw, the sound of church bells intermingled paradoxically with that of gunfire and artillery shells.

Bachner tried not to demonstrate too keen an interest in front of Kellner, but as soon as he was alone with Julek and Andrzej, he pressed them for all that they knew. Since news of what was happening to Jews at Treblinka had filtered back to the ghetto, the Germans had been meeting increasing resistance there. The Jews no longer cooperated in their deportation. The bodies Gerda had seen along the track in October were most likely Jews shot while trying to escape transport trains.

In mid-January, twelve Germans had been killed when they entered the ghetto to begin its final liquidation. The ghetto fighters seized rifles from fallen Germans to add to their tiny arsenal and continued to fight. For the next few months, the Nazis ceased the roundups, leaving the ghetto to starve.

Yet the pressure from Berlin to liquidate the ghetto continued. Bringing in reinforcements to deal with what they thought would once again be sporadic resistance, the Germans prepared to move in. Despite the fact that the ghetto inhabitants had been walled in, starved and systematically slaughtered for three years, these last few thousand Jews would not go without a fight. The final liquidation of the ghetto, like its initial creation, was deliberately set to take place on a Jewish feast day: Passover, 1943. Two thousand heavily armed troops entered the ghetto on the morning of April 19, to be met by five hundred Jews armed with small weapons, a few grenades and Molotov cocktails. Inside buildings and bunkers, thousands more prepared to die fighting rather than be deported.

In the midst of the tumultuous events in the city, Bachner managed to save two more former residents of Bielsko. He was going to visit Adolf and his wife. As he approached their apartment, he was startled to hear someone call his name softly. A couple emerged from the shadow of the building.

"Is that you, Willi?" The woman gave him a trembling, inquisitive smile. "Oh, God, is it really you?"

At first, Bachner was puzzled, but gradually, despite the intervening years and events, recognition dawned. "Mila?"

The woman nodded vigorously, "Yes. We came to see Ruth's father, Adolph. I had his address from before the war." She stopped and caught her breath as if unused to speaking to anyone. "Leon and I have come from Krakow. We have nowhere else to go." The tumult of words ended abruptly as she began to weep. The man beside her began to comfort her in a distracted way, never taking his eyes off Bachner.

"Come," said Bachner, taking the woman by the elbow. "Let's get inside."

Mila Bachner was a maternal cousin of Willi's. He had never met her husband, Leon Finder; the two of them had married after Bachner left Bielsko. Adolf's Polish wife accepted the arrival of two Jews with polite equanimity. She had long ago thrown in her lot with her husband's people, and, moreover, she knew that their relatively comfortable situation in Warsaw depended on the employment that Willi Bachner had provided her husband.

The tale that Leon and Mila told was familiar, but nonetheless disturbing. The Germans had moved in to liquidate the Krakow ghetto on March 15. Leon and Mila had managed to get out and had spent a few weeks in hiding before obtaining false papers. Mila had been friendly with Ruth Schwalbe before her marriage, and they saw Ruth's family as their last hope. They had not known that Bachner was in contact with the family.

Mila brought news of other relatives who had spent the last three years in the Krakow ghetto. Another Bachner cousin, Isidor and his wife Mania, as well as Jadwiga Finder, Leon's sister-in-law, had escaped and were in hiding. They lacked the money to purchase false papers. Jadwiga's daughter, Nina, only six years old, was in hiding with her mother.

Leon and Mila did not look particularly Jewish, but their papers were rather crude forgeries. Bachner was amazed that they had managed to get to Warsaw at all. He immediately arranged for the Kellner firm's chief forger, Julek, to make them new papers as Kellner employees. He also asked Julek to write up Marschbefehl, travel papers, for them in addition to new papers for his other relatives. He instructed the Finders to go to Krakow and get the others, then return to Warsaw in order to come to Novograd Volynsky on the next Kellner transport. The Finders, although reluctant to return so soon to Krakow, agreed, knowing that it might be their last chance to save the remnants of their family.

Bachner's stay in Warsaw was short; he left not knowing the final result of the revolt, but the news he took back to Kiev was heartening nonetheless. The Germans were not invincible, and the largest civilian rebellion against Nazi occupation in Europe had taken place in a ghetto, led by Jews.

Although sporadic resistance continued in the ghetto throughout the summer of 1943, the final crushing blow came on May 16, when the last building standing in the ghetto collapsed in a dust-filled cloud of brick and wood. By this time the transports to Treblinka were accompanied by so much gunfire that witnesses claimed it sounded like a full-scale battle going on along the tracks.

When Bachner returned to Kiev with stories of the revolt, he learned of some disconcerting events that had taken place in his absence. Cesia told him about a terrifying trip to Easter Mass with the Ukrainian housekeeper. She had gone to stay with the others in the Kellner house while Willi was away. Gerda was in Zitomir for the weekend and Kaethe Ostrowski was off with her husband. The housekeeper demanded that Cesia tell her whether or not she planned to attend mass on Easter morning.

"No self-respecting Catholic woman would miss mass on Easter," she declared. "Why, it would be a mortal sin!"

It wasn't like attending a Russian Orthodox mass. The Ukrainian Church, unlike its Russian counterpart, had never severed ties with Rome. The Nazis, while distrusting the church as a source of resistance, had allowed them to continue to function as long as they rigidly obeyed all Nazi directives.

Cesia reluctantly and apprehensively agreed to go, following the *chadziajka* to the cathedral. She frantically sought cues to behavior, learning that when she was greeted with the words, "Christ is risen," she was to respond, "He is truly risen." She struggled through the seemingly endless service, kneeling, standing, genuflecting, making the sign of the cross, while the dizzying smell of incense accompanied by the chanting of the priest and the choir made her head throb.

The *chadziajka* noted Cesia's uncertainty, but Cesia allayed her suspicions by convincing her that the Ukrainian ritual was different, unfamiliar.

"Oh, Willi," she told her husband. "I am so glad that most Ukrainians only go to church twice a year!"

Bachner laughed. "Yes, on Christmas and Easter. Praise God!"

Later, Heniek told him that he was not the only one to bring news of the ghetto uprising. Heniek had been sitting around the fire roasting potatoes with some of the other workers, when a new arrival from Warsaw launched into a tale of the revolt in the city.

"Most of them are already dead," the man said. "But the Gestapo picks people up at random on the street. If they are Jewish, they go straight to Treblinka or Majdanek."

One of the other workers had put his arm around Heniek and said, "Well, Kwiatkowski. That's at least one thing we can thank the

Nazis for. However bad things get, at least they have gotten rid of the Jews for us, eh?"

Heniek tried to say something. He felt as if his heart had stopped. So much hatred from so many. Why? He wanted to shout, to curse the Christians. To expose his identity and dare them to kill him. Luckily, someone else changed the subject and the matter was dropped before the bitterness spewed from his mouth.

A chill ran along Bachner's spine as his cousin's voice grew deeper with anger. What would he have done in Heniek's place? Would he have challenged the man's ignorance? Or silently ignored his prejudice? It was a dilemma he faced daily as he struggled to protect those he loved. Yet, like Heniek, he too grew weary of maintaining the façade.

*   *   *

Besides news of the ghetto revolt in the west, news of German setbacks on the eastern front filtered into Kiev. In fact, it was impossible to keep the news out of this important rail center. More troop transports passed through moving west, while fewer supply trains carried men and goods eastward. Kharkov, the fourth largest city in the USSR, was retaken by Soviet troops on February 15; Rzev fell on March 3, followed by Vajma on March 12. Soviet factories were now turning out huge amounts of equipment and ammunition at a rate the Germans were unable to match.

The Kellner work crews spent more time repairing partisan sabotage than constructing new projects for the Reich. Rail lines were a favorite target for Soviet partisans because charges could be set under cover of darkness and detonated from a distance. Railroad bridges were another favorite. Bachner felt exhausted as, day after day, saboteurs forced him to send crews out to do the same job over and over in an endless cycle.

In Kiev, there were many different reasons for a strained atmosphere, apart from the tension between German and Italian troops. Because of increased partisan activities, Ukrainians were no longer seen as lackeys by the Nazis, but as potential adversaries, with a consequent surge in arrests. German patrols seized people on the street; those taken were never seen again. Troubling rumors circulated of Polish Jews discovered hiding in Kiev and summarily shot.

Bachner discussed these events with some of the others and decided that it was time to split up the group. It had become too risky for so many Jews to be in such close contact with each other. The denunciation of one could lead to the execution of them all.

One difficulty in splitting up the group was that everyone would have to work at smaller sites, far from Bachner's watchful eye. It would also no longer be possible for large numbers of Jews to be on the Kellner payroll without doing any work. This danger was offset by the fact that these smaller outposts had less of an SS presence than Kiev; there would be fewer people deliberately searching for Jews in hiding.

Uncle Fabish was now the construction supervisor at Novograd Volynsky. Willi sent Heniek and his father there, hoping that Heniek and Uncle Fabish could protect the volatile, often uncooperative Papa Bachner. The particular lack of an SS presence in this small railroad junction had influenced Bachner's decision to choose it as a destination for Jews arriving from Krakow.

Nieczajuk, the Ukrainian engineer whose life Bachner had saved in Warsaw, was in charge of the Kellner Baustelle in Zitomir. Although Bachner had never told him that he was hiding Jews, he thought that Nieczajuk suspected it. However, he remained fiercely loyal to Bachner.

Gerda was also anxious to get out of Kiev, having heard numerous rumors of a crackdown on Jews in hiding. She said her "sixth sense" told her to leave. She was friendly with a relative of Ruth Schwalbe's, a pianist who lived in Zitomir, making her more than happy to go there as Nieczajuk's secretary. Her sister Halina went there as an employee of another German architectural firm.

Kazaniecki assumed bookkeeping duties in the small town of Spola, but also oversaw Kellner operations in Vinnizta and Dnepropetrovsk. Hania, Genia, the Ostrowskis and Moritz Stamberger were scattered among the Baustellen.

Bachner and Cesia remained in Kiev, living at the main office. Frieda Neuman, her son Georg and Richard Schwalbe, Julek's brother, stayed on at the Kellner boarding house.

A serious problem arose shortly after the group had been split up. With Gerda gone, Bachner was forced to rely more upon the Ukrainian secretary, Irina Kolomitchok. Irina eagerly assumed this new role. Indeed, it seemed to Bachner that she was too eager, too flirtatious. He became more and more uncomfortable as Irina's flirting became more blatant. He avoided calling her into his office to take dictation, and instead wrote out his letters longhand or dictated them to her in the main room.

Irina clearly saw Cesia, whom everyone took to be Bachner's mistress, as a rival. She glared at her every time she entered the office area, and tried to make Bachner see that he could do much better than this tiny, quiet wraith. Cesia feared Irina, Bachner knew, and he began to worry that Cesia's reaction would lead Irina to try to get rid of her by reporting some infraction. After all, being the mistress of the head engineer was an enviable position.

He solved the problem by posting Irina to another Baustelle for a few weeks. He hoped that the change would make it clear to her that he was not interested in her advances, and that the generous raise that came with the new position would make her unlikely to seek revenge.

A few weeks later, he heard that Irina had been arrested by the Gestapo along with a group of Ukrainians believed to be partisans. He tried to find out what had happened to her, but she simply disappeared, like so many in Kiev in the spring of 1943. At first, he braced himself for the knock at the door, for another SS interrogation about a partisan employee. But as the days passed and nothing happened, he assumed that Irina must not have had her Kellner work papers with her when she was arrested. For whatever reason, the identity of her employer had not become known.

He found himself a bit chagrined at the news of her partisan activity. Could it be she was more interested in the access being his mistress would have given her to carry out her resistance activities than in his charm and good looks? Well, he would never know. Gerda told him that Irina had made her hatred of the Nazis no secret and had once told her that "what Stalin had not been able to accomplish in 25 years, Hitler had done in one." He had completely subjugated the Ukraine.

Even though he was glad that the situation had been resolved, Bachner was sad to hear of Irina's disappearance. He knew that she had a mother and a young child in Kiev who relied upon her for their support. He let them know that they could continue to get food rations cards from him.

*   *   *

It was not just Ukrainians and Poles who found Kiev dangerous. Increasing partisan activity made it dangerous for Germans as well. By the summer of 1942, partisan forces had reached such a level of strength that they progressed from being an irritation to the German forces to presenting a real threat.

The strength of the partisan movement in the Ukraine was the result of two factors. First, Stalin, who had distrusted partisan fighters as too independent of his control and not worth assisting, had reversed his position. He now praised the movement as "a second front in the enemy's rear." The propaganda value, provided by the stories of heroic Soviets trapped behind fascist lines who refused to give up, was as important to Stalin as the actual damage caused by partisan activities. No longer abandoned, the partisans received supplies, ammunition and direction from Moscow.

Second, the Germans responded to increased partisan effectiveness by increasing their oppression of the Ukrainian people. They burned whole villages, shooting all the inhabitants for suspected partisan sympathies. Women and children were not spared. Hitler stated, "The partisan question can be solved only by force." Many German administrators in the occupied USSR saw this policy as suicidal. After all, the Germans depended on the local population for food supplies and labor. The German terror decreased the harvest, made labor more difficult to find and increased local sympathy for the partisans.

These two forces—partisan revolt and German suppression—fed upon each other. The more effective the partisans proved to be, the more ruthlessly the Germans tried to suppress them. As disaffection with the Nazis grew, the propaganda value of the partisans to Stalin increased. Local sympathies switched from somber acceptance of the Nazi overlords to active encouragement of the partisans.

Far behind the front, the partisans targeted supply lines, German personnel and Ukrainian collaborators. For Bachner, this meant the Kellner firm spent the majority of its time in a futile attempt to keep lines open to the east. While the military situation in the east continued to deteriorate, trains fully stocked with supplies lay waiting in Warsaw, unable to move east.

The water towers needed for steam locomotives continued to be a favorite target of partisan attacks. The vulnerable towers were easily damaged, and snipers rained fire down upon anyone attempting to repair them. Repairing these water towers was the task of the Kellner firm. Many of the towers were in remote locations and getting there was difficult, often deadly.

Mines laid along the track blew up so many trains that the Germans began riding in the rear cars, placing Ukrainian and Polish workers in the front of the car to act as a deterrent. The workers became so frightened that they refused to ride in the trains unless Bachner rode in the front with them.

The trains crept along at ten kilometers per hour, increasing the chance of partisan attack. Whenever Bachner rode in the front of a train, he would clasp his hands in his lap, keep his face impassive and try to ignore the frightened whispers of his workers.

"God," he would pray, "if you want me to die at the hands of partisans after I have survived the Nazis, at least take those damned Germans cowering in the back of the train along with me."

On one such trip, when Bachner was not present, a mine exploded, killing five workers. One of the workers, a Jew from Lwów, had come to Bachner in Kiev for help. The funeral had to be a Christian one, which to the worker's Jewish wife was almost as distressing as the death itself. Bachner spoke at the funeral, attended by nearly all the workers in Zitomir.

He felt the weight of all the Jewish deaths resting on his shoulders as he struggled to express his sorrow in Christian terms, with Christian words, words that tasted like bitter, foreign herbs on his tongue.

"Oh God," he began with a Psalm, "how long shall I harbor sorrow in my soul, grief in my heart day after day?" Tears formed in his eyes, clogged his throat and his voice deepened. He could not stop the next words that came from his mouth, words that would speak a private message to the Jews present, especially to the man's grieving wife.

"How many shall pass on? How many shall come to be? Who shall live and who shall die? Who shall see ripe age and who shall not? Who shall perish by fire and who by water? Who by sword and who by beast?" He voiced the words his father intoned each year on the morning of Yom Kippur, and all present, Jew and Christian alike, bowed their heads with a picture of the beast—the Nazi war machine—branded behind their eyes.

*   *   *

Travel between Kiev and the outlying Baustellen was becoming quite a trial. What used to be an hour-and-a-half trip became a day-long ordeal. Gerda came into the office one afternoon in early June, complaining about the trip from Zitomir. Kazaniecki had recently come from Spola and matched her horror stories on travel through partisan-controlled areas.

"Six hours, can you believe it? We were stopped dead for one whole hour, while they repaired the tracks."

Bachner, already at the office, was surprised to see both of them there. They looked at Bachner and immediately stopped talking, their eyes questioning. He gestured for them to follow him into his office.

"Willi, what has happened?"

"This morning, Richard Schwalbe and Georg Neuman were arrested at the bazaar," replied Bachner. He paused and added, "We found out from Frieda that Otto Feuereisen was arrested last night."

"Where is Frieda now?" asked Gerda.

"With Feuereisen's mother."

"I'll go see them now."

"Gerda, you must be careful. We all must. The SS could come here any minute," cautioned Bachner.

Gerda nodded silently and left.

"Do you think that's wise, letting her go like that?" asked Kazaniecki.

"Wise? If I were wise, I wouldn't have let her ever be seen with Otto Feuereisen. If Gerda were wise she wouldn't insist on taking chances like hanging around with people like him. She wouldn't have taken singing lessons at the Kiev conservatory. If we were all wise, we would all have gone to Palestine before this mess of a war got started."

He sat in silence for a few seconds, then said to his friend, "I'm sorry, Tadek. I shouldn't take it out on you. Sometimes I think I'm so clever, fooling the Nazis every chance I get. Other times I think they are just waiting to move in on me, that I am the fool.

"What about you, Tadek? Why are you doing this? Why do you risk your life for us?"

Tadek smiled. "I'm a fool, too. A fool for love."

"It's got to be more than that," Bachner countered. "It's not just Hania who you've helped."

"I don't really know, Willi." Tadek shrugged. "At first it was to help Hania, then to help her family. Then I met you and before I knew it, you were all like family."

Willi grasped Tadek's shoulder and squeezed. "I could never have done it without you, my friend. I just hope we can get through this latest crisis."

A sudden commotion from the outer office abruptly ended their intimate conversation. Bachner glanced at Tadek; all color had drained from his friend's face. Tadek started to speak, but Bachner put a finger to his lips, motioning for the other man to follow him into the outer office.

An SS officer and two stormtroopers stood in the middle of the room. The troopers carried rifles across their chests and the officer brandished a revolver. Bachner felt as if he had been punched in the stomach after eating a heavy meal.

"Which one of you is Bachner?" the officer demanded.

"I am. What do you want? You don't need to come in here with your guns and terrorize my workers."

"And I don't need a lousy little Pole to tell me what I need to do. Do you know Richard Stroynowski?"

"I believe he is one of my employees," replied Bachner.

"You believe?" the officer yelled.

"Yes, he is one of my employees. Why? Has he done something wrong?" asked Bachner innocently. The secretaries and Kazaniecki remained frozen, waiting for the German's response.

"He is a Jew! He is alive! That is his crime. What about Georg Mueller?"

"He is also an employee."

"He is also a Jew. What about Otto Feuereisen?"

"No. I don't believe I know him. He is not one of mine. Why, is he a Jew, too?"

"Don't get flip with me, Bachner." The officer raised his weapon once again. "We know you are hiding Jews here and we have come to root them all out."

So that was the extent of their knowledge. Bachner thought furiously. They didn't know who he was. So far, none of those arrested had talked, or they were shot before they had a chance to.

"Look, please come into my office and let's discuss this like gentlemen. There's no sense terrorizing these women." As he glanced around the room he saw that Kazaniecki was nowhere to be found.

The Germans appeared not to have noticed that the Pole had slipped out of the office. The officer and one of his men followed Bachner inside his office, while the other stood guard outside. Bachner politely gestured the officer to a chair and sat down behind his desk. The officer pointedly placed his gun on the desk with the barrel pointing at Bachner, who forced his hands to remain still upon the desk top as he pretended not to notice.

"Now," said Bachner, making a steeple out of his hands, and continuing in a reasonable voice, "I have been through this before with the SS. An Oberleutnant Mueller. Do you know him? No? Well, as I told him, I have over 800 men employed at twelve different Baustellen in the Ukraine. You know how this is. They come. They work for a few weeks, then they disappear. Where do they come from? Where do they go?" He shrugged his shoulders. Inwardly, he offered a silent prayer—*Dear God, please, not now, not after we have come so far.*

"So, you found out two of them were Jews. What am I supposed to do? They didn't look Jewish. They didn't have Jewish names. Their papers were all in order. So, what do you expect me to do? I need workers."

"Don't give me your excuses." The officer placed his finger on the trigger of the gun. His eyes narrowed to dark slits. "We know you are hiding more Jews!"

Bachner gathered all his energy, his anger, and his courage, then leaped to his feet. "If you think I am hiding Jews, then you find them! Where are they? Under my desk?" He looked under it in a theatrical gesture, then he walked to the closet. "Perhaps in here? Maybe I have ten Jews in my closet!"

Returning to his desk he seized a large stack of papers and slapped them down on the desk, where they spilled over the revolver. A few drifted into the lap of the officer and onto the floor.

"Do you know what those are?" he demanded. "Those are work requisitions for me and my workers. Train tracks, water towers, bridges, supply depots. All of them needed urgently. There are hungry soldiers on the front who have no food. Battles are being lost because they don't have ammunition or gasoline for tanks. And what am I doing here? I am answering questions about nonexistent Jews! Doesn't the SS have anything better to do?"

"The destruction of the Jewish vermin has been ordered by the Führer himself," the officer said, a bit defensively. "It is our duty."

"And mine is getting trains to the east," countered Bachner. "Go do your duty, but for Christ's own sake, let me do mine!"

The two men stared at each other for what seemed an eternity to Bachner. At last, the officer shoved the papers off his gun, put it in its holster and stood.

"I will be watching you, Bachner. You go and do your duty, but remember I will be watching you. Heil Hitler!" His arm shot upward, stiff with emotion. Then he turned on his heel and left the office with the two stormtroopers scurrying after him.

Bachner collapsed in his chair and put his head down on his desk. All energy drained from his body, and he felt as if he would never move again. Eventually, he heard whispering and raised his head. The two Ukrainian women peered cautiously through the door.

"Go home," he said gently. "It doesn't appear we're going to get much done today."

He went upstairs and found Cesia cowering in their bedroom. "Oh, Willi!" She sat up and reached for his hand. "I heard the commotion, but I didn't know what to do."

He patted her hand. It felt cold as a Russian snowfall, yet clammy with fear. "We will be all right," he said, "for now. But if they ever take me—"

Cesia gasped, clutching his hand. "Willi, I—"

He put a finger to her lips. "If they ever take me, you must try to get to Fabish in Novograd Volynsky."

They sat quietly sipping tea through the afternoon, waiting for word from the others. Kazaniecki returned first, proudly recounting his escape from the office. He had gone to all the Baustellen in the Kiev area and warned the few Jews remaining there to disappear until further notice.

Gerda returned in early evening, somber and shaken. She told them how she had gone to visit the mothers of the lost young men.

"Frieda met me at the door. She said, 'Gerda, I heard that they were caught. But she doesn't know, so don't say anything.' Otto's mother is in such poor health, Frieda was afraid it would kill her. Poor Frieda, first her husband, then her son, and now Georg."

"Gerda," said Bachner, "I want you on the first available transportation back to Zitomir. Stay out of Kiev. I don't know who denounced them, but you spent a lot of time with all three. The SS may be looking for you."

Gerda nodded, her eyes filling with tears. "It was Strelzov," she added matter of factly.

"What?"

"I can't prove it, but I know it was Yuri Strelzov who denounced him."

"Who is Strelzov?" asked Kazaniecki, alarmed.

"A Ukrainian friend of Feuereisen," said Bachner. "What makes you think it was him?"

"I never trusted him," said Gerda. "I always wondered why a former policeman wasn't in the Red Army or the Ukrainian militia. He always seemed too interested in Otto's activities. He probably got caught with black market goods and tried to save himself by denouncing Otto, Georg and Richard."

"But not you?" asked Bachner.

"Who knows," said Gerda wearily. "But one thing is for sure, Willi. You won't have to convince me to stay out of Kiev. I hope I never see it again."

*   *   *

The next morning Gerda and Kazaniecki returned to their respective Baustellen. Bachner anxiously awaited a return visit from the SS, but with each passing day he became more convinced that once again, with luck and bluster, he had managed to fool them.

As the summer progressed, Bachner got good news. Kellner made a trip to Kiev to visit the other Baustellen, and, before returning to Warsaw, announced himself pleased with operations. The Kellner firm was expanding its operations in other occupied areas—Norway, for one. Perhaps Kellner could see that behind the filtered news from the front, there were signs that the Germans' remaining time in the USSR was limited. He hinted as much to Bachner in his conversations.

Bachner also received good news from Novograd Volynsky. Leon and Mila Finder had arrived safely, along with six-year-old Nina Finder. Mania Bachner and Jadwiga Finder still remained in hiding, ready to follow in a few weeks' time. Mila praised Nina's behavior on the trip.

"Such wisdom in such a small girl," she said, shaking her head in wonder. "We had to get on a train in Krakow, then switch trains in Warsaw. No questions, no complaining. Once some Germans offered her chocolate. She smiled at them and thanked them ever so politely in perfect German."

"There's nothing like a ghetto to teach you manners," said Bachner's father sardonically.

"But Willi," said Mila, "with Isidor, we have a problem. His German is so bad, he has such an accent. I don't think he can make it."

"Where is he now?"

"Staying with Jadwiga in the home of a Polish woman. It has taken all of Isidor and Mania's money to pay her. That's why they couldn't leave with us. Mania is not happy at leaving him there, but it is the only way. He will have to stay in hiding."

"We will see," said Bachner, knowing how forceful his cousin Mania could be when she wanted something.

Leon and Mila joined the work force in Novograd Volynsky, Mila as a cook and Leon as a construction worker under the direction of Bachner's Uncle Fabish. After months of silent hiding in Krakow, Nina seemed happy just to have the chance to play with the children of other crew members. She spoke no Russian and they no Polish, yet within a few weeks she could hold her own in their conversations. With her blue eyes and blonde braids, no one ever questioned her ethnic background, and she, while only six, was careful not to give herself away.

About two weeks later, Jadwiga and Mania arrived in Novograd Volynsky, after a long dangerous trip from Krakow via Warsaw. As Bachner had feared, his cousin Mania, who also began to work in the kitchen, began pestering him to bring Isidor from Krakow. After some weeks of this, Bachner sent a young Jew named

Ludwig to fetch his cousin's husband. Ludwig was from Krakow and was blond, blue-eyed and spoke excellent Polish. When he found Isidor, he told him that he should play the role of his rather doddering old uncle, keep his mouth shut and follow instructions. Armed with this plan and some excellent forged papers from the Warsaw office of Johannes Kellner, Isidor and Ludwig made it back to Novograd Volynsky.

Despite his strong accent and Jewish appearance, Isidor had a valuable skill that made him welcome at the Baustelle. Trained as a dentist, he not only did manual labor, but also took charge of first aid for the crew. Despite the constant headaches, Bachner had to admit to himself that he was pleased to have gathered together so many from his extended family. Sometimes he found it hard to believe that his luck still held. God must have nothing to do but watch over Willi Bachner and his Jewish friends.

*   *   *

Things were not going well for Germany. The reality behind the optimistic propaganda dispatches from the eastern front was indeed grim. Although Stalingrad had been the turning point of the eastern war, the ebb and flow of military strength, fueled by the mistakes of the supreme commanders on both the Russian and German sides, brought the struggle to an impasse. Like a cresting wave just before it breaks, the opposing sides poised in momentary balance in the summer of 1943. Germany could not win; Russia could not lose.

In response, Hitler ordered his generals to prepare for a campaign that would demonstrate German superiority once and for all. Hitler called this move to crush the Red Army "Operation Citadel." Its target: the Russian city of Kursk.

Elsewhere in the Reich, news of other setbacks filtered in. On May 9, the Axis forces in North Africa surrendered to General Eisenhower. Just as the recapture of Stalingrad had signaled the beginning of the end of German control in the USSR, the battle of El Alamein, in November 1942, signaled the beginning of the end in North Africa. By summer 1943, the Allies were set to begin the liberation of Europe, preparing for the invasion of Sicily, while in the Reich itself, fierce allied bombings rained down on German cities and industrial centers with deadly frequency.

The decline of the Reich was evident: casualties filled the train stations; partisan activities slowed travel; and rumors swirled amid the mounting chaos in Kiev. The desperation of the Nazi commanders could be seen most clearly in the increasing frequency with which workers were rounded up to be sent west. The Ostarbeiter became more and more necessary as Germany tried to match the war production of the Allies. Initially, Hitler discounted the US entry into the war at the end of 1941, not realizing the advantage the Americans would give the Allies in equipment, weapons, ammunition and all the other accoutrements of war.

At first Ukrainians went willingly to Germany in search of higher wages and steady food rations. But as news of their ill-treatment made its way back home, volunteers became fewer and fewer. By 1942, the Generalbevollmächtigter für den Arbeitseinsatz, or GBA, under the direction of Fritz Sauckel, began forcibly collecting Ukrainians and sending them to Germany in unheated cattle cars, where they worked in conditions scarcely better than those of concentration camps. By summer 1943, there were two million Ostarbeiter in Germany, with urgent calls for millions more.

As they had during the anti-partisan campaigns, many civilian administrators tried to tell their leaders back in Berlin that such actions were counterproductive, that they served only to increase partisan support and decrease the ability of the civilian administration to assure the flow of supplies to the front. But Hitler gave the final word: if Germany could not win the war with new arms and munitions, then the Soviets would win it.

A new drive to collect Ostarbeiter, dubbed "Operation Sauckel," hit Zitomir in August of 1943. Hitler's forces swept through markets and movie theaters rounding up all able-bodied workers. Black-clad troops snatched adolescents from schools and dragged workers from their jobs.

When Zitomir supervisor Nieczajuk learned that most of the Kellner crew had been rounded up in such a sweep, he turned to the best German speaker in the office, Gerda Ferencz.

"Fräulein Ferencz, I must ask you to go and see if you can get our workers back," Nieczajuk said apologetically. "I would go myself, but you see . . ." He paused, embarrassed. "The SS, they terrify me." He shuddered. "I lose my tongue in front of them. Besides, my German is so bad. I hate to ask this of you, but you are our only chance."

"Of course. Just get me papers clearly stating that our firm is kriegswichtig. Get as many official stamps as you can—Reichsbahn, Civil Administration, Wehrmacht. Cover them with eagles and swastikas, then I will see what I can do."

Nieczajuk obtained the papers that Gerda requested and she took them to the rail yard. The scene at the station was nearly as bad as a selection at the Umschlagplatz in Warsaw. Hundreds stood under guard behind barbed wire, some as young as fifteen or sixteen. With tears streaking their dirt-smeared faces, they jostled one another, crowding close to the fence, calling for their parents, who reached through the wire, ignoring the barbs that ripped through clothing into skin, as they screamed the names of their children.

"Ivan! Misha! Anya!"

Mothers begged the guards to pass on the loaves of bread, chunks of cheese, crumpled shirts and faded trousers they had gathered. Gerda wanted to cover her ears, to drown out the wails of small children, to close her eyes against the anguish in their parents' faces. The German soldiers remained impassive, stirring only to batter people on either side of the wire with their rifle stocks when they failed to obey their orders to move back.

Gerda pressed a hand over her mouth. She could not believe the inhumanity before her. She had spent very little time in the ghetto, had only heard descriptions from others. Such cruelty, such disregard for the lives of people: Jews, Poles, Ukrainians, mothers and children. She realized then and there that the Germans would lose the war. They deserved to lose everything.

Near the entrance to the trains, a crowd had been assembled so that the Nazis could conduct a "selection." Each person was given a cursory examination by a German doctor to determine if he was fit for work, a very brief examination which nearly everyone passed. Gerda showed the stamped papers Nieczajuk had given her to every German official she could find. She was passed from one to another in an endless, nightmarish circle.

Finally, a harried official directed her to the examining officer. After close scrutiny of the papers and a heated discussion with two skeptical-looking German officials, he ordered Gerda to stand near him and listen as each worker gave his name. Any Kellner worker who could show a Kellner Arbeitskarte could be excused.

It took nearly all day, but in the end, Gerda rescued close to fifty Ukrainian and Polish workers who were allowed to return to their homes or the Kellner barracks. She returned to her apartment utterly exhausted and physically sick.

Nieczajuk was impressed with her success and apologetic for sending her into such a terrible ordeal in his place. The roundups continued in Zitomir, but the Kellner workers were left unmolested.

One evening near the end of August of 1943, Gerda wearily made her way back to her apartment. It had been a strenuous day, but the news from the east had been good, at least to her ears. The German offensive, Operation Citadel, had failed. Kursk had been liberated on August 22. The Germans lost 70,000 men, nearly 3,000 tanks and 5,000 trucks.

The Germans retreated toward the Ukraine, while the Red Army pushed west along all fronts. It seemed that more and more of the talk in the Ukraine turned to evacuation. It was no longer a question of how best to exploit the area, but of how to escape without losing everything.

When Gerda noticed people waiting outside her door, she groaned inwardly. The last thing she needed that night was visitors. But when she recognized Willi and Cesia, her fatigue left her.

"Hello, Gerda," said Willi, casually. "I wonder if you would mind having a couple of visitors? Things are rather hot in Kiev right now. I have to lay low for a few days."

Gerda opened the door and ushered them in. She followed Bachner, not needing to ask the now familiar question, "What has happened now?"

"It's Hania," he said. "Ostrowski came to see me this morning. Hania has been denounced in Spola."

10 THE REQUITAL OF THE WICKED

YOU SHALL NOT FEAR THE TERROR OF THE NIGHT
NOR THE ARROW THAT FLIES BY DAY;
RATHER WITH YOUR EYES SHALL YOU BEHOLD
THE REQUITAL OF THE WICKED.
                                    PSALM 91:5, 8

Bachner, Cesia and Gerda sat at the table long into the night, drinking tea, smoking and discussing the latest threat to their survival.

"It happened yesterday afternoon," Bachner began. "Genia came to Lonia right after it happened. She had been hearing whisperings in the kitchen that the supervisor's secretary looked Jewish. She warned Hania that morning." Willi shook his head. "Poor Hania was already in a panic. She was telling Tadek about it at the Baustelle when they spotted one of the Polish women coming toward them with some soldiers."

"Was the Pole one of ours?" asked Gerda.

"I'm afraid so," said Bachner. "We can no longer trust anyone. Not even the people who depend upon us to put bread on their tables." He blew on his tea, waiting for it to cool as he continued. "When Tadek and Hania saw the soldiers, they ran from the station into a cornfield next to the station. They ducked down between the stalks, but when the soldiers started shooting, Tadek jumped up. That man is crazy!" Bachner couldn't help smiling.

"Crazy for Hania," Cesia said. "He would do anything to protect her."

Willi sipped his tea and nodded. "Yes. He waved his arms and yelled, 'Here! Come and get me, you lousy Nazi bastards!' then took off with the Germans firing away at him."

"Dear God," Gerda's face went pale. "Did he make it?"

Bachner nodded. "According to Lonia, both Tadek and Hania made it back to the house where Genia is staying. Hania's landlady gave her some peasant clothes. Hania gave Genia all the things she had saved, including the last of the gold her brother had given her before she left the ghetto. She told Genia that she and Tadek were going back to Warsaw."

"Warsaw! But why?"

"Tadek thought that with his family and friends there it would be their best hope." Willi shrugged; his shoulders sagged as he lifted his teacup wearily. "The sad thing is, Lonia told me the soldiers came and searched Hania's room and found her papers, you know, as Bronka Kazaniecka. They were furious with the Polish woman for having wasted their time. Tragic. If Hania had not panicked, she might have gotten away with it." He rubbed a hand across his mouth, then sighed.

"Maybe yes; maybe no." Gerda waved away the cigarette smoke hanging over the table. "But if Hania was as frightened as you say, she could never have withstood an interrogation."

Bachner agreed. "The question now is, how will I be affected by all this? My last run-in with the SS was very close. Too close. When and if word comes from Spola that my supervisor and his secretary, who is his wife, ran away after being denounced as Jews!" Willi drew a rectangle with his hands above the table. "A very large red flag will be raised, no?"

"So, we came here," Cesia said quietly. She timidly touched Gerda's hand. "I hope we won't be too much trouble."

"Don't be silly." Gerda took Cesia's hand and gave it a squeeze. "After all you've done for me, the least I can do is give you a place to stay. What about Nieczajuk? Should I tell him?"

"No," said Bachner emphatically. "Not that I think he would turn us in, mind you. But as much as I like the man, I don't think he would be able to keep a secret that the SS wanted to get out of him. The less he knows the better."

When Bachner left Kiev, he had told his staff that he would be gone for a time to check on some Baustellen, but did not tell anyone where he could be reached. After a few days, he called Kiev on the pretense of checking on shipments of supplies. His matter-of-fact inquiries as to how things were going elicited no information of SS interest in his whereabouts. After a few days, he returned and resumed his usual activities.

In early September, Schwalbe got word to Bachner that Hania and Tadek had made it safely to Warsaw. They had taken a circuitous route by train, hitchhiked aboard Wehrmacht trucks heading west and were now staying with relatives of Tadek's in Praga, a suburb of Warsaw.

Unfortunately, Bachner had to send back bad news to Warsaw. Moritz Stamberger, Adolf Stamberger's brother, had committed suicide in Spola. Bachner learned of Moritz's death from Lonia when he went to oversee the work in Spola and Dnepropetrovsk.

There was an old German soldier who liked to come to the workers' barracks to play cards. As he got more friendly with the workers, he had asked more and more questions, especially of Moritz, who was close to his own age. Poor Moritz found it increasingly difficult to talk with this fellow without appearing nervous. After Hania was denounced, he became convinced that he would be discovered at any time.

He had stopped eating and sleeping; he paced the barracks all night, murmuring to himself, as if the tension of waiting for discovery made each moment an agony of terror. Finally, he could take it no more. Genia Teifeld had found him in a small room off the barracks, his wrists slit. His shirt sleeve was blood-soaked; he had slumped onto one side and rested there, close to death.

"Why?" Genia had asked him. "Why, when the end is so close? How could you give up now?"

But Moritz could no longer speak. He stared at her, his mouth moving slightly, his dark eyes haunted with questions of his own, questions no one could answer: Why? Why this war? Why this hatred? This preying of man upon mankind?

Genia held his limp hand, ignoring the sticky, sweet blood clotting between his fingers until the questions left his eyes. Then she slowly closed his eyelids.

*   *   *

Novograd Volynsky had become the largest Baustelle next to Kiev. The center of the far-flung repair operations that dealt with partisan damage to the rail lines, it now harbored the largest concentration of Jews in the Kellner firm. Jews continued to make their way to the Kellner firm, either by chance or by design. Bachner, although always glad to offer sanctuary to one more, could not quell the nervous worry that one more could spell disaster for them all.

One day, as he was overseeing the distribution of paychecks, one of these new arrivals made a potentially fatal error right under the nose of a Reichsbahn inspector. Routinely, the workers came up to the engineer and stated their names. Bachner checked each name against the roster, then had the worker sign before handing over paychecks and ration coupons. Bachner called out for the next man, who took a step forward saying, "Grossman."

Bachner looked up in surprise. The man had given his Jewish name, not his alias. As Grossman realized his mistake, the blood drained from his face. With a glance at the German inspector, who appeared not to have noticed, Bachner said in a calm voice, "Good day to you too, Wolniak, now just sign here."

Grossman hastily signed "Wolniak" with a trembling hand. Bachner handed him his pay envelope with a pat on his hand as if to say "Relax, no one noticed."

On another day, it was Heniek who panicked. He stepped up to the desk and gave his name "Kwiatkowski," then looked down at the list of Kellner employees. There he saw his real Jewish name, "Buchführer," plainly listed.

Drawing in a sharp breath, he whispered to Bachner, "Willi, my name. How did they find out my name!" He had looked at the roster and seen the designation "Buchführer," which means "bookkeeper," under another worker's name.

He started to look around frantically, but Bachner said calmly, "Come now, Kwiatkowski, we haven't all day. Just sign your name." His eyes told Heniek to relax and in a moment the young man realized his mistake.

"Yes, Panie Bachner," he said. Chagrined, he walked off shaking his head.

Willi's biggest headache in Novograd Volynsky was keeping an eye on his father, who had been assigned to the kitchen to help with cooking and carrying water. A typical family patriarch, he resented the fact that his nieces Mania and Mila told him what to do. So he often refused to cooperate. He sometimes came up to Bachner, casually asking for a cigarette, regardless of who might overhear. Exasperated, Bachner would slip him his whole pack.

"Please, Papa," he would beg, "you must not do such things." But Papa Bachner would simply retort, "If a father cannot ask his own son for a simple smoke, who can he ask?"

One day, Bachner journeyed to Novograd Volynsky. After taking care of Kellner's business with his Uncle Fabish, he went looking for his father. The kitchen workers told Bachner he could find the old man out behind the building. Behind the kitchen and barracks, a small wooded area formed a peaceful glade next to the stream they used for drinking water.

Bachner stepped out the back door. Through the sparse stand of trees, he glimpsed a figure seated by the stream. He walked toward his father but stopped suddenly when he realized what his father was doing: he held a small prayer book in his hands; quietly praying in Hebrew, he rocked his upper body back and forth.

Bachner shook his head with exasperation and hissed, "Papa, what are you doing!"

The elder Bachner stopped and looked over his shoulder at his son.

"So, what does it look like I'm doing?" He turned back to his book. "I'm saying my prayers."

"Papa." Willi strode forward, reaching for the book. "You can't do this. You put all of us at risk. How long have you had that prayer book?"

"Since 1928," he said mischievously, holding the book just out of his son's reach.

Willi saw that his father had crudely taped brown paper over the book's embossed leather cover. Its pages were stained and yellowed with use.

"It's a very small prayer book," he said. "See, it fits right in my coat." He tucked the prayer book into his pocket.

"I don't care how small it is!" Willi kept his hand outstretched. "If anyone finds it or sees you using it, you'll be dead. For God's sake, Papa! Use some sense."

"Wilhelm, not you, not those two nagging nieces in there," his father's greying brows formed an arch over his sparkling eyes, "not even Hitler himself will keep me from preparing for Yom Kippur."

"Yom Kippur!" Willi's hand fell to his side. "Oh God, I had completely forgotten. I missed Rosh Hashana completely."

"That's not surprising, the way you seem to feel about praying."

"Look, Papa," said Bachner in a conciliatory tone. "I know that your prayers are important to you. But, please, be a bit more discreet. God will still hear you, even if you whisper. Pray in your room, not out where anyone can see you."

He led his father back toward the building, all the while wondering if his words had had the slightest impact. But evidently their impact was limited. A short time later, Heniek told Bachner about another incident involving his father, who had gone into the barracks one afternoon, when everyone else was still at work. Sitting on his bunk, he brought out his beloved prayer book and began to pray quietly. Suddenly, someone stirred in the bunk above him. He stopped and was silent. It was Stanislaw, an older Pole, who, like Papa Bachner, did minor light work at the Baustelle.

"Don't mind me," said Stanislaw. "Go right on with your praying."

When Papa Bachner told his nephew of this incident, Heniek spoke with Stanislaw, hoping to determine if his uncle had gone too far this time. Without really coming out and asking the Pole, Heniek probed for information. The older man gave no indication that he posed any danger, but Heniek promised Bachner he would continue to keep an eye on Stanislaw and his Uncle Heinrich.

Willi's father was not the only one who behaved suspiciously during this treacherous time. Jadwiga Finder was also suspected by some of the other kitchen workers. She told Bachner she had fasted on Yom Kippur and had been questioned by one of the Ukrainian kitchen workers. Jadwiga told her she wasn't hungry, that she had an upset stomach. "Well, that's quite a coincidence, seeing that today is the Day of Judgement." Jadwiga had looked at her with a puzzled expression as if she did not know what she meant. Bachner decided that the woman was too suspicious to be in a kitchen with four Jews, so he told her that they needed a cook in Zitomir, gave her a raise and she left willingly.

*   *   *

The news from the front, though grim to the Germans, was naturally greeted with joy by the Jews and people in the occupied territories. The Red Army continued to push the forces of the Reich back in a slow, methodical, bloody fashion. By late September, Ukraine was no longer behind the front. Artillery fire could be heard at Dnepropetrovsk. To the north, the Red Army pushed even further westward and Smolensk, about 300 miles north of Kiev, was retaken by the Soviets on September 25.

Earlier, during the summer, the Germans had halfheartedly toyed with the idea of trying to get the Ukrainians to ally themselves with Germany, to join them in fighting the Communists. Similarly, the Germans considered using the propaganda tool provided by the defection of a prominent Soviet general.

Andrei Andreyvich Vlasov had been captured by the Germans in July 1942. After his capture he became convinced that Germany could help the people of Russia overthrow Stalin. Nazi propagandists proclaimed the formation of the Russian Liberation Movement, headed by Vlasov. But the Führer's inner circle, and indeed Hitler himself, saw Vlasov as a danger. The Slavs were to be exploited, not liberated. Hitler believed that any talk of Russian nationalism would only cause problems in the occupied areas. Control must be left firmly in the hands of the Aryan race.

But by the fall of 1943, keeping the reins in German hands was no longer possible. Even the SS was not immune to the changes necessitated by the loss of personnel. As SS members were either killed in battle or withdrawn to other areas, a manpower shortage developed in the Ukraine. Estonians and Latvians, considered Aryan by the Nazis, had been allowed earlier into the military wing of the organization—the Waffen SS. By mid-1943, plans were made to recruit 3,500 Ukrainians, integrating them into the campaign to stop the Red Army.

Hitler, by now having silenced the military specialists, and ever more convinced of his military genius, was confident that the Soviets could be stopped before winter set in. He gave the order to hold on to every inch of Russian territory. The Russians pressed on, crossing the Dnieper north and southeast of Kiev.

The war was now four years old. Germany had been defeated in North Africa, and was losing in Italy and in Russia. Day and night, American and British forces bombarded German cities, creating panic throughout the Reich. Germany had also lost the battle for control of Atlantic shipping lanes. American-made war material streamed into Great Britain in preparation for an assault on the Continent.

The Germans no longer had any real hope of holding Kiev, or any of the Ukraine for that matter. The city was in chaos. At the train station, civilians, businessmen and wounded soldiers fought for space on trains heading west. The trains crept out of the station at a snail's pace, jammed with passengers. Once they left the city the trains were at the mercy of the thousands of partisans who now controlled large portions of the countryside.

Johannes Kellner had come to Kiev to oversee the closing of the office and its evacuation to the west. The Kellner Baustellen in Dnepropetrovsk, Spola, Nikolayev, Odessa and Poltava had been abandoned and evacuated. The Ukrainians stayed behind, awaiting liberation, along with some of the Polish workers and Jews who chose to remain.

Lonia Ostrowski, who was born in Russia, decided that he and his wife, Kaethe, would have a better chance for survival if they stayed in the Ukraine. Hania's sister Genia would also remain. While Bachner agreed that their prospects for survival were better if they remained, he was reluctant to set loose those who had been under his protection for so long.

Kellner decided that Bachner should go to Novograd Volynsky and take most of the office equipment with him. Kellner would personally oversee his remaining Ukrainian operations from Lwów. All the paperwork and records from the Kiev office were hastily boxed up and sent there.

When the evacuees from Kiev reached Novograd Volynsky, they watched the train continue westward. As the Reich forces retreated, a host of would-be colonists preceded them: all the bureaucrats, businessmen and tradespeople who had hoped to profit from the Nazi hunger for conquest. With this evacuation, the pace of work at Novograd Volynsky slowed. There were no new construction projects, only repairs necessitated by partisan-inflicted damage. The Germans seemed distracted, the Ukrainians and Poles surly.

The Jews, from long practice, simply melted into the crowd, trying to avoid notice; they could not yet relax their wary vigilance. The SS's manpower shortage had resulted in a decision to allow Ukrainians into its previously pure Aryan ranks. These new recruits demonstrated their loyalty by attempting to root out any Jew who might have escaped previous extermination efforts.

Nieczajuk and Gerda helped one such individual escape from Zitomir. Gerda had been eating her lunch in a park near the Kellner office one day when she saw two Gestapo men accost another employee, an accountant, outside the office. She knew that the man was Jewish and that, somehow, the Germans must have found out. She went back to the office to speak to Nieczajuk, who had seen the whole thing.

As the two debated what to do, the worker returned. He had managed to stave off arrest but said he had to disappear. Nieczajuk and Gerda prepared Marschbefehl for the man, instructing him to make his way eastward where he would be liberated. Bachner realized that even though he had never spoken to Nieczajuk about his or the others' secret identities, the Polish engineer no doubt knew he had Jews hidden among his workers.

Grossman was not as lucky as Nieczajuk's accountant. He, Heniek and a Ukrainian bricklayer were at work one day when a German vehicle arrived with two plain-clothes Gestapo agents and a large Ukrainian.

"You!" One of the Germans pointed at Heniek. "What is your name?" he asked in German.

"Henryk Kwiatkowski," replied Heniek, attempting a friendly grin.

"Where are you from?" demanded the German.

"From Krakow, Mein Herr," he replied. The smile froze on his face.

"What about you?" The Germans said, turning to Grossman.

"Wolniak, Janusz Wolniak, from Warsaw," said Grossman, his eyes wide with fear.

The large Ukrainian got out of the car and walked over to Grossman.

"Get in the car," he said flatly in Ukrainian.

"But I can't," protested Grossman, his voice quavering and rising in pitch. "I am working, I cannot leave my job."

The Ukrainian pulled a revolver out from beneath his coat, "In the car, now!"

Grossman made his way toward the vehicle. The Ukrainian pushed him into it and they sped off.

The Ukrainian bricklayer turned to Heniek and said, "You turned as pale as milk when they dragged him off. What are you afraid of, what are you hiding, Kwiatkowski?"

"You bastard. You turned just as white as I did. What are *you* hiding?" Heniek retorted.

The Ukrainian turned and spat on the ground, then went back to laying bricks.

Grossman was never seen again. Fabish made inquiries and found out he had been taken a few miles outside of town and shot.

Fabish told Bachner that he was fairly sure that the bricklayer had denounced Grossman to the Ukrainian SS. There was little Bachner could do. Since the workers were divided between only two sites now, he no longer had the flexibility to move people around to protect the Jews in his care.

The day after Grossman was shot, a young man approached Heniek during a break in the work.

"I heard what happened to Grossman," the youth said. He waited, his arms folded across his chest, as if expecting a response from Heniek.

Heniek continued to sip his coffee, saying nothing.

"Look, I know you are Jewish."

Heniek's cup stopped halfway to his lips.

"But, you see, I'm Jewish too," the boy continued.

Heniek hadn't known, but he still gave no reply.

The boy looked at him, hoping for a response. Finally, he said, "Well, I'm not staying. I'm going to join the partisans. I hear they're just over in those woods. I'd rather die fighting."

Heniek didn't look at the boy, but gazed off at the horizon. "Look, I'm not Jewish," he said at last. "But you do whatever you think is right."

When he said nothing more, the boy walked away. The next morning he had disappeared.

Cesia, too, came under scrutiny in Novograd Volynsky. Although she kept a low profile and seldom interacted with the other workers, she did assist Willi on payday. Heniek reported to Willi that he had heard two workers talking at mealtime that day. One of the workers said, "You know the woman who helps the engineer on payday? She is a Jewess."

The other had said, "No. She couldn't be. She is the mistress of the chief engineer! Why would he take such a chance as having a Jew in his bed?"

The other worker just shrugged and said, "Who knows why. Maybe she's worth it in bed. But I know a Jew when I see one."

In this case, Bachner had an option. Both men were Poles and many Poles were anxious to return to Warsaw. He called the two men into his office the next day.

"Here." He handed each a train ticket and several documents. "These travel papers will get you back to Warsaw." The suspicious Pole smirked at Bachner as though sharing a secret, but Bachner ignored him.

The other one winked as they left the office, whispering to his companion just loud enough for Bachner to hear, "You see, I told you she had great talents."

Willi half rose, then stopped himself. They could think what they wished, as long as they forgot the "Jewish mistress" when they returned to Warsaw.

The unrest caused by the retreating army continued. Soldiers needed lodging behind the front lines; housing became a problem in the town. The Reichsbahn barracks that the Kellner firm had been using were requisitioned by the army. To provide lodging for the displaced workers, the Reichsbahn moved into Novograd Volynsky Bauzüge, rail cars equipped with workshops and sleeping quarters.

Ever since the invention of the railroad, trains had been seen as an important logistical tool for war; yet the Nazi use of the railroad was unprecedented. Use of trains as mobile repair shops and construction units was an innovation. At first this construction was overseen by a variety of organizations, but eventually the Reichsbahn, and subsequently the Bauzüge, were placed under the direction of the Reichswehrministerium. As in the case of the rebuilding of the Kiev railroad station, the Reichsbahn contracted out to large organizations such as Organization Todt, which in turn subcontracted out to groups like the Kellner firm.

The Reichsbahn had used Bauzüge since the beginning of the war. They converted cattle cars into units equipped with sleeping quarters, kitchens and workshops. Initially, the units transported crews to remote locations where they would repair locomotives and other equipment necessary to the smooth functioning of the war machine. The flexibility provided by rail-based units enhanced the ability of the army to function far ahead of established civilian administration. During the early period of occupation, transports with as many as thirty cars sped toward the east from the central facility in Berlin, bringing fresh supplies and replacement workers on a regular basis.

However, by late 1943, the grand plan was undermined by the lack of supplies and spare parts and by partisan interference with rail lines. By that time, the Reichsbahn had 150 of these rail-based workshops throughout the occupied areas, fighting a losing battle against partisan damage to rail lines. Bachner and his workers were familiar with the Bauzüge; but they had, for the most part, stayed in fixed locations. The assignment of the crews to the railroad cars was a strong admission that, for the time being, they were unlikely to stay in any one place for long. Their home would be Reichsbahn Bauzug 1001. Given the news from the front, it was obvious that their stay in Novograd Volynsky would be temporary. The remaining Jews working for the Kellner firm had to decide whether to stay behind or return to Poland. Despite the fact that he was married to a Ukrainian woman, Uncle Fabish decided to return to Poland with his relatives, rather than remain behind. Nieczajuk, however, informed Bachner and Kellner that he'd had enough of the Reichsbahn and would remain in Zitomir.

Gerda and her sister were offered another choice. Kellner, who had always been impressed with Gerda's efficiency as a secretary and bookkeeper, suggested she return with him to Lwów. All the records from the Kellner installations were still boxed and unsorted. The Reichsbahn still owed the firm large sums of money, none of which would be forthcoming without the proper paperwork. Gerda agreed and left Zitomir as the sounds of approaching artillery grew closer.

Heniek couldn't decide what to do. He wanted to stay with Bachner and the others. But his cousin encouraged him to remain behind.

"Look, Heniek, when the war is over, I will find you. Or you will find me. All you will need to do is get back to Bielsko. But if you go west, who knows? At any time we could all be dead."

"But, Willi," Heniek protested, "you need me, too. I am your eyes and ears in the barracks. How will you know what the workers are saying if I'm not there? They trust me. I'm one of them."

"That's just it." Bachner reached up to put a hand on his cousin's broad shoulder. "They like you. You work with them and drink with them. You'll be safer here, Heniek. The Russians will be here any day now."

"But where can I stay?" protested Heniek.

"From what I hear, you have someone more than willing to take you in." Willi grinned, his moustache twitching mischievously.

"Who told you that?" Heniek's Slavic face took on a ruddy cast.

"Rumor has it that there is a woman at the marketplace who has her eye on you."

Heniek looked embarrassed, "Well I don't have my eye on her. For God's sake Willi, she has to be at least ten years older than me. She outweighs me too, she must weigh 100 kilos. It's gotten so I dread going to the market. She is there at her stall and she calls out to me. 'Come to me, you handsome thing.'" Heniek shuddered. "She's married! Her husband is off fighting the Germans and here she is inviting men to her house."

Bachner laughed at his cousin's discomfort. "Heniek, at least she won't be asking you to marry her. It isn't a matter of months or even weeks. The Russians will be here within days. Then you will be a free man. Every day we stay with the Germans is a day we risk our lives. Isn't freedom worth a few days as the object of a robust lady's affection?"

Heniek had to grudgingly admit that his cousin was right. "But what do I do?"

Bachner clasped his hands behind his back and thought for a moment.

"The next time you go to the market," he said after a moment, "smile at the woman. Make idle chat."

Heniek pulled a face. "Please, Willi. I'll do what I must, but let me put it off until it is absolutely necessary."

He didn't have long to wait. On November 26, the front was at Korosten, a mere twenty kilometers from Novograd Volynsky. The Kellner crews were greeted early that morning with an order to evacuate the town before noon. While the evacuation had been anticipated, no one expected it so soon. There was insufficient time to load all the equipment and supplies, so only the essentials were piled onto the trains.

The Ukrainians and Byelorussians made it clear that they would remain behind. Heniek slipped into their midst, the only "Pole" to do so. He searched the departing crowds for his cousin; when Bachner saw him standing head and shoulders above the crowd, he smiled and winked. He wished that his cousin felt as comfortable with this choice as he did. The big man's face saddened as the train pulled out of the station. Since he knew that Heniek saw him as a life-preserver, Bachner sent up a silent prayer that God would keep his cousin from feeling alone and adrift in this sea of foreigners.

That afternoon, Heniek went to the market and told the Ukrainian woman about his circumstances. This time he acquiesced to her invitation to come home with her. With the evacuation of the Bauzug, Heniek's work papers were worthless. But his admirer had a solution for that as well. She worked at a sawmill near the railroad station and asked the owner of the mill to hire Heniek. Thus, he was given new work papers and found himself a prisoner of love to a rotund Ukrainian.

The lady had a four-year-old daughter, and within a few days, she instructed the child to call Heniek "father." At the end of one week, she broached the subject of marriage. It bothered her that she was living in sin, she said. She was sure her husband was dead, so why shouldn't they just get married?

Heniek balked at the suggestion. He found himself listening closely for the sound of artillery that would tell him the front was near. The Soviet assault had stalled near Korosten. The days dragged on and on. Heniek found himself wrestling lumber all day at the sawmill and fending off the woman's amorous advances at night. He was not altogether successful.

Ten days after the evacuation of Novograd Volynsky, a locomotive and six cars came from the west. On the train were Reichsbahn Inspektor Pichelmeyer and a number of Kellner workers, including Mania Bachner and her husband, Isidor. Heniek had the misfortune to be near the station when they arrived and was seen by the German railroad official.

"You!" he called out as Heniek tried to slip away. "We have been looking for you. Why did you not evacuate with the rest of us?"

Heniek hung his head and responded in deliberately atrocious German. It was his lady friend, he explained. She had hidden all of his things because she didn't want him to leave. By the time he got them together, the train had already left.

The inspector sighed and shook his head. "A likely story. Well, never mind. Now we are here, and so are you. Get back to work. We have only two days to strip this godforsaken station of anything valuable. Go. Join the others."

Heniek dutifully joined the other Poles. He was pestered with questions about why he had stayed. Why would he want to remain with the Ukrainians and Byelorussians? Didn't he want to go home? His cover story earned him a lot of ribald laughter and a lot of jokes at his expense, especially from those who knew of the lady in question.

After two days, poor Heniek was once again faced with the choice of leaving or returning to the Ukrainian woman and waiting for liberation. He sought the advice of his cousin Mania.

"Look, I can't tell you what to do," she said distractedly as she packed up the kitchen. "You will have to make your own decision. That's the way life is."

As it turned out, the other workers made the decision for him. They took Heniek's suitcase and placed it on the train as it started to move out of the station. Heniek stood by irresolutely as the train whistle blew. Then, over its fading shriek, he heard a shriller cry.

"Henryk!"

Heniek turned. There, hurrying toward him, was the Ukrainian woman carrying her child. He decided in a moment, and leapt into the open door of the last car.

The woman ran after the train calling out to Heniek. She told her daughter, "Your father is leaving!"

The little girl began to cry and call out for him. As the train gained speed, the distance between them lengthened. Heniek's last view was of the two of them, standing in the middle of the tracks weeping. Heniek felt horrible. He didn't like to hurt anyone's feelings, especially a child's. The workers continued their merciless teasing all the way to Kovel.

After all of that, Heniek had to endure Bachner's chiding once he arrived in Kovel.

"What are you doing here?" he demanded. "You were supposed to remain behind."

Heniek halfheartedly tried to explain, but Bachner realized that he just didn't have the energy. Seeing his young cousin's glum mood, Bachner did not press the issue. He put his arm around Heniek and told him to find a place to sleep in the Bauzug. Wearily, Heniek left to join the other Poles in one of the cars that served as sleeping quarters. Two days later, word came that Novograd Volynsky had been liberated.

The Bauzug stayed at Kovel until just before January of 1944. During most of that time, the workers were engaged in a half-hearted attempt to repair the station, which had recently been bombed. But the Germans always had a worried eye turned eastward. The order soon came to leave, along with a locomotive to take them to Minsk.

*　　　*　　　*

If the partisans had easy access to the German forces in Ukraine, they had an even easier time in Byelorussia. The large forested areas of the republic provided more cover for attacks and sabotage, making it much more difficult for the Germans to round up partisans.

Bachner and the others knew nothing about the fate of the Jews in Byelorussia and Minsk, but they had heard rumors of Jewish partisans in the woods. Between July 1941 and October 1943, over five thousand Jews from the Minsk ghetto had been smuggled out by its well-organized underground and had fled to the surrounding forests. Of these, most had been killed on their way or in German partisan sweeps of the forests. But others had joined Soviet-backed bands. One such band, commanded by Shlomo Zorin, was made up of Jewish fighters who fought the Germans while protecting nearly six hundred women and children in a hidden camp in the forest.

The final liquidation of the Minsk ghetto occurred in October of 1943, when the last two thousand Jews in the Minsk labor camp were rounded up and killed in pits outside the city. Several had escaped even this final assault and were hidden by sympathetic Russians.

Bauzug 1001 was stationed at the Minsk railroad station. The railcars were detached from a locomotive and placed on a side track. No mention was made of finding more permanent lodgings. Although the Ukraine was now in the control of the Red Army, the front held fast at Smolensk. The work of repairing tracks and towers seemed more and more futile to both the workers and their superiors, yet it continued at a pace that, while not energetic, was at least efficient.

Bachner used his contact with Julek in Warsaw to try to get information on those who were no longer with him. Tadek and Hania were still in hiding. Gerda, having completed the task of closing books on the Ukrainian operations at Lwów, with a resulting healthy profit for Johannes Kellner, had been asked by him to assume bookkeeping duties at the Kellner operation in Norway. She and her sister had left Warsaw.

In February 1944, a supply shipment brought along another message from Julek, this time through a Jewish lawyer, Jakob Filinski. Filinski, his wife and daughter had been living under false identities in Warsaw since the creation of the ghetto. The daughter, Stefania, only 17, had been recognized as a Jew on the street by Polish police. By the spring of 1944, very few Jews survived in Warsaw. Any that were found were immediately shot.

The police demanded 5,000 zlotys to refrain from turning Stefania and her parents in to the Gestapo. Julek and his father-in-law scraped together the money, then sent the family to Willi on the next transport. Carefully avoiding the watchful eye of the Reichsbahn inspector, Bachner integrated the family into his crew.

They soon got used to Bauzug living. Kellner and Inspektor Pichelmeyer each had a whole car to himself. They lived in relative luxury, tended to by their Polish mistresses. Willi and Cesia had half a car; the other half was lined with three-tiered bunks that provided beds for the other workers. Some other family groups were given additional space.

Food was not provided directly by the Reichsbahn. The workers were given ration coupons by the Bauzug kitchen. Heniek, who proved to be an ingenious shopper, gradually assumed most of the responsibility for obtaining the foodstuffs to be prepared in the communal kitchen staffed by Mania, Mila and Jadwiga, with Bachner's father as kitchen helper.

Cesia spent most of her time caring for Jadwiga's daughter, Nina, although she continued to assist her husband with the payroll. All in all, life was not unpleasant. A seed of anticipation had begun to grow in the Jews and Byelorussians, while the Germans' confidence withered away to an uneasy apprehension.

$$*\qquad*\qquad*$$

On March 13, 1943, the Führer himself flew over Minsk on a return flight from Army headquarters at Smolensk. One of the bags on the plane harbored a bomb, placed there by high-ranking German generals who had decided that Hitler must be killed to end the war. The bomb malfunctioned and did not go off. At least six attempts on Hitler's life failed over the next few months, as dissatisfied military leaders continued to plot assassination attempts and coups. Still, the war dragged on. Hitler continued to foil all attempts to remove him from power.

In early April 1944, Kellner, who had returned to Warsaw, notified his crew that they would be evacuated east once again. They would go this time to Bydgoszcz, commonly known by its German name, Bromberg. The Poles celebrated, but the Jews had mixed feelings about returning to Poland. Only Bachner truly realized the danger involved.

He knew that trains returning from the occupied east would have to pass through Warsaw, for medical examination and delousing. With over thirty Jews scattered among the crew, Bachner knew that a thorough medical exam would reveal their circumcisions and expose them as Jews. Once the men were exposed, the women would be implicated as well. Somehow, he had to bypass Warsaw if they were to survive.

Willi's first step was to talk with Pichelmeyer.

"Herr Inspektor," he began, "do you know what is going to happen if we go through Warsaw? We will lose nearly every Warsaw man on this train. They will return to wives and girlfriends. It will be you and me on this train when we get to Bromberg. If we could go straight there, we could avoid this."

"Engineer," Pichelmeyer replied, "what is this? You know the rule. Everyone returning from the east must be examined and treated in Warsaw before they are allowed to enter the Reich. You exaggerate. We may lose a few workers, but we can replace them in Bromberg." The inspector made it clear that the discussion was ended and Bachner was dismissed.

Bachner fumed and worried for a few hours more, before coming up with a plan. Going to the Reichsbahn office in the train station, he placed a call to Warsaw and asked to speak to the Reichsbahn Oberbaurat in charge of Bauzüge transport. When the official answered the phone, Bachner began to rant in his most officious manner.

"This is Bauzugführer Wilhelm Bachner, calling from Minsk. We have been ordered to go immediately to Bromberg, to begin an important construction project. But I find we are supposed to go to Warsaw first. Do you know what will happen when I take all these Polish workers to Warsaw? No? Well, I will tell you." He did not wait for the official to answer, but drew a deep breath and continued. "They will disappear, that's what. Nearly half of my crew is from Warsaw.

"They have one thing on their minds and it's not construction. Even if they do come back, they'll be so hung over, I won't get any work out of them. Are you willing to take responsibility for our Bauzug not having enough workers to complete this important project?"

Bachner held his breath through the considerable hemming and hawing at the other end of the line.

"All right," the Oberbaurat said at last. "I will look into the matter. But I promise nothing. Is that understood?"

Bachner rang off and stormed out of the office under the startled gaze of the other employees. The bravado he had demonstrated in the office dissipated as soon as he stepped outside. His legs felt like boiled noodles and he put one hand against the building to steady himself as a wave of dizziness washed over him.

Throughout the afternoon he caught the worried glances of his Jewish workers as they loaded equipment and supplies. Most now realized what a trip through Warsaw could mean to them. He tried his best to silently communicate the assurance that Willi Bachner, as always, had everything under control. But he didn't feel in control. He felt as if he had already boarded a train that was hurtling toward his death. He wished that he could confide in someone, but didn't dare share with his wife how dangerous the situation was.

The next morning the workers assembled for a final roll call and then reboarded the trains. A locomotive was connected to the Bauzug and Pichelmeyer was given the all-clear to proceed. As he left Bachner to enter his own living quarters, the inspector stared at the engineer with an expression that led Bachner to ask him if there was anything wrong.

"No. Nothing wrong, Herr Bachner." He held up a telegram he had placed on top of the Bauzug roster. "I was just thinking about our conversation yesterday. It's such a coincidence. This morning I received orders to proceed straight to Bromberg. We are to bypass Warsaw." He gave Bachner a knowing glance and stepped up into his quarters to join his mistress for the trip west.

11 Survivors of Zion

THE REMAINING SURVIVORS OF THE HOUSE OF JUDAH
SHALL AGAIN STRIKE ROOT BELOW AND BEAR FRUIT
ABOVE.
FOR OUT OF JERUSALEM SHALL COME A REMNANT,
AND FROM MOUNT ZION, SURVIVORS
ISAIAH 37:31-32

Bauzug 1001 entered the Reich near Bromberg without incident. The furor over the change of travel plans had occurred earlier at the small rail junction at Pilawa. Instead of turning northwest toward Warsaw, the train continued east to Zyrardów. Workers made their way to Bachner's car, demanding to know why they were not stopping in Warsaw.

"I have no idea," replied Bachner innocently. "I thought we were going there, too. You must ask the Reichsbahn inspector when we stop."

There was little chance that the workers would dare to question a uniformed German, especially one who always carried a loaded revolver at his side. The workers grumbled, but returned to their cars. Bachner was sure that many of them would leave anyway, as soon as they set foot on Polish soil, but that mattered little to him. The important thing was he had escaped the entlausung.

The part of Poland that had been incorporated into the Reich seemed foreign to them. All the signs had been changed to German, and the presence of the invader was much more prominent than in the occupied USSR.

The Kellner Bauzug was deposited on the side track at a rail station just outside of Bromberg. They found themselves on a flat plain that was just beginning to emerge from the bleakness of the winter.

Their work in Bromberg seemed a throwback to an earlier time. They were to build a series of barracks for Germans returning from the east. It was as if the Reich had acquiesced to the loss of its "colonial empire" but was determined to take a stand at its borders. The area of Poland that had been annexed by the Reich was seen as rightfully belonging to Germany. The building of military installations in central Poland was designed to underscore that fact.

The construction was not hampered by partisans to the degree that it had been in the east. The Polish underground, divided between the western-backed Armia Krajowa, the Home Army, and the Soviet-backed Armia Ludowa, spent almost as much time fighting each other as they did the Germans.

Weeks passed without incident. The Kellner workers seldom went into town and rarely did anyone from the city venture out to the construction site. They were a self-contained community and work proceeded as planned.

Heniek gradually assumed responsibility for keeping the kitchen supplied with food and cooking supplies. Papa Bachner also worked in the kitchen, helping his nieces with cooking and bringing in water. He was now sixty years old. The war, with its hardships and losses, had taken its toll. He spent very little time working and a lot of time telling the others what they should be doing. Mania, Mila and Jadwiga were afraid to speak up to him and tended to do the tasks themselves rather than try to get their uncle to cooperate with them.

Heniek, braver than the others, would occasionally remind him gently, asking, "Panie Godewski. What about the water?"

To Papa Bachner, this was the last straw. He would walk up to Heniek and say, "Shut up, or I'll box your ears."

The situation became increasingly awkward when some of the other workers noticed.

"Why do you put up with the old man, Kwiatkowski? Why don't you tell him to go fuck himself?"

Heniek mumbled something about harmless old men and shrugged it off. But Papa Bachner was developing a reputation among the workers.

At the end of May, 1944, the Kellner firm completed the barracks at Bromberg. The Reichsbahn ordered them next to Gdynia, just north of Gdansk, which the Germans had renamed Danzig. They were to build a similar installation there. Johannes Kellner came from Warsaw shortly before their departure to discuss the job with Bachner and the ever-present Inspecktor Pichelmeyer.

After they had gone over the blueprints and specifications, Kellner asked to speak with Bachner privately. They went to the car that was reserved for Architekt Kellner, arranged as his private living quarters and office.

"Herr Engineer," began Kellner, with his hands folded against his chin. "It seems to me that a move of this sort is a good time to get rid of some of our less efficient workers. I'm sure you know which individuals I mean."

Bachner protested. "Herr Kellner, I hardly think that is necessary."

Although he didn't dare tell his employer, he felt that as long as his workers didn't pose a risk to himself or the others he was hiding, they could sit on their behinds all day.

"Come, come, Bachner. I know you are a soft-hearted fellow. Don't think I haven't noticed. Oh, yes. Even to my family. I received the thank-you notes from my children for the package of food sent from the Ukraine last Christmas." Kellner continued, somewhat chagrined, "You take better care of my family than I do."

"It's just that I knew you were so busy, Herr Kellner." Bachner modestly inclined his head. "I knew you would have sent them something if you didn't have so many things on your mind."

"Yes, well." He cleared his throat. "I appreciate your attention to these matters, just the same." He took out a silver cigarette case, flipped it open and offered Bachner a smoke. When the other man declined, he continued.

"As for our situation here, this isn't a charity we are running. That old man in the kitchen, what's his name?"

Bachner's heart sank. "You mean Godewski?"

"Yes, that's him. The man can't even do a decent job of carrying water. It's time to let him go."

Bachner protested, but Kellner remained adamant. Bachner's mind raced through mental calculations as he tried to guess how Kellner would react to the truth. He came to the conclusion that he had no choice.

"Godewski is my father," he said. The words hung in the air, as though frozen. Kellner just sat there looking puzzled.

"Your father. Well . . . that's ridiculous. Why in the world have you been hiding your own father under a false name? Or is it your name that is false?"

"No," replied Bachner. "His name is Heinrich Bachner." He took a deep breath and pushed the words out. "He is a Jew."

Kellner was speechless. Expressions of anger, surprise, fear and incredulity passed over his face.

Bachner answered his unspoken question, "Yes, I am a Jew, too. I came to your office that first time straight from the Warsaw ghetto. I had no other choice, Herr Kellner. It was the only way I could survive."

The clock on the desk ticked away as the sounds of the work outside filtered into the otherwise silent railcar. It seemed an eternity before Kellner spoke again.

"So, Herr Bachner, just how many of my employees are Jewish?"

"Do you really want to know?"

"No." He crushed out his cigarette in an ashtray. "I don't want to know. Look, Bachner, I have been very satisfied with your work. I could never have made this firm a success without you. But don't expect me to come to your aid if they find out." He spoke as though he could erase any knowledge of what had just passed between them.

"You needn't worry about me turning you in. It would be disastrous for me as well, if they learned my work crew was full of Jews. But don't expect me to lift a finger to help you or any of your kind."

"Yes, Herr Kellner. Of course." Bachner nodded, then added tentatively, "But about my father . . . ?"

Kellner heaved a weary sigh. "Oh, let the old man stay."

"Yes, Mein Herr." Bachner dared to let a smile cross his face. "Thank you. Thank you very much." He held out his hand. Rolling his eyes toward heaven, Kellner grasped the engineer's hand and shook it.

$$* \quad * \quad *$$

The Bauzug left Bromberg, heading due north to the port city of Danzig, then on to Gdynia. There, around mid-June, they heard the news of the Allied invasion at Normandy. At first, it seemed like just another war rumor, that staple of idle but hopeful conversation. But the rumors persisted, becoming more detailed as the days passed.

The long-awaited second front had been established and was pushing the Germans back from the coast. Germany was now trapped between the Soviets in the east and the Anglo-Americans in the west. In the south, two days before the Normandy invasion, the Allies entered Rome.

One story made it to Gdynia, untarnished by rumor. On July 20, a group of German officers launched an unsuccessful coup, hoping to end what they saw as the senseless slaughter of German forces as well as to seek peace with the Allies. A bomb placed in Hitler's "Wolf's Lair" in East Prussia left the Führer only slightly injured. This latest attempt on the Nazi leader, like the previous ones, failed as the conspirators fumbled in their attempts to take over the government. They were quickly captured and executed. Some of the Kellner workers who overheard the Führer's broadcast announcing the failed coup told the others that Hitler had claimed that his escape was proof that divine Providence was on his side.

But even the "divine" ability of the Führer to escape certain death did not deter the stirrings of hope in this small group of Jews. They could never all assemble as a group, but spoke one-to-one in whispers, calculating how much longer the war could possibly last.

Sometimes they longed to return home; at other times, they planned to emigrate to Palestine, or even to the United States. After long years of never looking beyond the next day, it seemed that they might have a future after all. Simple things they once took for granted, which had become impossible luxuries, now seemed once again within their grasp.

"I tell you what I'm going to do," said Heniek. "I'm going to find a huge feather bed, two feet thick, with clean white sheets and a goose-down comforter. I'm going to climb in, pull the covers up under my neck and sleep for a week."

"Will that be before or after you eat all the chocolate left in Europe?" inquired his Uncle Heinrich.

"I know what I want," said Cesia quietly. "A bathtub filled with hot water and bubbles. It's been so long since I really felt clean."

Parties, food, the theater—each held on to some post-war fantasy as though it were a talisman to get them through the remaining time. But a huge expanse of German territory lay between the Allied forces. And, despite the urgings of his generals, Hitler refused to consider an end to the war. Despite the ever-more lethal bombing of German cities, despite the mounting casualties and the inability of the Reich to adequately supply her armies, he insisted that the Allies would be driven back. He placed his hope on the introduction of new war technology such as the V1 rocket, used for the first time against civilian sites in Britain.

In the east, it seemed that the war presented a mirror image of the events of June, 1941. On June 23, a new Russian offensive opened, reflecting the determination to drive the Nazis from Soviet soil. Minsk fell July 3, Vilna July 8, Lwów July 27. By the end of July, 1944, the Red Army had entered Poland and was headed for Warsaw.

On August 1, 1944, a second uprising broke out in Warsaw. Although better supplied than the Jewish ghetto fighters, the Armia Krajowa was hopelessly outgunned by the German forces. Believing that the Red Army would immediately begin an attack on the city from the east, the partisans emerged from basements and doorways, swarming into the ruined streets like wasps from a damaged hive. But the AK's tactics were fatally flawed; they had failed to establish communication with the Red Army forces before they began their uprising.

Hitler brought in SS Obergruppenführer von dem Bach-Zelewski, who had overseen the anti-partisan campaign in the east, giving him free reign in the streets of Warsaw. The resulting slaughter ruthlessly targeted Polish civilians, regardless of their membership in the AK.

Meanwhile, the Red Army faced a formidable German force which had been pulled from other areas and sent to defend Warsaw. At the very time that the AK was calling for assistance from the outside, the outside forces were being pushed further and further away from Warsaw.

The Polish underground, along with its representatives in Moscow and London, called upon the Allies to come to the assistance of the beleaguered AK forces. The only aid forthcoming was dropped from the air; much was lost to the Germans in the close quarters of the city.

It took over a month for the Soviets to clear the southern suburb of Praga. Many said that the Soviets sat on their hands outside Warsaw waiting for the Germans to destroy the AK. While it is true that Stalin had no love for the anti-Communist AK, he held back on the advice of his generals, unwilling to risk the high casualties they claimed would result from an assault on Warsaw. The city would not be liberated until January of 1945, long after the Germans had crushed the AK uprising, leaving nearly half of the AK forces dead. Over 10,000 men died as German forces decimated Warsaw, leaving the air heavy with dust, the streets littered with bodies.

Word of the uprising came to Gdynia along with an influx of Polish workers who had fled the city and were looking for work wherever they could find it. Bachner received more personal news in the form of a letter from Julek, delivered by Johannes Kellner, when he evacuated Warsaw in September.

Julek's letter was full of grim tidings. His father had left home one day early in August and never returned. Hania had come to the office in a panic a few days later. She and Kazaniecki had fled to the city from Praga and sought shelter with Tadek's relatives. He, too, had left one morning to search for food and never returned. Adolf and Tadek became two of the 200,000 civilians killed during the merciless suppression by the Nazis.

Julek wrote that he had not been able to do much to help Hania. She had stayed at the Kellner office for a few days. But when the office closed, he could do nothing for her. She vanished into the smoldering ruins of the city. Julek ended his letter with a sad farewell and a promise to make contact when the war ended.

The new workers from Warsaw proved to be a rough lot. Many had criminal records and had fled Warsaw to get away, not just from the Germans, but from the police. Among them were a few who seemed even better than most Poles at spotting Jews. When orders came that the Bauzug would be going west, the order was given that all workers would have to undergo entlausung. Supervisors like Bachner and Uncle Fabish, were exempt. But the others had no choice but to go. German soldiers controlled the water flow from the showers. The Jewish men placed themselves as far from the others as possible, trying not to let their hands shake as they assumed a false modesty, hoping to hide their circumcisions.

Heniek turned this way and that, but found one Pole staring at him, with a nasty smile on his face.

"Now, Kwiatkowski," he whispered with a malicious smile, "now you cannot deny that you are Jewish."

Heniek turned and faced the wall, as water dripped from his body. He dared not turn around and face the man who knew his secret.

"Hey, Kwiatkowski," he continued. "Don't worry, I won't tell those bastards. Why should I help them, anyway? As long as my belly stays full and the police stay away from me, your secret is safe."

But the man found great amusement in whispered teasing of Heniek. Just when Heniek would think the man his friend, he would make it clear that Heniek's life was in his hands. When one of the workers suggested they all go swimming, the Pole turned to him and said, "See those hills, Kwiatkowski? See those beautiful hills?

You better run. Swimming's not for you. Better you should go hiking in the mountains." Then he laughed and walked away, leaving Heniek to worry all over again.

$$* \quad * \quad *$$

They left many of the Poles behind when the Bauzug was directed to Stettin in October of 1944. From there, they moved on to Eberswalde, then to Wittichenau, southeast of Berlin, and finally to Cottbus. When the train pulled through the Cottbus station to the assigned side track, the Bauzug crew stared out through partially opened doors. They noticed women working on the tracks, clearing debris. They wore the striped uniforms of concentration camps, which hung on their skeletal forms. Whispers rippled like waves through the crew: "Jews." Heniek and the others turned away, unable to watch.

When the Bauzug went to Bautzen, in Saxony, Kellner decided to leave a portion of the train there. He left its crew under the direction of Uncle Fabish. Leon and Mila Finder remained behind. After a bittersweet farewell with the other members of the crew, all promised that they would assemble in Bielsko when the war was over.

Bachner noticed Kellner watching this final exchange with Fabish. He looked at Bachner with an inquisitive look, as if to say, "Him too? Another relative?"

Bachner smiled sheepishly and nodded his head. Kellner sighed, shook his head and boarded the train.

And so the Bauzug meandered across Germany, dragged from one spot to another by a locomotive which would deposit them on a side track, then disappear. There was little work at this point, only the occasional repair of bomb damage or removal of debris and track repair. They would sometimes remain idle at one location, then be ordered to move on to another. The Reich continued to function like an automaton but there was a hollowness to it; its activities were largely without purpose.

On December 15, at the Führer's orders, the German Army launched an offensive in the Ardennes forest. Catching the Allied High Command unprepared, Hitler's army penetrated their front on several locations. But by the first week of January, 1945, the inability of the Germans to resupply their forces and the clearing of the weather allowed the vastly superior Allied air force to target German positions.

By mid-January, just one month after the offensive started, the Germans had been pushed back to where they started, suffering massive casualties—120,000 men—and a tremendous loss of planes, tanks, trucks and ammunition.

Things in the east looked even more grim. On January 12, 1945, the Red Army launched its assault on the Reich. Warsaw was finally cleared of Germans on January 17. Krakow and Lodz followed soon after. Although important symbolic victories, the recapture of major Polish cities did not have the strategic impact of the seizure of Silesia in southwest Poland. The Soviets were careful not to damage this important industrial basin, which had supplied sixty percent of Germany's coal.

The locomotives needed to pull Bauzug 1001 were forced to save their coal for more important trips. In late January the Kellner workers were on their way to the Thuringian city of Erfurt and were directed to pass just south of Berlin. The prospect of passing so close to the capital of the Nazi state was unnerving, to say the least. Bachner was even more distressed when the Reichsbahn decided they needed the locomotive and directed the Bauzug to make its way to the central station of the capital. There they were left on a side track and told to wait until a locomotive could be found to continue them on their way to Erfurt. Pichelmeyer and Kellner disappeared into the city, leaving the crew—mostly Polish, but with some very nervous Jews—sitting just outside the station. That night a fearsome bombing raid began. The sirens started to wail and the lights blinked out.

The Reichsbahn workers along the rails shouted for everyone to leave the train and enter the station bomb shelter. The crew emerged from the trains and ran across the multiple tracks toward the main station building as falling bombs whistled and explosions shook the yard.

Bachner took Cesia by the hand, but she refused to leave the train. She said, "Willi, I can't."

He didn't know if she was paralyzed by fear from the bombs or by the prospect of spending several hours in a bomb shelter filled with Berliners, but she would not run across the yard. Grabbing a blanket from their bed, he said, "Come on. We won't go to the shelter, but we have to get out of the train or we'll be killed."

Still she hesitated. He shouted over the cacophony of the raid, "Cesia, I didn't get us this far only to be killed by the Americans. Come. Now!"

Once outside, they crawled underneath the train. Bachner spread the blanket on the ground and they rolled up in it. There, from ground level, they watched the Allied bombers rain down their fury. With each impact, the ground shook; they clenched their teeth and covered their heads. It seemed that it would never end. Then it was over, leaving only the plaintive wail of the sirens.

Cesia clung to Willi and cried. "I'm sorry, Willi. I'm sorry I'm not brave like the others. But going into a room with all those Germans, I just knew they would know what I am."

Bachner mumbled reassurances and pulled her out from beneath the train. The others filtered back when the all-clear sounded and found the two of them standing by the train, still wrapped in the now-muddy blanket.

"So you just didn't want to miss the fireworks?" asked his father with a grin.

"It was quite a show. Sorry you couldn't see it," Bachner retorted.

The crew spent a nervous twenty-four hours in Berlin before a locomotive arrived to take them to Erfurt. They began to anticipate the nightly bombings, but they were never able to get used to them. On February 22, the Anglo-American forces launched a massive air campaign against the German rail system, called Operation

Bugle. Luckily, the Allies targeted main rail junctions; because of its low priority, Bauzug 1001 was usually relegated to side tracks in small towns.

One day, however, as they crossed an open area between Leipzig and Weimar, fighter planes swooped down and began firing on the train.

"Everyone off!" Bachner shouted, waving his workers toward the exits.

They spilled down the metal train steps, tripping over one another as they ran through the fields to the surrounding woods. One plane swooped so low, Bachner could see the pilot zeroing in on him from the cockpit. His short legs pumped; his breath came in ragged gasps as he pushed Cesia ahead of him.

"Hurry, Cesia. Run!"

He glanced back, just before they reached the shelter of the trees. The pilot's face registered a look of surprise, and the plane suddenly broke off the attack, climbing steeply, its engine whining. Bachner watched the smoke spiraling upward as the plane gained altitude.

"Willi? What happened?" Cesia held his arm and sagged against him.

"The pilot." Willi slowly exhaled. "He saw the women and children. And . . . he stopped shooting."

Cesia dropped to the ground. Her shoulders heaved as she began to weep. After the brutality they had all experienced in the east, where there was no distinction between soldier and civilian in the eyes of the Nazis, this show of humanity broke through the wall of numbness she had built. Willi sat down beside her and gathered her into his arms.

"Perhaps," he said, "God has at last remembered the Jews."

They made it to Erfurt, where they stayed a few days, clearing bomb rubble from the station before being ordered east to Gera. There seemed to be no sense to their assignments. It was easy for anyone to see that the Reich was dying.

By March 7, 1945, the Red Army had progressed to the Oder and Neisse rivers on the east. Allied forces under Eisenhower's command pushed the Germans back to the Rhine. Because of Hitler's determination to fight for every square inch of ground, the German forces in the west had been severely weakened. They now held at the Rhine, but it was clear that once the line was breached, the front would collapse. Germany held territory only 300 miles wide.

From the east and west, POWs and concentration camp victims were forced to march to the interior of the Reich to prevent them from being liberated by the advancing Allies. Hundreds and thousands who had managed to survive until then succumbed on these forced marches.

Nor was the German population to be spared either. Hitler, having failed to conquer the world, turned his wrath upon the German people. He claimed that if the German people failed it was because they were weaklings and thus deserved destruction. He ordered the destruction of all factories, electrical facilities, trains, ships, railroads and bridges. The only thing that prevented total decimation was the refusal of German officials, like Albert Speer, to carry out the Führer's orders.

The Bauzug had been sent to Plauen, but there was no longer any pretense that there was work to be done. All that remained was to wait for the end to come. Some Germans disappeared, but Kellner and Pichelmeyer decided to stay.

Kellner spoke to Bachner about his decision. "Well, Herr Bachner, it looks like you will make it."

"Yes, Herr Architekt." Bachner allowed himself a smile. "It does look that way."

"So, tell me. Who are the Jews?"

Bachner hesitated, then with a shrug said, "Myself, of course. My wife."

"Your wife!" Kellner clicked his tongue. Like the others, he had always assumed the pretty blue-eyed Miss Dambrowska to be Bachner's mistress.

Wilhelm felt the color rush to his face. "Yes, my wife. Her name is Cesia. My father, you already know. Uncle Fabish. Heniek, you know as Kwiatkowski, who gets the food." |

Kellner's bushy brows rose higher and higher as Bachner continued.

"The cooks, Mania and Mila, and their husbands. Jadwiga and her little girl . . ."

"The blonde one with the pigtails? I never would have guessed," said Kellner. "Go on." He waved his hand.

"Let's see," continued Bachner. "Gerda and her sister."

"Gerda!" Kellner exclaimed. "The best bookkeeper I ever had. She is Jewish?"

"Yes, and Bronka Kazaniecka, she was actually Hania Teifeld. There were others. Too many to mention, really. Most are still alive, some. . . ." His voice trailed off as he smoothed his moustache, shaking his head.

"What an amazing fellow you are, Bachner." Kellner clapped his hands once, then rubbed them together.

"I couldn't have done it without you, Herr Kellner, even if you didn't know you were helping me."

The architect inclined his head, acknowledging Bachner's implicit gratitude.

"I'm just glad its over," said Kellner. "God, it's been so long since things were normal. This Nazi shit. Ever since 1933, it seems like the whole country has been crazy. Now, maybe we can put our lives back together."

"For some of us, that will not be possible," Bachner reminded him gently. "My mother, brother, sisters, hundreds of relatives and friends are dead. For no reason but that they were Jewish."

For the first time, Kellner's eyes misted, and he leaned forward, elbows on his knees, head bent. After a long silence, he said somberly, "I would consider it an honor, Herr Bachner, to be liberated with you."

Bachner nodded and bade his employer good day.

During the third week in April, the locomotive engineer split up the Bauzug once again. Half the cars were taken just outside

Plauen. On these cars were Jadwiga and Nina, Mania and Isidor Bachner, and Frieda Neuman. The remaining cars, with the rest of the crew, Pichelmeyer and Kellner, were pushed onto some dead-end tracks in a forested area near the village of Muldenberg.

The Americans met the Red Army at the Elbe river on April 11, 1945. The area around Plauen was controlled by the US First Army, which entered the city on April 25. For the crew that had remained there, the long ordeal was over. Others, not so fortunate, were still behind German lines.

On May 5, a German officer approached Heniek at the Bauzug.

"Who are you?" he asked. "What is your purpose here?"

Heniek nervously explained that they belonged to a Reichsbahn crew, and that they were awaiting orders for their next assignment.

The next day, Willi sent Heniek on what was to become his last dangerous trip. They had received a requisition form for thirty-two pairs of leather boots, available from a shoe factory in Falkenstein, just a few kilometers from where they were. He sent Heniek, along with one Polish and one Latvian crew member, on bicycles to get the shoes. Who knew when they would have another chance to get badly needed footwear?

The three men made their way to Falkenstein without incident and got the shoes, which they divided up and hung over the handles of their bicycles. As they headed out of town, cannon fire suddenly erupted.

"This way!" Heniek waved to the others, peddling as fast as he could. In his haste to outrun the explosions rocking the buildings on either side, he took a wrong turn and they soon found themselves in the middle of a forest.

Suddenly, two soldiers with rifles emerged from the woods. "Halt!" one of the soldiers commanded, aiming his rifle at Heniek's forehead.

The three men raised their hands and slowly shifted off their bicycles. The soldiers motioned with their rifles for Heniek and the others to precede them into the woods, where they were brought before the German commander of the area. All around, soldiers in trenches trained machine guns upon the road. Heniek spotted a few tanks along with some heavy artillery, strategically hidden among the trees.

"What are you doing here?" the officer demanded, slapping his gloves against his leg.

Heniek explained, in deliberately fractured German, who they were; then he showed the officer his copy of the requisition form. After the man perused it, he ordered that the three be taken to head-quarters for questioning.

They rode to the headquarters, bikes and shoes piled in the back of a transport. The noncommissioned officer guarding them asked Heniek jovially where he was from.

"Krakow," replied Heniek.

"Me too," said the man. "Volksdeutscher."

Luckily, the trip to headquarters was short, and Heniek was spared more probing questions.

When they arrived, they were taken inside a large building filled with soldiers sitting behind desks shouting orders into tele-phones. Heniek sat with the Pole and the Latvian, drumming his fingers nervously on his knees as he waited for a very long time. All around them, Germans engaged in a manic, futile effort to conduct a war they could no longer control.

This is wonderful, thought Heniek. After all he'd been through, he was liable to get shot at the last minute. Hitler could be dead, the war could already have ended. But these Germans were probably going to kill him over some shoes.

When they were called in for questioning, the officer-in-charge was the same man who had spoken to Heniek at the Bauzug the day before. He recognized Heniek. In addition to the requisition papers that Heniek showed the officers, he and his two companions were wearing the distinctive blue caps with the red stripe worn by Reichsbahn employees.

The officer waved them toward the door.

"You are free to go," he said, bowing stiffly, but the men who had been guarding the bicycles and shoes had other ideas. As soon as they were out of sight of their commanding officer, they told Heniek they were confiscating them for the army.

Heniek protested. Although he now wished he had never seen the stupid shoes, he knew that the trip back would be very long and dangerous without the bicycles. He decided to try Willi's method. Straightening himself to his full height, he looked the solider in the eye.

"You cannot confiscate these bicycles," he said gruffly. "They are Reichsbahn property!"

The Latvian and Pole exchanged a frightened glance, as if wondering whether Heniek had lost his wits. An officer from inside heard the commotion and came out.

Heniek spoke up before the soldiers could open their mouths.

"Your commanding officer has ordered these men to release us, and they are trying to confiscate Reichsbahn property." He locked his hands behind his back. "Which of you wishes to accompany me back inside to report this?"

The officer quickly took in the situation.

"Release these men immediately," he instructed the soldiers. "Get back to your posts while I decide what disciplinary measures are in order."

The two soldiers scurried back inside the building, and the officer winked at Heniek. "On your way." He waved his baton.

Heniek and the others did not waste a moment straddling their bicycles and peddling away, as if Hitler himself were at their heels.

They encountered many Germans on the road back to the Bauzug, but the once-mighty Wehrmacht had more important things on their minds than shoes and bicycles. They were seeking some form of escape from the advancing troops.

It was almost dark by the time the three reached the Bauzug. They were met by Pichelmeyer, who demanded to know what had taken them so long. While they were explaining breathlessly, Bachner arrived, and, oblivious to the Reichsbahn inspector, embraced his cousin, apologizing for sending him on such a trivial errand.

"It was nothing," Heniek assured him. "And look at all these great shoes." Heniek managed a feeble grin, but his hand trembled as he gestured toward the bicycles. Willi put his arm around his cousin and guided him inside.

"Come," he said. "I think we both could use a drink."

The war really was over by the time Heniek returned to the Bauzug. The final piece of news received by Hitler in his Berlin bunker was that his old ally, Mussolini, had been executed, along with his mistress, in Milan. The next day, Hitler committed suicide.

Like a train that could not stop itself after the engineer's death, the war chugged on for seven more days. Early on the morning of May 7, 1945, in a red schoolhouse at Reims, where Eisenhower had set up his headquarters, the Third Reich surrendered unconditionally.

A few days later, on May 10, at about ten o'clock, the Americans entered the village in their strange-shaped green vehicles with machine guns mounted on the back. They seemed very nervous at first, but as the crowd roared, with the Bauzug members cheering the loudest, the liberators began to smile and wave. They drove to the center of town where they began to set up their headquarters, with a river of smiling, tear-drenched faces flowing around them. The crew returned to the train in high spirits. It was a sunny morning. The most beautiful morning, Bachner thought, God had ever granted.

Heniek went to fetch some water to brew coffee. A smiling Johannes Kellner greeted him in the kitchen. He stood beside the stove with his arm around his young blonde mistress.

"Congratulations, Kwiatkowski. Or what should I call you now?" He winked.

"Buchführer, Herr Kellner. Heniek Buchführer." He lifted his chest proudly.

Heniek was even more startled when the imperious Pichelmeyer came into the kitchen and shook his hand. The inspector had been advised by Willi to bury his ever-present revolver, and seemed to be trying to be as friendly to the crew as he could.

When the Ukrainian worker who had followed the Americans to the center of town came back, complaining that they had taken his watch, Bachner decided that perhaps a more official envoy should be sent to greet the liberators. He asked Kellner if he wanted to come, but the architect seemed no more eager to meet Americans than he had been to meet the SS. Pichelmeyer also declined, deciding it would be wise to keep a very low profile.

Bachner turned to his young cousin, who had been with him through so much and who had never lacked for courage or resourcefulness. "Come, Heniek. Let's go see these Americans."

Behind them they heard Papa Bachner proclaiming to the incredulous workers, "That's right, the engineer is my son. And that youngster with him is my nephew. My name is Heinrich Bachner. We are all Jews!"

Smiling to himself, Bachner went to meet the Americans.

$$*\qquad*\qquad*$$

As he walked down the middle of the street, Willi tried to convince himself that it was really over. It was difficult to accept the arrival of an event that had for so long been a fervently hoped for but seemingly unattainable goal. Here and there, in the streets of the village, the remnants of gardens, left untended in the last months of the war, showed only glimpses of color, as if the plants were reluctant to emerge from winter until they, too, were sure that the war was really over.

As Bachner neared the center of the village, he saw the first signs of activity in the streets. The Americans stood in clusters with their rifles slung across their chests, trying to assess the mood of the curious villagers. Groups of German soldiers stared from behind the barbed-wire fence hastily erected on the square in front of the village hall. The Americans had chosen this imposing structure as their temporary headquarters.

Bachner straightened his Reichsbahn uniform and smoothed his hair. He had tried to make himself as presentable as possible, washing, shaving with his last dull razor, shining his boots to re-move all traces of the mud ground into them beneath the railroad car during the American bombing. He knew he did not cut an im-pressive figure in his stained blue Reichsbahn uniform with its miss-ing buttons. Still, it was the best he could do and someone had to make contact.

Out of the corner of his eye, he noticed two Americans ha-rassing a well-dressed citizen of the village. The taller of the two soldiers pointed to a gold ring the man wore on his left hand. When the German shook his head and tried to walk away, one American pulled a knife from a sheath beneath his overcoat and ran his thumb along its edge. Bachner tensed as the German slowly pulled the ring from his finger and thrust it at the soldier. The tall soldier tossed the ring in his palm, laughing as the man hurried away.

Heniek took a step toward the soldiers, but Bachner stop-ped him with a hand on his arm. He motioned to his cousin to wait and proceeded toward the American headquarters, wondering if they had merely substituted one oppressor for another. Would the spoils of war be extracted from only the Germans? Would the Ameri-cans be able to distinguish between those who had suffered at the hands of the Germans and those who had perpetrated the injustices of war?

As he made his way up the steps, he failed to notice the tem-porary barricade with its off-limits sign until the shadow of a tall American MP fell over him, and he looked up from his reverie. Bachner, at only five foot four, found himself on eye level with the MP's arm band. He stared at the black letters on the white back-ground. He had seen so many arm bands in the last five and a half years: glaring red ones with black swastikas, worn with arrogant pride by the German SS; dull grey ones, worn out of necessity by Bachner and his crew of Reichsbahn workers, the disguises which allowed them to survive; and humiliating white ones with the single blue six-pointed star, worn reluctantly by the Jews, which marked them for extermination. The history of the war could be told through patches of cloth.

Bachner shook his head, trying to clear the haze of color from his mind as the soldier's guttural commands began to penetrate the fog. He looked up to find the MP's rifle inches from his chest. Although he couldn't understand the words, the hate in them struck him like a physical blow.

Bachner reeled, nearly losing his balance on the step as he realized that the soldier thought he was German. Have I made it all this way only to be shot because I can't tell him who I am? At any other time, the irony of the situation would have made him laugh, but the strength fed by determination which had seen him through the war suddenly drained out like water from a tap running dry. His legs would no longer hold him, and he sank to the step at the American's feet. As he sat shaking uncontrollably on the steps of city hall, foreign words he had learned in school long ago miraculously formed in his head.

"Sir, I am not a German," he said wearily in English. "I am a Jew."

For a moment, the MP continued to stare down the barrel of his rifle, his eyes uncertain, fingers locked on the trigger. Then, incredibly, he lowered his rifle and yanked open his shirt. A gold chain with a Star of David caught the sunlight where it hung next to the dull silver of his dog tag. Bachner stared at the golden star, overwhelmed to find a Jew among his liberators. A swell of emotion washed over him; he felt the protective walls he had maintained over the long years of war crumbling around him.

Gold and silver filled Bachner's vision, blending until he saw only grey. A shrill whine like the whistle of falling bombs filled his head and the MP's face dissolved into the greyness. Bachner forced himself to speak the Hebrew words recognizable to all Jews, regardless of their country: "*Sh-shema Israel . . .*" He took a shallow breath and began again.

"*Shema Israel Adonai,*" he managed to mumble. As he crumpled forward, the black shine of the MP's boots rushed toward him. For Wilhelm Bachner the war, at last, was over.

EPILOGUE

Bachner revived to find himself surrounded by soldiers speaking a mixture of English, German and, amazingly, Yiddish.

The soldiers were astounded at the story that Bachner told them. Many had seen the camps after liberation and could not believe that so many Jews had survived under the very noses of the Germans.

Bachner returned to the Bauzug with American medics and a large supply of army rations. There, an impromptu liberation celebration was held. After a few days, a locomotive was brought to move the train to Oelsnitz, where a displaced persons camp was located. In the camp they were reunited with the Jews from the other half of the Bauzug who had remained in Plauen.

Bachner and the others had thought they were the only Jews who survived. When they met others in the DP camp, they became obsessed with finding out who else in their families were still alive. Lists of survivors and their towns of origin were circulated. Ads were placed in papers across Europe in the hope that family members would surface. Few did.

When that part of Germany came under Soviet control, they returned to Bielsko in Poland. There, Bachner was reunited with his youngest sister Hilde, who had miraculously survived alone.

However, Bachner and his family soon found the growing repression of Communist rule in Poland and the continued anti-Semitism to be intolerable. They returned to Bramberg, West Germany. In 1951, Willi and Cesia Bachner emigrated to the United States and settled in Oakland, California. They had no children; Cesia's abortion had caused her to become sterile.

Heinrich "Papa" Bachner died in Bamberg, Bavaria, Germany in 1948.

Heniek Buchführer now lives in Ramat Gan, Israel.

Johannes Kellner settled in Munich, West Germany, after the war. During the difficult post-war years, Willi Bachner sent him food and money.

Heinrich Fabiszkiewicz, "Uncle Fabish," was liberated in Bautzen, Germany, along with his Ukrainian wife, Luba. They emigrated to Brazil after the war. Fabisz died in 1977.

Hania Teifeld was sent as an Ost worker to Germany in December, 1944. She survived, and was liberated by Russian forces in April of 1945. She emigrated to Israel and then to the United States. Hania lives in Southfield, Michigan.

Genia Teifeld was reunited with her sister soon after the war ended. She, too, emigrated to Detroit to join a sister already living there.

Tadeusz Kazaniecki, "Tadek," was never seen after the morning he disappeared. He is presumed to have been killed by German forces during the Warsaw uprising.

Gerda Reichenbaum and her sister Halina were liberated in Norway. Gerda emigrated to Australia where she lives today. Halina died in 1957 in Norway, shortly before she was to leave to join her sister.

Leon and Mila Finder were also liberated in Bautzen. They emigrated to Mexico, had a daughter and lived in Mexico City until their deaths: Leon in 1970, Mila in 1974.

Isidor and Mania Bachner were liberated in Plauen. They settled in Dusseldorf, West Germany. Isidor died in 1975 and Mania in 1990.

Jadwiga Finder and her daughter Nina were liberated in Plauen. They returned to Bielsko where they lived until 1965, when they emigrated to Israel. Nina Hudzik is now a physician in Afula, Israel. Jadwiga lives in Afula, Israel, near her daughter, Nina.

Julek and Ruth Schwalbe spent the remainder of the war in hiding in Warsaw. After the war, they settled in Cologne, West Germany, where Ruth still lives. Julek died in 1991.

Jakob, Felicia and Stefania Filinski, who joined the group in Minsk, were liberated along with the Bachners and emigrated to São Paolo, Brazil.

Frieda Newman, who was liberated at Plauen, remarried after the war and settled in Peterborough, England. She died in 1984.

Kaethe and Lonia Ostrowski survived in the Ukraine. They reunited with Bachner following the war and emigrated to Montreal, Canada. Lonia died in 1979 and Kaethe in 1984.

Willi Bachner led a quiet life as an engineer in the San Francisco Bay area until his retirement. He continued to keep in contact with those he had saved from the Holocaust. He helped many of them emigrate and establish homes far away from the painful memories of Europe. In 1989, some of the survivors joined Willi and Cesia when they celebrated their fiftieth wedding anniversary.

Cesia Bachner died in November, 1990. She was followed by her husband Willi just four months later. Up until the day of his death, Wilhelm Bachner continued to care for those around him, doing volunteer work with senior citizens and always watching over those who had survived the Holocaust through his actions.

GLOSSARY

Aktion: Action; round-up of Jews (*German*)

Amchu: Are you Jewish? (*Hebrew*)

Appell: Rollcall (*German*)

Arbeitsamt: Labor office (*German*)

Arbeitskarte: Worker's identification card

Armia Krajowa: Territorial army—Non-Communist Polish Partisans (*Polish*)

Armia Ludowa: Peoples' army; Polish Communist Partisans (*Polish*)

Bauleiter: Building inspector (*German*)

Baustelle: Building site; plural: **Baustellen** (*German*)

Bauzug: Construction train; plural: **Bauzüge** (*German*)

Bauzugführer: Construction foreman (*German*)

Blitzkrieg: Lightning war (quick conquest) (*German*)

Buchführer: Bookkeeper (*German*)

Chadziajka: Housekeeper (*Ukrainian*)

Chazak Veamatz: Be strong and brave (*Hebrew*)

Chevra-Kadisha: Jewish burial society (*Hebrew*)

Der mann ist tot: The man is dead; also, the husband is dead (*Hebrew*)

Deutsche Technische Hochschule: German University of Technology

Einsatzgruppen: SS units designated to murder (mobile killing units) (*German*)

Einsatzkommandos: Members of the **Einsatzgruppen** (*German*)

Entlausung: Delousing (*German*)

Generalbevollmächtigter für den Arbeitseinsatz: Person in charge of the workforce (*German*)

Generalgouvernment: Nazi-established government in Central Poland (*German*)

Gestapo: Secret Police (*German*)

Goldfasanen: Nickname for Civil Administration in occupied USSR because of their yellow insignia. Literally means "golden pheasant." (*German*)

Goy: Gentile; plural: **goyim** (*Yiddish/Hebrew*)

Judenrat: Jewish Council in the ghettos (*German*)

Judenrein: Free of Jews (*German*)

Kapo: Enforcers of discipline for the Germans (*German*)

Kriegswichtig: Important to the war effort (*German*)

Kripo: Acronym for criminal investigation department of the SS (*German*)

Lebensraum: Living space—term used by Hitler for eastern territories to be settled by Germans (*German*)

Leutnant: Second Lieutenant (*German*)

Luftwaffe: Air Force (*German*)

Luftwaffen Bau Dienstelle: Building office of the Air Force (*German*)

Marschbefehl: Marching order—travel papers (*German*)

Mein Kampf: *My Struggle* (*German*)

Mein Polnisches schwein: My Polish pig (*German*)

Mensch: Exclamation to a familiar person (*German*)

Oberbaurat: Head office council (*German*)

Obergruppenführer: Major group leader (*German*)

Oberleutnant: First Lieutenant (*German*)

Oberstabsfeldwebel: Chief warrant officer (*German*)

Oberstürmführer: Colonel (*German*)

Organization Todt: German construction organization named for its director, Herr Todt (*German*)

Orpo: Order Police (*German*)

Ostarbeiter: Worker(s) from the east (*German*)

Ostministerium: Ministery for Eastern affairs (*German*)

Panie: Mister (*Polish*)

Reichsbahn: German railways (*German*)

Reichsbahn Direktion Ost: Railway administration east (*German*)

Reichsbahn Direktor: Director of railways (*German*)

Reichsbahnoberbaurat: State railroad surface construction council (*German*)

Reichsdeutsches Bauunternehmen: German building enterprise (*German*)

Reichskommissar: State commisioner (*German*)

Reichswehrministerium: The ministry of railway construction (*German*)

Schatchen: Matchmaker (*Yiddish*)

Schutzstaffel: The SS blackshirted Nazi stormtroopers (*German*)

Shema Israel Adonai: "Hear O Israel my Lord" (section of a prayer) (*Hebrew*)

Shtetl: Small Jewish town (*Yiddish*)

Sipo: Security police (*German*)

Sitzkrieg: Period of inaction from the time the Allies declared war on Germany until the "Blitzkrieg" began (*German*)

Stürmführer: SS Major (*German*)

Szmalcownik: Taker of bribes (venal person) who denounced Jews for money (*Polish*)

Umschlagplatz: Transshipment site—loading area where Jews were assembled for deportation (*German*)

Uranus: Soviet code word for counter-offensive at Stalingrad (*Russian*)

Verdammtes gesindel: Damned mob (*German*)

Vernichtungslager: Extermination camp (*German*)

Volksdeutscher: Member of the German nation; used to refer to Germans who lived in other countries (*German*)

Wehrmacht: German army (*German*)

Zydowska Organizacja Bojowa: Jewish fighting organization in the Warsaw Ghetto (*Polish*)

NOTES

PREFACE

Page 13: The Altruistic Personality Project's results were published in Oliner, *The Altruistic Personality: Rescuers of Jews in Nazi Occupied Europe.*

CHAPTER ONE: THE DEVICES OF THE WICKED

Pages 17–18: Descriptions of the bombardment of Warsaw: interviews with Willi and Cesia Bachner, and Gerda Reichenbaum. Also Lifton, *The King of the Children*, 248–50; and Hilberg, et al., *The Warsaw Diary of Adam Czerniakow*, 73–77.

22: Accosting Jews on the streets of Warsaw: Hilberg, et al, 77–78.

23: Nazi view of the Jews: Rubenstein and Roth, *Approaches to Auschwitz*, 92–125.

24: Appointment of Hans Frank: Sloan, ed., trans., *Notes from the Warsaw Ghetto*, 348. Background on Frank: William Shirer, *The Rise and Fall of the Third Reich*, 268. Order to turn over radios to the Germans: Hilberg, et al., 34–35, 85. Closing of schools and churches from Sloan, 248; and Gilbert, *The Holocaust*, 111.

25: Description of Bachner's wedding: interview with Willi and Cesia.

26: Warsaw census: Hilberg, et al., 79–91. The arm band decree: Gilbert, 98.

27:   Korczak's refusal to wear the arm band: Lifton, 252. Fines for not wearing arm band: Hilberg, et al., 107.

27–28:   Incident with Heinz Hoinkes: interview with Hilde Bachner.

28–29:   Incident of Germans harassing a Warsaw family: Gilbert, 106.

29:   Conditions in Warsaw early in the occupation: Hilberg, et al., 108–28; Gilbert, 100–117; and Sloan, 7–28.

30:   SS organization: Hilberg, et al., 29, 49.

30–31:   Conflict between SS and Civil Administration: Hilberg, et al., 31.

31:   Description of early ghettos: Gilbert, 89.

CHAPTER TWO: THE YOKE OF FOREIGNERS

Page 33:   Construction of the ghetto walls: Hilberg, et al., 136.

33–34:   Description of parents' arrival and the work situation in Warsaw: interview with Willi and Cesia.

38–42:   Arrival and story of Heniek: interview with Heniek Buchführer.

42:   Work on the Italian Embassy: interview with Heniek. Situation in August 1940, and reprimand of Czerniakow: Hilberg, et al., 182–83.

46–47:   Continued adjustments to the ghetto boundaries: Sloan, 80. Population transfer in and out of the ghetto: Gilbert, 127–29.

47–48:   Situation in the ghetto in October 1940: Mogilanski, ed., *The Ghetto Anthology*, 309–10; and Hilberg, et al., 211.

48:   Poles shot for trying to get food into the ghetto: Sloan, 82–89. Korczak's arrest: Lifton, 265.

49–50:   Bachner's decision to find a way out of the ghetto: interview with Willi and Cesia.

CHAPTER THREE: OUT OF CAPTIVITY

Page 51:   Ghetto census, December of 1940: Mogilanski, 310. Food rations in the ghetto: Hilberg, *Destruction of the European Jews*, 168. Role of the black market in augmenting food supplies: Sloan, 97. Typical ghetto diet: Hilberg, et al., 55.

52:   Description of the ghetto in December 1940: interview with Willi and Cesia.

53:   Description of the ghetto marketplace: Lifton, 268–70.

54–56:   Annia Meyer and her story: interviews with Willi, Cesia, Hilde and Heniek.

58–60:   Bachner's meeting with Johannes Kellner and description of his first job: interview with Willi and Cesia.

63:   Hiring of Stamberger and Schwalbe: interview with Willi and Cesia.

63–64:   German sightseers in the ghetto: Sloan, 97, 181. German abandonment of public works projects: Mogilanski, 311.

65: "If we want to rule . . .": Dallin, *German Rule in Russia*, 7–9. German objectives in the west; and reaction of the German Foreign Service: Dallin, 11–14; 14–19.

66: "The Red Army is leaderless"; "triumph of preconceptions"; German attack on the USSR; and "Cowards and deserters . . .": Erickson, *Road to Stalingrad*, 15–49; 73–98; 118–25; 142.

67: German victories in the summer of 1941: Erickson, *Road to Stalingrad,* 146–79. "Our India . . .": Dallin, 20–43.

CHAPTER FOUR: THE SNARES OF EVILDOERS

Page 69: Use of Kazaniecki as a go-between: interviews with Willi, Cesia and Heniek.

70–73: Nieczajuk incident: interview with Willi and Cesia.

74: Kellner as subcontractor to the Luftwaffe: interview with Willi and Cesia.

75–77: Hans Gregor incident: interview with Willi and Cesia.

77–81: Descriptions of the first wave of exterminations and Bachner's learning of it: interviews with Willi, Cesia and Heniek; and Gilbert, 154–99.

81: Mass exterminations in the wake of the Nazi invasion of the USSR: Rubenstein and Roth, 126–33.

82: Jewish victims in the first five weeks of the German invasion: Gilbert, 175. Jews as slave labor: Rubenstein and Roth, 132.

82–83: Description of the killing squads and Jewish resistance in the USSR; and description of Babi Yar: Gilbert, 184–86; 201–4. Search for a more "efficient way to exterminate the Jews": Rubenstein and Roth, 137.

84: "Our Children Must Live": Sloan, 234. Execution order for Jews leaving the ghetto: Sloan, 353; and Gilbert, 242.

85: Suspension of food packages entering the ghetto: Mogilanski, 311. Typhus deaths; and delousing policies: Hilberg, et al., 310; 274–75.

CHAPTER FIVE: HARBOR OF SORROWS

Page 89: Description of the transport to Kiev: Wilhelm and Cecile Bachner interview; and Marian Pretzel, *Portrait of a Young Forger*, 140–46.

90: Description of German civilian administrators: Dallin, 84–101. Goldfasanen: Dallin, 102–3.

91: Exploitation of the Soviet populace: Dallin, 45–58. Effect of spring thaw on troop movements: Erickson, *Road to Stalingrad,* 335; Kreidler, *Railroads in the Sphere of Influence of the Axis Powers*, 120, 249; and Rohde, *Das Deutsche Wermachttransportwesen*, 169. Additional information on

CHAPTER SIX: DELIVERANCE AND DESTRUCTION

168: Rescue of other Bielsko residents: interview with Willi and Cesia.

169–71: Description of Otto Feuereisen: interview with Gerda, and Pretzel, 55–57.

171–72: Gerda's admission to Kiev Conservatory: interview with Gerda.

173–75: Wilaski incident: interviews with Willi and Cesia, Hania, Gerda and Heniek. Hania, who knew Wilaski best, said she never saw him as a threat, that his insults were just the result of his drunkenness. Gerda agreed, but said that his frequent drunkenness presented a threat to the group.

176: Description of Yuri Strelzov: interview with Gerda.

177–78: Night at the Kiev Opera House: interviews with Gerda and Hania.

179: Attack on Stalingrad: Erickson, *Road to Stalingrad*, 400–44. Hitler's order prohibiting retreat from Stalingrad: Erickson, *Road to Stalingrad*, 471. German casualty figures at the beginning of 1943: Erickson, *Road to Berlin,* 1–3. "Authoritarian anarchy . . . and mutual throat cutting": Dallin, 670.

180: Uta Frischler and Erich Pollak story: interview with Willi and Cesia.

CHAPTER NINE: THE WORK OF THEIR OWN HANDS

Pages 183–87: Incident involving painting the SS offices: interview with Willi and Cesia.

187–88: Description of Kellner's mistress: interview with Gerda.

188–89: Events in the Warsaw ghetto in January 1943: Gilbert, 523–25.

190–91: Cesia in church on Easter: interviews with Willi, Cesia and Gerda.

192–93: Conditions on the eastern front in spring 1943: Erickson, *Road to Berlin,* 53–60.

194–95: Irina Kolomitchok story: interview with Willi and Cesia.

195: "Second front in the enemy's rear"; and German response to partisans: Dallin, 209; 210–11.

196: Repair of watertowers and damaged tracks: interviews with Willi, Cesia and Gerda.

198: Arrest of Richard Schwalbe and Georg Neuman: interviews with Willi, Cesia, Gerda and Heniek.

199–201: Bachner's interrogation by the SS: interviews with Willi, Cesia, Hania and Gerda.

203: Arrival of Leon and Mila Finder in the Ukraine: interview with Jadwiga Finder and Nina Lurie.

204: "Germany could not win; Russia could not lose"; and Operation Citadel: Erickson, *Road to Berlin*, 85; 97.

205: Operation Saukel: Dallin, 430–35.

206–7: Incident of Gerda being sent to retrieve Kellner workers: interview with Gerda.

207: German losses at Kursk: Erickson, *Road to Berlin*, 120–21.

CHAPTER TEN: THE REQUITAL OF THE WICKED

Pages 209–10: Story of Hania and Kazaniecki's escape from Spola: interview with Hania. Bachner's coming to Zitomir: interview with Gerda.

211–12: Suicide of Moritz Stamberger: interviews with Hania, Willi, Cesia and Heniek.

212–13: Heniek thinking he saw his real name on the pay roster: interview with Hilde.

213–15: Bachner's troubles with his father: interviews with Willi, Cesia and Heniek.

215: Jadwiga fasting on Yom Kippur: interview with Jadwiga.

215–16: Vlasov movement: Dallin, 553–86.

216: Military situation in October 1943: Shirer, 1006–7. Ukrainian SS: Dallin, 598–600.

217: Jews escaping from Zitomir: interview with Gerda.

218: Arrest of Grossman: interviews with Willi, Cesia and Heniek.

219: Incident of Jewish worker leaving to join the partisans: interview with Heniek.

219–20: Workers recognizing Cesia as a Jew: interview with Heniek.

220–21: Information on the Bauzüge: Kreidler, 137. Role of the Bauzüge in the eastern campaign: Poltgiesser, *Die Deutches Reichsbahn in Ostfelsung, 1939–1944*, 43, 54.

221–25: Heniek's remaining behind in Novograd Volynsky: interview with Heniek.

225–26: Jewish resistance in Minsk: Gilbert, 619–20.

226–27: Rescue of the Filinskis: interview with Heniek.

227: Attempt on Hitler's life in Smolensk: Shirer, 1020.

228–29: Incident of Bachner managing to bypass Warsaw on the way to Bromberg: interview with Willi and Cesia.

CHAPTER ELEVEN: THE SURVIVORS OF ZION

Page 232: Armia Krajowa and Armia Ludowa: Erickson, *Road to Berlin*, 258–59.

233–35: Bachner revelation to Kellner that he is Jewish: interview with Willi and Cesia.

236: Hitler's refusal to consider a negotiated end to the war: Shirer, 1036–40. Soviet position at the beginning of the Warsaw uprising: Erickson, *Road to Berlin*, 286.

237: Soviet refusal to attack Warsaw: Erickson, *Road to Berlin*, 287.

238–39: Heniek's stories about showers and swimming: interview with Heniek.

240: Ardennes offensive: Shirer, 1092–96. Loss of Warsaw and Silesia: Erickson, *Road to Berlin,* 450; and Shirer, 1099.

240–41: Bombing raid on Berlin: interview with Heniek.

242: Attack on the Bauzug: interview with Heniek and Jadwiga.

243: Military situation in March 1945: Ambrose, *Eisenhower and Berlin,* 17–18. Hitler's turning on the German people: Shirer, 1102.

245–48: Incident of Heniek and the shoes: interview with Heniek.

248: German surrender: Shirer, 1139.

249–51: Bachner meeting Americans: interview with Willi and Cesia.

BIBLIOGRAPHY

Ainsztein, Reuben. *Jewish Resistance in Nazi Occupied Eastern Europe.* New York: Barnes and Noble, 1974.

Ambrose, Steven. *Eisenhower and Berlin, 1945: The Decision to Halt on the Elbe.* New York: W.W. Norton, 1986.

Dallin, Alexander. *German Rule in Russia: 1941–1945: A Study in Occupational Policies.* New York: Octagon Books, 1980.

Erickson, John. *The Road to Stalingrad: Stalin's War with Germany, Vol. 1.* New York: Harper and Row, 1975.

————. *The Road to Berlin: Continuing the History of Stalin's War with Germany.* Boulder, Colo.: Westview, 1983.

Gilbert, Martin. *The Holocaust: A History of the Jews in Europe During the Second World War.* New York: Henry Holt, 1985.

Hilberg, Raul. *The Destruction of the European Jews.* New York: New Viewpoints, 1973.

Hilberg, Raul, et al. *The Warsaw Diary of Adam Czerniakow: Prelude to Doom.* New York: Stein and Day, 1979.

Kreidler, Eugen. *Railroads in the Sphere of Influence of the Axis Powers During the Second World War: Applications and Accomplishments for the Army and War Economy.* Frankfurt: Musterschmidt Gottingen, 1975.

Lifton, Betty Jean. *The King of the Children.* New York: Farrar, Straus and Giroux, 1988.

Mogilanski, Roman, ed. *The Ghetto Anthology: A Comprehensive Chronicle of the Extermination of Jewry in Nazi Death Camps and Ghettos in Poland.* Los Angeles: American Congress of Jews from Poland, 1985.

Oliner, Samuel P. and Pearl M. *The Altruistic Personality: Rescuers of Jews in Nazi Occupied Europe.* New York: The Free Press, 1988.

Poltgiesser, Hans. *Die Deutsches Reichsbahn in Ostfelsung: 1939–1944.* Postdam: Bundesarchiv, n.d.

Pretzel, Marian. *Portrait of a Young Forger.* St. Lucia: University of Queensland Press, 1989.

Rohde, Von Horst. *Das Deutche Wermachttransportwesen im Zweiten Weltkrieg.* Stuttgart: Deutsche Verlags-Anstslt, 1971.

Rubenstein, Richard L., and John K. Roth. *Approaches to Auschwitz: The Holocaust and Its Legacy.* Atlanta: John Knox Press, 1987.

Shirer, William. *The Rise and Fall of the Third Reich: A History of Nazi Germany.* New York: Simon and Schuster, 1960.

Sloan, Jacob, ed., trans. *Notes from the Warsaw Ghetto: The Journal of Emmanuel Ringleblum.* New York: Schocken Books, 1974.

Tape recordings of interviews with the following survivors are on file at the Altruistic Personality and Prosocial Behavior Institute, Arcata, California:

Wilhelm and Cecile Bachner	Jadwiga Finder and Nina Lurie
Hilde Bachner	Gerda Reichenbaum
Heniek Buchführer	Hania Teifeld

INDEX OF PROPER NAMES AND PLACES